Children's Literature

Volume 26

Children's Literature

Volume 26

Annual of
The Modern Language Association
Division on Children's Literature
and The Children's Literature
Association

Yale University Press

New Haven and London

1998

The editors gratefully acknowledge support from Hollins College.

Editorial correspondence should be addressed to The Editors, *Children's Literature,* Department of English, Hollins College, Roanoke, Virginia 24020.

Manuscripts submitted should conform to the style in this issue. An original on non-erasable bond with two copies, a self-addressed envelope, and return postage are requested. Yale University Press does not accept dot-matrix printouts, and it requires double-spacing throughout text and notes. Unjustified margins are required. Writers of accepted manuscripts should be prepared to submit final versions of their essays on computer disk in XyWrite, Nota Bene, or WordPerfect.

Volumes 1–7 of *Children's Literature* can be obtained directly from John C. Wandell, The Children's Literature Foundation, P.O. Box 370, Windham Center, Conn. 06280. Volumes 8–26 can be obtained from Yale University Press, P.O. Box 209040, New Haven, Conn. 06520-9040, or from Yale University Press, 23 Pond Street, Hampstead, London NW3 2PN, England.

Set in Baskerville type by Tseng Information Systems, Inc., Durham, N.C.
Printed in the United States of America by Vail-Ballou Press, Binghamton, N.Y.

Library of Congress catalog card number: 79-66588
ISBN: 0-300-07415-8 (cloth), 0-300-07416-6 (paper); ISSN: 0092-8208

A catalogue record for this book is available from the British Library.

The paper in this book meets the guidelines for permanence and durability of the Committee on Production Guidelines for Book Longevity of the Council on Library Resources.

10 9 8 7 6 5 4 3 2 1

Contents

From the Editor

In introducing volume 26 of *Children's Literature,* there are many people whom I would like to thank, welcome, and reluctantly bid farewell. First, I am grateful to U. C. Knoepflmacher and Mitzi Myers for editing last year's splendid volume on cross-writing child and adult. I was just enough involved in the project to know how hard the co-editors worked for a period of more than two years, and I had little enough to do with the final product to be able to join in the chorus of praise that I am sure it has inspired. The co-authored introduction to the volume alone should do much to stimulate dialogue and debate as to what constitutes children's literature, its relation to the adult literary canon, and the contribution the study of children's literature can make to cultural studies in general. Anyone who attended the packed session at the end of the 1996 MLA meeting, at which U. C. Knoepflmacher and three other scholars discussed the politics of children's literature within the academy, can confirm that such issues as those raised in *Children's Literature* 25 are vital for our community.

I would also like to thank retiring book review editor John Cech for his fifteen years of service. When I assumed the editorship with volume 22, I relied on John for continuity and support, and I have greatly enjoyed our collaboration over the past five years. Replacing John will be Christine Doyle, who teaches in the English department of Central Connecticut State University. Chris served as an editorial associate for volumes 19 and 20, while in graduate school at the University of Connecticut, and she co-edited volume 21 with fellow graduate students Anne Phillips and Julie Pfeiffer. Thus in a sense continuity is preserved. It is equally gratifying to announce that Julie Pfeiffer has become my colleague at Hollins College and that she will be helping to edit what I hope will be the many volumes of *Children's Literature* yet to come.

Next I would like to offer special thanks to Pamela Harer, who volunteered to prepare the twenty-five-year cumulative index for next year's volume. As long-time subscribers know, *Children's Literature* has published a five-year index at regular intervals, the last appearing in volume 21. A few years ago Pamela wrote to me, offering to send an index for volumes 1–21 for use in Hollins's children's literature M.A.

program. She sent me another for volumes 1–23, and these proved so useful to our students that, as the time approached for another index to appear in *Children's Literature,* I thought its readers would also appreciate a cumulative index. Its publication will be cause for celebration of founding editor Francelia Butler's extraordinary vision and of all the contributors, reviewers, editors, and consultants who have enabled it to flourish over the years—in short, of the hundreds of people whose names appear in the index.

Finally, I would like to thank the *fifty-two* consultants who have made the present volume possible. Forty-four manuscripts were submitted for consideration, and a number of them were revised and resubmitted. Many consultants read more than one manuscript or read two or more versions of the same manuscript. In a few instances, the consultants worked directly with the contributors in what became a collaborative effort. I am grateful to both consultants and contributors for their patience and hard work.

In contrast to last year's special-topic volume, *Children's Literature* 26 is a kind of carrier bag, to borrow a term from Anne Lundin's piece on Kate Greenaway's autobiography. Its contents have been painstakingly gathered, but they point to no unifying theme, raise no series of related questions. Several essays are carrier bags themselves in that they are surveys—gatherings or collections—of works that have heretofore escaped close examination. But the size and shape of these bags—and the ground over which the scavenging activity takes place—vary greatly. Gillian Adams only begins to gather what she hopes may eventually require a very large bag: literature of the Middle Ages written for or especially attractive to an audience of children; Jane Parish Yang fills her bag but covers a more limited (but to most of us an equally unfamiliar) terrain: Chinese children's literature since World War II; Jeanie Watson's bag bulges with long-discarded nineteenth-century schoolbooks that contain the poetry of Samuel Taylor Coleridge; and Tina L. Hanlon's bag, although both it and its contents may have come from Barnes and Noble, contains a surprisingly varied collection of Jane Yolen fairy-tale heroines.

Other essays, like Hanlon's, explore the works of a single author or a single work, though placing these in a broader context. John Rieder examines poetry at the opposite end of the spectrum from Coleridge's, though both Lear's limericks and Coleridge's mystery poems appeal to a dual audience, perhaps because elements in both defy rationality. Naomi J. Wood offers a fresh reading of Lear's contemporary, Robert Louis Stevenson, by placing his classic *Treasure Island* in the context of contemporary controversy over the gold standard. Yoshida Junko, like Jane Parish Yang, is concerned with a changing society, but whereas Yang surveys a wide selection of children's books in order to document changing Chinese attitudes toward the family, Yoshida sees Robert Cormier's *The Chocolate War* as contributing to the debate in our society begun in the 1970s over models of masculinity. Finally, Paula T. Connolly places Julius Lester's "Where the Sun Lives" in the context of nineteenth-century slave narratives, demonstrating the sophistication with which this young adult story treats both racial and gender oppression.

The contents of this carrier-bag issue are not only varied; they also have been gathered from several different cultures. In addition to a selection on the Chinese family and one contributed by a Japanese scholar, we have Emer O'Sullivan's unusual piece, which in itself represents three European countries. O'Sullivan, an Irishwoman living in Germany, has contributed an essay originally published in German (translated here by Anthea Bell). To make matters even more complicated, the subject of O'Sullivan's essay is the losses—and, more interesting, the gains—involved in translating British writer Aidan Chambers's children's books into German. The inclusion of O'Sullivan's essay alone would make this volume the most international of those I have edited. However, J. D. Stahl's review of *Aspects and Issues in the History of Children's Literature,* a collection of essays from the Ninth Congress of the International Research Society for Children's Literature, contributes further to the international flavor of the volume.

Other reviews, like the essays and the "varia," examine the contents of carrier bags or are carrier bags themselves. Alida Allison reviews a book—Suzanne Rahn's *Rediscoveries in Children's Literature*—that retrieves nine authors of children's books from undeserved obscurity. Jan Susina describes a new biography as "a gathering together . . . of Cohen's previous Carroll research." Ledia Dittberner and Ian Wojcik-Andrews bring together three new works on children's literature and critical theory. And, finally, I review two works from Twayne's ever-growing list of critical books on children's authors. Recently someone remarked to me that few of these books, most of them written by members of ChLA, are ever seriously reviewed. I hope that in the next few years reviewers will be encouraged to gather the more interesting of these books into the carrier bags of omnibus reviews.

As you are reading this volume, we are beginning to gather essays for volume 28 (2000). We hope that volume 28 can somehow salute the new century and millennium; thus we would welcome reflections on the future of children's literature and children's literature studies as well as on their development in the century that is now drawing to a close.

Elizabeth Lennox Keyser

Articles

Medieval Children's Literature: Its Possibility and Actuality

Gillian Adams

Years ago, while taking a graduate course in medieval Latin, I was struck by the wide disparity in the difficulty of the works that were assigned, a disparity that often did not coincide with other variables such as the historical period or the author's social class, profession, or region. In that course it was assumed that all the texts we addressed, whatever their degree of difficulty, were written for adults. I concluded at the time that there must have been a substantial number of adult readers with literacy skills below the third-grade level. I have since become convinced that some of the works we were looking at were written not only or even initially for semiliterate adults, a group often equated with children in the earlier periods, but for children.[1] In order to support my claim that such works should be considered children's literature I draw on evidence provided by cultural and literary historians to dispute two widely held convictions that have hampered previous critical and theoretical studies. The first is the nonspecialist belief that there can be no medieval children's literature because a conception of childhood as we know it did not exist in the Middle Ages. The second is the specialist assertion, typified by the medievalist Bennett Brockman, that "the Middle Ages made no provision for a separate literature for children, apart from pedagogical texts designed to teach them to read, to write, to cipher, and

An earlier version of this essay was read at the Second Biennial Conference on Modern Critical Approaches to Children's Literature, Nashville, Tennessee, April 10–12, 1997. I wish to thank Claudia Nelson and Marilynn Olson for their ideas for clarifications, transitions, and rephrasings; Ruth Bottigheimer and Elizabeth Scala for their bibliographical suggestions; and my two anonymous readers for further assistance. All translations in this essay are my own.
Children's Literature 26, ed. Elizabeth Lennox Keyser (Yale University Press, © 1998 Hollins College).

to behave civilly" ("Juvenile" 18). Finally, I discuss the ways in which some medieval works and their contexts indicate a child audience and why such works warrant further exploration as children's literature.

I

First it is necessary to dispose of the myths about medieval children that have prevented scholars from seriously considering that a literature for them might exist. There are three initial barriers, primarily hypothetical, to recognizing medieval children's literature. To begin with, there is the still-widespread belief in the "Ariès thesis," in brief that childhood was "discovered" in the seventeenth century (according to Philippe Ariès) or the eighteenth century (according to some other researchers). Ariès, as he admits in his introduction to *Centuries of Childhood,* was not a specialist in the periods for which he claims that "the idea of [*sentiment,* a separate feeling about] childhood did not exist" (128), and in fact, if his book is deconstructed, it is evident that there was a cognizance of childhood throughout those earlier periods. What his thesis amounts to is that previous centuries thought quite differently about children than did seventeenth-century France. A statement of this nature is true for any time and for any region even today: for example, the conception of childhood is different for the first half of the twentieth century and the second; for the rich, the urban poor, and the comfortable, usually suburban, middle class; and most notably for Americans and those who live in countries where poor children go to work in factories at six or seven and parents sell children into prostitution and even slavery.[2] Nevertheless, Ariès's insistence on the social construction of childhood and on not naively reading the past in terms of the present is an essential contribution to the study of past children's literatures. His work has informed many subsequent critical and historical studies and has given rise to the examination of specific works within a wide-ranging sociohistorical context that includes nonliterary texts.

It was not long after the Ariès book appeared (in 1960 in France and in 1962 in English translation) that specialists in the medieval and early modern periods began to point out what was wrong with its ideas and with the data used to support them. As early as 1975 Meradith McMunn wrote in *Children's Literature,* on the basis of her examination of the description of children in French medieval literature, that Ariès's claims are "not supported by a close look at medieval literature" ("Children" 54). She was followed by C. H. Talbot, who asserted in *Children's Literature* in 1977 that "anyone who is at all conversant with the biographies of the saints; with the lives of abbots, monks, and nuns; or with the chronicles of monasteries and cathedral churches written between the eighth and the twelfth century will realize that such a theory [as Ariès's] is untenable" (17). Books criticizing Ariès soon followed: recent works accessible to nonspecialists and available in paperback are John Boswell's *The Kindness of Strangers* (1988, see particularly 36–38), Shulamith Shahar's *Childhood in the Middle Ages* (1990), and Barbara A. Hanawalt's *Growing up in Medieval London* (1993).[3] By 1995, Hugh Cunningham can comment in *Children and Childhood in Western Society Since 1500* that disproving Ariès is "an easy goal" and that what is needed is greater attention to "the contradictions and changes over time and place in medieval thought and practice" (40). In short, medieval and early modern scholars are unanimous in discarding the Ariès thesis, in spite of the interest of many of his observations; it is time for children's literature scholars to do the same.

Ariès's claim that childhood as we now think of it did not exist before the seventeenth or the eighteenth century as well as his chapters on the ages of life, the discovery of childhood (in art), and children's dress have resulted in two additional barriers to locating medieval children's literature. The first is the idea that parents did not love (or were afraid to love) their children because infant and child mortality was so high. One finds this claim made, in spite of ample evidence to the contrary, for periods ranging from antiquity through the eighteenth century. Such a claim is logically absurd; for the greater part of human existence, life for most has been nasty, brutish, and short. Death rates have often been almost as high for adults as for children, particularly in the case of childbearing women and warriors, yet there is no lack of early literature about love. In fact, a high value was placed on children and on parental love (see Boswell, Hanawalt, Shahar, and Talbot passim), although often on a sliding scale: some children—for example, male heirs of the wealthy and powerful—were more valuable than others, and a separate literature for them was more likely to develop and to survive.

The second and more damaging idea, as far as children's literature studies is concerned, is based primarily on Ariès's discussion of medieval dress and art and his claim that children were viewed as "miniature adults." Ariès was not an art historian, and his interpretation of the evidence he presents is flawed, given that for the period he discusses artists were not interested in realism as we conceive of it. There is other medieval art, notably sculpture and manuscript illustration, that better represents the child as distinct from the adult. In Ariès's day, in contrast to the present, European children and sometimes adolescents were strongly differentiated by their clothing (for example, short pants and school smocks), so it would be natural for him to be struck by the similarity of adults' and children's clothing in medieval art. Moreover, Ariès's claim that childhood was not viewed as a separate stage of life is not supported by the ample evidence of the interest shown during the Middle Ages in discussing and defining the ages and characteristics of *infantia* (birth to six or seven years), *pueritia* (seven to twelve for girls, to fourteen for boys), *adolescentia* (the period between biological and social puberty and legal and social majority), and *juventus* (see, for example, Shahar 22 and notes; Hanawalt, passim).

Nevertheless, these myths about medieval children persist. For example, in the most recent edition of *The Pleasures of Children's Literature* (1996), although Perry Nodelman cites Pollock's and Shahar's studies, he continues to assert that in the earlier periods "a *different* conception of childhood operated, [and] that conception required no special literature for children" (70, emphasis in original).[4] If we contend that a society whose conception of childhood is alien to our own is incapable of developing children's literature, we should also argue that there could have been no children's literature in the eighteenth and nineteenth centuries in England and the United States either, since the ideas operative then about the "innocent" child and about family structure, clothing, age- and gender-appropriate activities, and social status are not identical to today's. In fact, there is no logical reason why societies with constructions of childhood that differ widely from our own (for example, China) should not develop literature for children, whether or not they actually do. To assert that only *our* conception of childhood can result in children's literature, a literature that only we are able to judge as literature in terms of its literary value (which for some reason must include "entertainment"), is the kind of cultural imperialism and ideological colonialism that modern critics, Nodelman among them, often seek to avoid (see Nodelman's often-cited essay "The Other: Orientalism, Colonialism, and Children's Literature").

II

Even if we admit, then, that the period roughly from the sack of Rome (410) to the invention of printing had different conceptions of childhood from those current in most of Europe and America today, such conceptions do not logically preclude the possibility of a literature for children. More problematic is the narrowness of vision of those who do recognize and write about medieval and early modern texts for children and youth as exemplified by the quotation from Brockman with which I began this chapter. Brockman makes two claims: first, that there is literature but that it is "pedagogical," and second, that apart from this literature there is no separate literature for children (i.e., that it was a part of adult literature that children shared with adults). Brockman is not alone; on the basis of the scholarship that I have seen to date, the only medieval texts recognized as exclusively for children are considered nonfiction: instruction manuals and courtesy books. The idea that this sort of work is all that exists is fostered by bibliographies, collections of excerpts such as that edited by Patricia Demers and Gordon Moyles, and the early chapters of F. J. Harvey Darton's *Children's Books in England*.[5]

Like Brockman, most children's literature specialists who are also medievalists address themselves to a shared literature whose content or circumstances may indicate a child audience, or they tell us how good or poor a job modern children's literature does in portraying the medieval period. I find particularly distressing the essays on medieval children's literature in volume 1 of *Children's Literature*.[6] Although Hugh Keenan's piece on Old English children's literature is suggestive, mentioning not only Aelfric's *Colloquy* (ca. 1000) but also the Exeter and Cotton gnomes, the McMunns' essay, in spite of some excellent citations, writes off the fourteenth-century French *Book of the Knight of La Tour-Landry* (translated into English in the fifteenth century) as "an encyclopedic catalogue of anecdotes, each with a very explicit moral" (23); Brockman terms its stories "crudely manipulative" ("Medieval" 40). Anyone who has read this work knows that it contains fascinating narratives of some length, some readily accessible to students today. Nothing has changed in volume 4 of *Children's Literature,* where William McMunn asserts in his introduction to the four papers from the MLA panel "Children and the Middle Ages" that "all of us on the panel agree that 'children's literature' did not exist in the Middle Ages" ("Literacy" 36).

Why will these scholars not consider as children's literature "the pedagogical texts designed to teach [children] to read, to write, to cipher, and to behave civilly" (Brockman, "Juvenile" 18) or the "entertaining stories [that] were used in programs of instruction" (McMunn and McMunn, "Children's" 22)? I believe that there are two reasons, and the case of the McMunns' and Brockman's condemnation of *The Book of the Knight of La Tour-Landry* provides a clue to the first. It seems to be the belief in the romantic notion, based on Darton's 1932 definition of children's literature, that didactic works do not count, are not truly "literature": "By 'children's books' I mean printed works produced ostensibly to give children spontaneous pleasure, and not primarily to teach them, nor solely to make them good, nor to keep them *profitably* quiet" (1, emphasis in original). Such a narrow definition of literature has been repudiated by a number of scholars, ably led for some years now by the new historicist Mitzi Myers, whose groundbreaking review of Geoffrey Summerfield castigates his book for its "presentism" and espousal of "Romantic values" (108). Brockman's essay on medieval poetry, in spite of valuable observations on lullabies and on different types of medieval didacticism, is a sad example of such "presentism." Recently Patricia Demers in *Heaven upon Earth: The Form of Moral and Religious Children's Literature, to 1850,* which begins its study of children's literature with Erasmus's 1540 *Sermon of the Chylde Jesus,* has provided a telling critique of Darton's antididactic position.

In fact, in certain countries and periods, among them medieval Europe, didacticism has been highly valued (as it is by many education students today); typical is the classical poet Horace's proclamation in his *Ars Poetica* (often part of the medieval curriculum) that *Scribendi recte sapere est et principium et fons* [The source and first principle of good writing is wisdom] (l. 310). In a dictum often referred to by medieval theorists, Horace adds, *omne tulit punctum qui miscuit utile dulci / lectorem delectando pariterque monendo* [he has won the day who has mixed the useful with the pleasurable / equally delighting the reader and instructing him] (ll. 343–44). In Horace's own work the needle was closer to *dulci* on the continuum between *utile* and *dulci;* in most medieval literature, it tended to be closer to *utile.* Thus the works of the great literary figures of the High Middle Ages, for example, Dante and Chaucer, are explicit about the lessons to be drawn from their fictions. Yet their situation as stars of the literary canon—along with that supremely didactic work, the Bible—has never been denied. Of course, as Marxist and other ideological critics often remind us, all literature has an agenda, however carefully disguised.

I suspect that the second reason for refusing to believe that anything connected with pedagogy could be literature has to do with the need perceived by many American academic children's literature specialists to divorce themselves from the fields of education and library science. Nevertheless, from its beginnings in the ancient world, children's literature has been intimately related to pedagogics and remains so today (see Adams). European scholars appear much more comfortable with the connection than we do, on the evidence of Maria Nikolajeva's introduction to the essays in *Aspects and Issues in the History of Children's Literature* and many of the essays themselves. There is no logical reason why texts used for educational purposes should not also qualify as literature, whether they appeal to us or not. The history of education demonstrates that poetry, drama, and narrative have been used to supplement nonfiction in the schools from their beginning, whether adult material used and sometimes adapted for children or material created especially for them and whether used in ways that seem familiar to us or alien. To investigate fully the possibilities of medieval children's literature, then, we must begin with medieval education and the texts used within or as supplements to the curriculum.

III

Once we have disposed of the mythologies and prejudices that have prevented specialists and nonspecialists alike from admitting that medieval children's literature may exist, two important barriers to an accurate, scholarly assessment of that literature remain, and they have to do with the nature of medieval education. The first concerns what was once thought to be the low percentage of the population for whom literacy was deemed necessary or even desirable, the second the admittedly high price of codices. Of late, scholars have been revising literacy figures upward, led by Rosamond McKitterick for the earlier periods; for the later periods see the historical studies mentioned at the beginning of this essay. The Middle Ages are not monolithic, and certain groups of people placed a high value on literacy: the Jews (the people of the book), whose males were required by religious law to be literate enough to read the Scriptures;[7] the church (monks, nuns, and the secular clergy); royalty and the high nobility (and the clerks and legal experts who served them); and, beginning with the twelfth century, those engaged in commerce. Of course, the situation in urban areas was different from that in the countryside, and some regions were more learned and literate than others. For example, many parts of Italy, particularly the regions under Arab and Byzantine influence, never lost a respect for learning. Once most of Spain came under Muslim domination, high culture flourished. Southern France was ahead of northern France until the Renaissance of the twelfth century; there were pockets of culture in Germany; and England tended to lag behind, even with respect to Ireland. But because of the high value placed on books—both as objects sometimes worth enough to hold for ransom and as containers of text that was also highly esteemed—they, and the ability to read them, were indicators of power and status. Literacy was not only useful but necessary for upward mobility.[8]

But it is exactly the high value of a book before the invention of printing, and even for a time afterwards, that most scholars assume makes it unlikely that any but a child from a wealthy family would actually have possessed a book of his or (even more rarely) her own; if there were books for children in a household or school, they would be shared and as likely to be heard as read. There obviously could be no children's book trade in the modern sense, although there is plenty of evidence of the buying and selling of codices: as early as the eighth century certain ecclesiastical establishments depended on the money they gained from copying (see McKitterick, "Nuns' Scriptoria"; *Carolingians* ch. 4), and books for children must have been part of this trade.

Nevertheless, some children did learn how to read, whether taught in schools run by monks and nuns or by the secular clergy, at home by parents, or at court by tutors. Exactly how this teaching was done is detailed by Suzanne Reynolds in *Medieval Reading: Grammar, Rhetoric, and the Classical Text.* Although her account is based on a description in a twelfth-century English text by Alexander Neckham, *Sacerdos ad altare accessurus,* scholars agree that the general shape of the curriculum as Neckham describes it is characteristic of the whole medieval period. The student began with the alphabet, perhaps inscribed on an object in daily use such as a bowl or a belt (8), and went on to the proper pronunciation of Latin syllables by memorizing the Paternoster, the Creed, and perhaps parts of the Psalter. Much of this learning would be done by rote at a level of "uncomprehending reiteration" (10).[9] Texts were also written on parchment attached to wooden paddles or in large letters glued to a wooden board (Shahar 189). Many institutions had extremely large service books that could be seen at a distance by a number of readers, and books were often chained to bookstands so that they could be read seriatim.

Reynolds emphasizes the orality of education, arguing that students "do not read (in our sense of the term) the text at all, for it remains at all moments and in all senses in the teacher's hands. . . . This is a communal reading, communicated orally. . . . Reasons of economy and availability make it very unlikely that individual students, even if they could write, would have had access to copies of the text. If they did write, it was probably on wax tablets. . . . [And] the wax tablet of *memoria* is fundamental in medieval literacy" (29). On the other hand, in her studies of the Carolingian period, McKitterick emphasizes the dominance of the written text and of writing from the earliest periods. Talbot (22) and R. H. and M. A. Rouse describe the slates framed in wood and the wax-covered wooden *tabellae* on which students did their first writing exercises (4–5), usually, according to Reynolds, short or long paraphrases (21). It seems probable that the balance between memorized and written text varied according to time, place, the institution and its resources, and the status of its pupils.

The next text in the learning sequence was a grammar book, usually the Donatus *Ars Minor* or part of the *Ars Maior,* with local variants, which was used from the fourth until at least the fifteenth century;[10] its question-and-answer format is characteristic of other medieval master-pupil dialogues specifically designed for children. At least one child owned his own copy of Donatus, a ninth-century schoolboy named Sado, "who wrote in a mixture of rather straggling capitals and minuscule . . . with a notably shaky command of grammar" across the top of the page: "*Sadoniis iste liber est sua mater dedit illi Magnum onor illa sit qui dedit hunc librum*" [this book is Sados his mother gave it to him may she be greatly honored who gave him this book] (McKitterick, "Ninth" 228). In her study of this manuscript, which is "rather inferior quality vellum" and gives other indications of an attempt at economy (for example, leaves erased and reused), McKitterick details the ways in which it has been prepared for "a learner's eye": it has clearly punctuated sentences, section headings in "rustic capitals," and "extravagantly wide margins" (227), some of which have been ruled with narrow lines for the "annotations of the struggling student" who has written (incorrectly) on one of them, *stultissimo grammatica* [extremely stupid grammar] (228). McKitterick concludes, "Phillips 16308 in fact contradicts a frequent assumption that books in the early Middle Ages were too costly and scarce to be owned by the ordinary schoolboy" (228). The multiple copies of Donatus in the library lists of monasteries known to have flourishing schools, and the many copies that still survive, are further confirmation of McKitterick's claim.

A second work found in multiple copies, falsely attributed to the Roman philosopher Cato and universally coupled with Donatus in the elementary curriculum, is the *Catonis Disticha* [Cato's distichs]. It is a third-century collection of 152 moral couplets in four books, prefaced by a short introductory epistle and about fifty-four very short sentences, some as little as two words. The introduction addresses a child, "Cato" 's son: *Nunc te, fili karissime, docebo quo pacto morem animi tui componas* [Now I will teach you, dearest son, how you can put your mind in order] (T. Hunt 9). The work ends with *Hic finit Cato dans castigamina nato / ostendens quare mundum non debet amare* [Here Cato finishes admonishing his son / showing how he ought not to love this world].[11] From the tenth century onward "Cato" was the first item in an elementary reading book, the *Liber Catonianus.* Tony Hunt gives a full account of how the selections in this reading book varied according to location and period, but three items in addition to "Cato" were constant. First there were fables, usually Avianus's expansion of those by Babrius; then something about the Trojan war—in the earlier period the *Ilias Latina,* a shortened version of the *Iliad* from A.D. 65, which was later replaced by the medieval version of Statius's *Achilleis,* valued for its account of how Achilles obeyed his mother Thetis, her concern for him, and his upbringing by Chiron (Hunt 69). The third item was usually the *Eclogues* of the tenth-century author Theodolus, a debate between Truth and Falsehood about Christianity and paganism that owes much to Virgil's third and seventh eclogues and that was viewed as preparatory to his study. None of the works Hunt mentions, aside from "Cato" and Avianus, was originally composed for children; rather, all were appropriated (and glossed, often heavily) for and by them. Donatus, "Cato," the fables, and some of the other texts exist in multiple versions and variants with interpolations and excisions; I cannot emphasize their fluidity too strongly.

It was at this point, before the serious student went on to Virgil's *Eclogues* and the fixed texts of the classical and late Latin *auctores*

(Cicero, Horace, Ovid, Lucan, Terence, and others), that according to Alexander Neckham, he was to read "*quibusdam libellis informationi rudium necessariis*" [certain shorter works necessary for the instruction of the unlearned] (Reynolds 7).[12] And, I would argue, it is at this point that we should find, between the elementary texts and the medieval equivalent of Shakespeare and other works in today's high-school canon, the optional material in a curriculum otherwise dominated by classical and late Latin texts: the poems, fables, and stories adapted or specially written for children, the "separate literature" that, according to Brockman and others, does not exist in the Middle Ages.

IV

Now that I have established that there is no reason why medieval children's literature—even material with an agenda covert enough for critics such as Brockman to accept as literature—should not exist, and that there is a place in the curriculum for such works, I would like to name a few candidates and the genres in which they occur. Most of the examples that I describe below happen to be in Latin; I am convinced that further material is available not only in Latin but in the vernaculars. Because there are medievalists who have no interest in children as an audience, indeed to whom the idea of children as a potential audience might seem utterly foreign, it is important to find as many indications as possible that a text has a connection with child readers or auditors. To discover features that indicate a child audience, absent the kind of smoking gun that McKitterick finds in Sado's grammar book, I ask the following questions: in terms of the text itself (internal evidence), is there a dedication to a named child or introductory material indicating that the work is intended for children or younger students? What is the language like—is it very simple or simpler and more direct than that in other works by the same author clearly directed at adults, and is the language in the prefatory material more complex than the language in the body of the text? Is a child directly addressed or portrayed as a major character? How is he or she presented? What is the appearance of the manuscript or manuscripts of the text? Are there explanatory glosses directed at inexpert readers, as in the case of Sado's grammar and the *Liber Catonianus*? Does the calligraphy of some versions indicate inexpert copyists? If there are illustrations, what do they reveal about an implied audience, keeping in mind that the primary audience for illustrated material was an adult one? Are the manuscripts inexpensively produced, or are they so lavish that they imply a princely owner?

In terms of external evidence, what is the nature of the scriptoria from which the earliest examples come? What establishments owned the manuscripts? Are they also the sites of schools? What do we know about the author, whether actual or ascribed (for example, "Cato" or "Aesop")? How popular is the text and how fluid? Does it exist in multiple versions, or in Latin and the vernaculars? With what other works is it bound? (For example, works bound with "Cato" or the popular grammars are more likely to be directed at children). What is the historical and cultural context of the work, its period and location? Do selections from it appear in *florilegia,* collections of excerpts for use in the schools? Is it referred to in other texts as somehow connected with children or with education?

I have already mentioned that fables, usually about animals, were a curriculum standard for young readers. They were often grouped with *aenigmata* (riddles) by Symphosius, Aldhelm, and others, also used in the schools from an early period (see Ziolkowski 40–46). The best-known fables are found in collections such as "Aesop" and those by Babrius and Phaedrus in versions known as Avianus and Romulus (see Ben Edwin Perry for an extended discussion of various versions and their use). On the basis of what has survived, apart from classical fable material, narratives containing speaking animals begin with ninth-century animal poems by Alcuin of York and others who were members of Charlemagne's palace school; Alcuin's poem "The Cock and the Wolf" is the earliest known analogue of Chaucer's "Nun's Priest's Tale."[13]

These and other short poems are followed by *The Ecbasis Captivi,* an eleventh-century Latin frame tale intended on one level to serve as a warning to young novices against attempting escape from the monastery (a major problem, according to Boswell). The inner story is about a calf (*vitulus*), a common term for a novice, who is imprisoned by a wolf, rescued by a fox, and taken to the court of the lion king. The work is a cento; that is, it is made up of multiple short quotations, which may be intended as embellishment, parody, or a kind of contextual gloss, from the set texts that children would have encountered in their studies. It is bound with school texts in the two surviving manuscripts. The *Ecbasis* is followed in turn by animal epics such as the twelfth-century *Ysengrimus* (attributed to "Nivardus"), which is the first fully worked-out version of the Reynard the Fox material. On the basis of its complex structure, difficult language, learned jokes, and inclusion of a smutty passage, it was probably intended for an audience of ecclesiastics. The questionable passage, however, was early removed for a presumably younger audience in a version of the manuscript that comes from a teaching establishment, and selections from the *Ysengrimus* found their way into *chrestomathies* and *florilegia* bound together with grammatical and other teaching texts.[14]

Although nonspecialists will be familiar with the medieval Reynard cycle and its offshoots only from modern versions, the association of medieval children with drama, both as actors and as part of the audience, should be common knowledge (see, for example, Brockman, "Children"; Hanks; and M. and W. McMunn). In the second half of the tenth century Froumund of Tegernsee refers to using props and animal masks to get the attention of his pupils; Ziolkowski suggests that some animal poems "were perhaps scripts for schoolroom performances in which pupils donned animal masks" (5, see also 147–52). But I know only one dramatic corpus specifically written for children: the plays of Hrotswitha of Gandersheim, a late-tenth-century nun who taught in an establishment limited to female children of the German royal family and important nobility. Her series of playlets, written in simple Latin with short, snappy, often amusing dialogue and some slapstick, celebrates the victories of prepubescent girls—the major characters—over threats to their chastity and integrity. The language of the plays is totally unlike the grandiose rhetoric of works by Hrotswitha dedicated to the king and to other important adults, and there are additional internal and external features that indicate a youthful audience. The plays are still performed today, primarily in academic situations.[15]

In the later periods there appear didactic works intended for the young containing fictional narratives among their moral precepts; a prime example is the *Fecunda ratis* of Egbert of Liège. An early-eleventh-century collection of Latin verse texts of varying lengths and degrees of difficulty written and compiled for Egbert's young pupils, it is a "gallimaufry of proverbs, fables, fairytales, and anecdotes" (Ziolkowski 42–43). Among its treasures is the first known version of "Little Red Riding Hood," complete with moral (see Berlioz; Lontzen).

Whereas Egbert, to my knowledge, has not been translated into English, a medieval best-seller, the *Disciplina Clericalis,* has two fine translations. It is by Petrus Alfonsi, a Spanish Jew who converted to Christianity in 1106. Written in very simple Latin at a time when the language often reflected Ciceronian splendors, this collection of stories primarily from Semitic and Arab sources, is, on the evidence of Alfonsi's ornate preface and an addressee in the text ("a little boy like you"), especially intended for young students. Termed "the oldest story book of the Middle Ages" (Beeson 84), its tales are usually short, as are its easy sentences; there is much dialogue, and the anecdotes are far less didactic than one would expect given both the agenda the author promotes in the preface and the genre: wisdom literature.[16] From slightly later in the same period comes a frame tale enclosing similar stories, Johannes de Alta Silva's *Dolopathos,* or *The King and the Seven Wise Men.*[17] Versions of Alfonsi's stories appear in the *Gesta Romanorum,* Marguerite of Navarre's *Heptameron,* Boccacio's *Decameron,* and other later collections; both his and Alta Silva's tales are quite familiar to folklorists.

Jonathan Nicholls sees the *Dolopathos* and *Disciplina Clericalis* as forerunners of the somewhat later courtesy books, observing that the teaching of courtesy as a part of the grammar course began in the twelfth century, when these works were written and when the nobility became more universally literate (58). Courtesy books are the one medieval genre that has been recognized as primarily directed at children or adolescents by children's literature scholars. But readers of the McMunns' "Children's Literature in the Middle Ages" or Ann Hildebrand's helpful study of the relation between courtesy books and the *Babar* stories would be ignorant of the fact that courtesy manuals contain more than just short, basic precepts of table etiquette. The narrative material they include may be part of the reason for their wide popularity; it certainly bears further investigation.[18] Allied to the courtesy books are the "mirrors for princes," handbooks for those expected to be in positions of power, for example, the manual that Dhuoda wrote for her sixteen-year-old son, arguably an adult by Carolingian standards, when he set out for Charlemagne's court (see McKitterick, *Carolingians* 223–25).

Religious texts are another popular medieval genre that scholars who write about children's literature seem reluctant to include as true children's literature, probably because they are didactic and thus presumably not entertaining. But when Chaucer's Prioress begins her sad tale of Little Hugh of Lincoln she is embarking on a topic, if not an actual story, no doubt well known to and enjoyed by most of her audience from their childhoods. Stories about exemplary children abound throughout the history of children's literature, and stories about child saints in simple language, especially when bound with school texts, would repay close examination. In a letter of 25 February 1997, Ruth Bottigheimer suggests for consideration as children's texts the narratives taken from the Vulgate by Peter Comestor, the author of the best-selling twelfth-century *Historia Scholastica* (see Bottigheimer, *Bible* 14–23). The stories in John the Monk's fourteenth-century *Liber de Miraculis* are another possibility. And Milla B. Riggio notes that in the fifth century Claudius Marius Victor's paraphrase of Genesis, *Alethia,* was "expressly written to train the young" (48).

Neither space nor the limits of my investigations to date permit addressing the possibility of medieval children's literature in the vernaculars. Geoffrey Chaucer's *Treatise on the Astrolabe,* written for his ten-year-old son Lewis, is an obvious example of nonfiction (see T. and K. Jambeck). On the basis of manuscript evidence, Mary Shaner has discussed the ways in which a medieval romance was revised for a child reader, and Brockman argues that *Sir Orfeo* is an example of shared, or family, literature because of its internal accessibility for children and the content of the codices in which the three surviving manuscripts of it are contained ("Juvenile"). Brockman has also examined how the Robin Hood narratives were transformed from an entertainment shared by adults and children into one exclusively for children, and Harriet Spiegel has looked at the way Marie of France's *Fables* work as shared literature since "[they] not only seem well suited to children but directly address them or their well-being," and "some present a child actually being taught by a parent" (29). More work needs to be done along these lines, and perhaps in the course of scholarly explorations, more compelling evidence on the order of Shaner's discoveries will be found to connect vernacular fiction directly with children. It seems likely that examples of cross-written or threshold literature—for example, the *Morall Fabillis* of Master Robert Henryson or *Aucassin and Nicolette*—will be more frequent in the vernaculars because of their less intimate connection with education.

Thus the works that I have argued are clearly children's literature are in Latin, although there came to be vernacular versions of some of them (for example, the stories in Petrus Alfonsi, the Reynard the Fox stories, and most of the fables). This is because most education was conducted in Latin throughout the European Middle Ages, and if a text is associated with a church or a secular school, there is a strong likelihood that it was used for its pupils. The fact that the extant translations are often in extremely stilted, even pretentious, English has helped to disguise the true nature of these works. Moreover, the little excerpts of medieval Latin published for Latin students in textbooks such as *Fons Perennis* tend to lead to the conclusion that medieval Latin is a simple language—thus a simple text is just as likely to be for adults as for children. But in actuality medieval Latin comes in a wide variety of styles and complexities. It has its Dr. Seusses, Virginia Woolfs, and James Joyces, just as other languages do. If a text is short and in very simple Latin, it is proper to ask why this is so. What evidence exists that it is written for semiliterate adults as opposed to children learning how to read? Is there, for example, a more difficult, perhaps more "adult" version extant?

If we wish to certify such texts as children's literature, however, we must examine their use of language, the local meaning of terms such as *infans* (infant or child), *puer* (boy), and *puella* (girl), the literary and legal evidence for what constituted a child at that time, location, and situation, other possible audiences, and the textual criteria that I mentioned at the beginning of this section. All of these matters, one might object, are just old-fashioned philology and not a legitimate literary pursuit. But philology is no longer old-fashioned; the "new philology," according to Leah Marcus, constitutes the new frontier of modern literary studies (*Renaissance* 22–30, passim).[19] What the new philological approaches add to the old philology is a greater interest in and ease with textual instability in its material context, just as new historicism has brought a special appreciation of literary works within their cultural context. Such methodologies should help us strip away as much as possible our preconceptions, in this case of what a child and children's literature *ought* to be, and take a look at what fiction was actually written for children and what they actually read. It is a good bet that the works that I have cited above were both valued and enjoyed, because if such had not been the case, the costly material on which they were written would have been erased and used again.

I hope that younger scholars who do not suffer from misconceptions about children as unloved and as miniature adults or participate in the presentism of earlier critics will join me in the exciting search for medieval children's literature. We need fresh eyes, better scholarship, more lively translations, and new children's books reworking the old texts. In addition, I hope to begin a process whereby the many books and articles about children's literature that are operating on incorrect assumptions or that are simply wrong will be changed in subsequent editions. We also need to avoid in the future theoretical constructs built on inaccurate information such as Zohar Shavit's attempt at a historical model for the development of children's literature.

And finally, I hope to counter the current wave of ahistoricism among some children's literature scholars. They seem blind to the fact that, like readers at the end of the Middle Ages, we face a radical transformation in both the way that words are transmitted and, according to some observers, the way that children are constructed (see Cunningham 179–90). At the children's literature conference in Charlotte in 1996, a critic with a distinguished publication record asked me why the existence or nonexistence of medieval children's literature should matter. "It is so long ago," he said. Peter Hunt has written several pieces recently along similar lines; for example, in his column "Passing on the Past: The Problem of Books That Are for Children and That Were for Children," he distinguishes between "live" books and "dead" books, which he claims concern no one except historians. He challenges the view that all books for children are connected and that "we in the present can learn from the past about books and children" (200). Although Hunt claims that "different skills" are required to read books from earlier periods (202), no different skills are needed for the imaginative works that I have mentioned when they are well translated.

Moreover, such works are not "dead." I would argue, on the contrary, that, with the exception of Hrotswitha and apart from the nonfiction, most of the material in the texts that I cite in the last part of this essay is an integral part of "the sea of stories" and continues to be found in the modern period in works now generally agreed to be children's literature. The *Ecbasis Captivi* and the *Ysengrimus* were discovered and copied by Jacob Grimm in the Bibliothèque Nationale during his researches there in the 1830s; material from them is alive today in various versions of Reynard the Fox and in some of Joel Chandler Harris's Uncle Remus stories. At the same time, Grimm copied shorter medieval texts that he included in his *Kinder- und Hausmärchen* and that are now classed as fairy tales (for example, in the Jack Zipes translation, nos. 73 and 146). Grimm could recognize a fine story when he saw one, and some of the originals he transcribed continue to be a good read. We need to recognize similar medieval narratives, plays, and poems for what they originally were: fictions provided to children, most probably initially for educational purposes. But they are a far cry from *Fun with Dick and Jane.* They are children's literature.

Notes

1. For the semiliterate adult–child equation see, among others, Ruth Bottigheimer's "The Child-Reader of Children's Bibles" (45). Children's literature is not a tidy genre: the boundary between it and adult literature is indeterminate, as the Perry Nodelman–Michael Steig exchange in the *Children's Literature Association Quarterly* (spring 1993) makes clear. All children's literature is shared with adults (if only parents and teachers) to a greater or lesser degree; some works read by children remain popular with adults; some adult literature has become children's literature (often in special versions for them); some literature is marketed simultaneously to adults and to children with the same text presented in different formats (see Sandra Beckett) or with a different target audience in another country (*Watership Down*); a work marketed as children's literature may be claimed by adults (*The Adventures of Huckleberry Finn*); some children's literature is "cross-written" (see the 1997 special volume of *Children's Literature*); some authors claim that they let their editors decide whether their work is for children or for adults; and even picture books, once thought to be for children only, are now enjoyed by and used for teaching young adults and adults. For the purposes of this essay, I am defining children's literature as texts that, on the basis of internal or external evidence, are written with a child audience in mind or for which a child audience actually existed.

2. Readers of the international journal *Bookbird: World of Children's Books* and its reports on the state of children's literature in non-Western countries are familiar with the often striking differences between Western and non-Western constructions of children and the impact of these differences on the literature to which those who are literate are exposed. Rosamond McKitterick notes the similarities between the situation of the medieval Carolingians and that of contemporary multilingual countries seeking to develop a literature apart from that of their former English or French colonizers (*Carolingians* passim).

3. Also important are the first chapter of new historicist Leah Marcus's *Childhood and Cultural Despair* (1978), Linda Pollock's *Forgotten Children* (1983), and most recently, the first two chapters of James A. Schultz's *The Knowledge of Childhood in the German Middle Ages* (1995). The bibliographies and footnotes of these works cite numerous studies in learned journals critiquing Ariès's theories, however much their interests and conclusions may differ. Talbot offers tantalizing leads to potential children's literature, but his references are so sketchy that it is impossible to follow them up. Shahar concentrates on the central and late Middle Ages (roughly from the twelfth century on) and devotes the second half of her book to education in "the second stage" (*pueritia*), roughly ages seven to fourteen. Although Hanawalt occasionally draws in material from other countries and periods, she divides her book according to the stages of childhood and provides a picture of each stage on the basis of evidence found in court records, wills, and other archival, as well as literary, sources from fourteenth- and fifteenth-century London. Schultz bases his study on the way aristocratic children are portrayed in Middle High German texts by poets who sought to please the German aristocracy and would thus be conservative in their views; he is closer to Ariès, concluding that these children are viewed as separate from adults but "deficient" and that their attempts to play adult roles are deemed inadequate. There is a split between scholars who emphasize the biological (nature) and those who emphasize the cultural (nurture); for example, Schultz criticizes Shahar's book for its "confident sentimentality" and the too-easy identification of medieval with modern children (6). Neverthe-

less, Schultz agrees that medieval society saw childhood as a separate stage and that medieval children were loved.

4. I mention Nodelman's book in particular, although there are many similar examples, because it is arguably the best of the general books likely to be used by students and graduate students in children's literature studies. Roderick McGillis in *The Nimble Reader* (1996) is more judicious: "As nearly all the handbooks and histories of children's literature state, literature for children as we know it—a distinct body of works written and published for the edification and enjoyment of children—only came into being in an organized way in the eighteenth century" (52). But McGillis, like many others, is by implication defining children's literature in terms of its commodification; the idea that its very existence as a separate entity is tied to commercial interests was pointed out by Francelia Butler long ago in her introduction to *Children's Literature 1.* Nevertheless, the researches of scholars such as Gillian Avery and Margaret Kinnell into the children's literature of the early modern period in England have already established the existence of "a distinct body of works" prior to the eighteenth century. German scholars have pushed even further back, as Theodor Brüggemann and Otto Brunken's bibliography of 484 books and broadsides intended for children with accompanying essays and commentary demonstrates; it begins with Ulrich Boner's 1461 *Der Edelstein.*

5. Jane Bingham and Grayce Scholt's annotated bibliography, limited to England, includes works for adults by Boethius, Bede, Geoffrey of Monmouth, and others, appropriated in whole or in part, they argue, for children. Among such works they list *Beowulf,* which, according to David Howlett, was originally children's literature: "I see *Beowulf* as Boethius for babies, teaching the young king [Aethelstan] how to behave in a time of extreme danger. . . . But the establishment will resist the idea that the national epic was written for a little boy" (qtd. Dugdale 51).

6. For example, in his essay on *Aesopica,* Robert G. Miner Jr. claims that "none of these editions [of Aesop] were for children (children, of course, were not invented until the seventeenth century)" (10). That fables and fable collections were associated with children throughout the classical and medieval periods is well known. For a recent discussion of the use of fable texts in the education of children during that time span see Jan M. Ziolkowski's *Talking Animals* (21–24). For Caxton's *Aesop* and later fable versions see the special issue of the *Children's Literature Association Quarterly* 9, no. 2 (Summer 1994).

7. For an introduction to the topic of Jewish literacy see Stefan Reif, particularly 149–55. For those with the linguistic skills, the topic of medieval Jewish children and any material that may have been written for them would be a rich, and apparently uninvestigated, field.

8. McKitterick claims that an esteem for books and their contents—and a literacy level much higher than originally thought for the laity as well as the church—are as characteristic of the so-called Dark Ages as the High Middle Ages; see particularly her *Carolingians and the Written Word.* William McMunn also argues for a higher literacy rate than was once thought ("Literacy"). In her fourth chapter, "The Production and Possession of Books," McKitterick details the high cost of the many skins, the binding, and the pigments used for an illuminated book (*Carolingians*).

9. Reynolds emphasizes that even at this early stage, learning to read is learning to read in a foreign language, Latin, and it is the Latin pronunciation of the alphabet that is learned. McKitterick argues, however, that in the Frankish regions, through the Carolingian period and even extending beyond it, students were learning the learned version of their own language (perhaps on the order of standard English and "ebonics"); this practice was even more widespread in Spain and Italy (*Carolingians* passim).

10. McKitterick notes the shortcomings for elementary educational purposes of the

original "Donatus" (by a fourth-century Roman grammarian), which dealt only with the parts of speech. She discusses some of the additions, variants, and substitutes made for it, even as early as the Carolingian period, in order to meet local needs (*Carolingians* 13–20).

11. The short phrases at the beginning commence with *Itaque deo supplica* [And so pray to God], *Parentes ama* [Love your parents], and *cognatos cole* [honor your relatives] (i, nos. 1–3). The longer couplets in the second section are along the lines of *Plus vigila semper nec somno deditus esto / nam diuturna quies vitiis alimenta ministrat* [Always devote yourself more to waking than sleeping / since long repose gives nourishment to the vices] (ii, no. 2). Jonathan Nicholls comments that "such was the popularity of the original idea that, in translation and paraphrase, [Cato] reached an enormous public in every country in Europe" (64). The distichs were still popular enough in the early modern period for Benedict Burgh's fifteenth-century English paraphrase to be one of Caxton's earlier productions, *Cato,* in 1477; it went into a second edition within a year and a third in 1481 (Childs 176). For the most accessible original and translation see [Cato]. After the second half of the twelfth century the anonymous *Facetus,* "a disorganized collection of precepts that dealt with moral welfare, points of etiquette, and semi-proverbial wisdom," is often found together with the distichs (Nicholls 182).

12. For the many shifts in the upper-division classical curriculum in the medieval period, see Ernst Robert Curtius's chapter "Curriculum Authors" (48–54). He notes that "medieval reverence for the *auctores* was so great that every source [of their texts] was held to be good. The historical and the critical sense were both lacking" (52).

13. Ziolkowski provides a detailed analysis of this poem (48–53). Alcuin spent the first half of his adult life in York and was head of the cathedral school there. At the International Research Society for Children's Literature conference at York in August 1997 I presented a paper on Alcuin and his writing for children in which I argued that his poem was an example of a work "cross-written" for a dual audience of children and adults.

14. It is a shame that Zeydel's English translation of the *Ecbasis Captivi* is so unreadable; for an analysis that emphasizes the work's religious symbolism and connection to Easter, see Ziolkwoski 153–197. Mann's prose translation of the *Ysengrimus,* on the other hand, is clear and direct and has excellent notes. For the most recent work on medieval animal literature in general see Ziolkowski's authoritative book, which is sensitive throughout to the possibility of a child audience and mentions when the works he addresses are bound with school texts.

15. Hrotswitha has not been well served by the English translations, which obscure the vividness and immediacy of her text. The two most recent ones I have seen, by Larissa Bonfante (1979) and Katharina Wilson (1989), are no exception; Bonfante's is slightly preferable.

16. I presented a paper on this text, "A Medieval Storybook: The Urban Tales of Petrus Alfonsi," at the Children's Literature Association Conference in Omaha, Nebraska, in June 1997.

17. The original audience for *Dolopathos* is not easily specified because there is only one manuscript from a time (about 1200) and location close to the author; the other five that the editor Alfons Hilka cites are from the fifteenth century (vii–x). There are also later vernacular variants. Although it is dedicated to Bertrand, the bishop of Metz, I believe that this work had a youthful audience. The framing story is a rousing account of how a fourteen-year-old pagan, Lucinius, is saved from the lust of his wicked stepmother and from being burned to death by a series of tales told by seven wise men; the secular frame concludes with a tedious account of Lucinius's conversion to Christianity later in life, added no doubt to get the bishop's approval. *Dolopathos* has been well translated by Brady B. Gilleland and is an excellent read.

18. For a detailed description of each of these medieval courtesy books in Latin,

Anglo-Norman, and English with all known texts and preferred editions, see Nicholls, Appendix B (179–97).

19. The introductory chapter to Marcus's study of problematic early modern texts, *Unediting the Renaissance,* applies to critical approaches to literary works of all periods and should be required reading for graduate students who plan to deal with the material text as a network or force field linked to a wider historical and cultural matrix.

Works Cited

Adams, Gillian. "The First Children's Literature? The Case for Sumer." *Children's Literature* 14 (1986): 1–30.

Alfonsi, Petrus. *Die Disciplina Clericalis des Petrus Alfonsi (das älteste Novellenbuch des Mittelalters).* Ed. Alfons Hilka and Werner Söderhjelm. Shorter edition. Heidelberg: Carl Winter, 1911. Trans. Joseph Ramon Jones and John Esten Keller as *The Scholar's Guide: A Translation of the Twelfth-Century Disciplina Clericalis of Pedro Alfonso.* Toronto: Pontifical Institute, 1969, and P. R. Quarrie as *The Disciplina Clericalis of Petrus Alfonsi.* Berkeley: University of California Press, 1977.

Alta Silva, Johannes de. *Dolopathos sive De rege et septem sapientibus.* Ed. Alfons Hilka. Heidelberg: Carl Winter, 1913. Trans. Brady B. Gilleland. *Johannes de Alta Silva: Dolopathos, or The King and the Seven Wise Men.* Binghamton, N.Y.: Center for Medieval and Early Renaissance Studies, 1981.

Ariès, Philippe. *Centuries of Childhood: A Social History of Family Life.* 1960. Trans. Robert Baldick. New York: Vintage, 1962.

Beckett, Sandra. "Crosswriting Child and Adult: Henri Bosco's *L'Enfant et la rivière.*" *Children's Literature Association Quarterly* 21, no. 4 (winter 1996–97): 189–99.

Beeson, Charles H. *A Primer of Medieval Latin: An Anthology of Prose and Poetry.* Chicago: Scott, Foresman, 1925.

Berlioz, Jacques. "Un Petit chaperon rouge médiéval? 'La petite fille épargnée par les loups' dans la *Fecunda ratis* d'Egbert de Liège (début du XIe siècle)." *Merveilles & Contes* 55 no. 2 (December 1991): 246–63.

Bingham, Jane, and Grayce Scholt. *Fifteen Centuries of Children's Literature: An Annotated Chronology of British and American Works in Historical Context.* Westport, Conn.: Greenwood, 1980.

Boswell, John. *The Kindness of Strangers.* 1988. New York: Vintage, 1990.

Bottigheimer, Ruth B. *The Bible for Children: From the Age of Gutenberg to the Present.* New Haven: Yale University Press, 1996.

———. "The Child-Reader of Children's Bibles, 1656–1753." In *Infant Tongues: The Voice of the Child in Children's Literature.* Ed. Elizabeth Goodenough et al. Detroit: Wayne State University Press, 1994. Pp. 44–56.

———. Letter to the author. 25 February 1997.

Brockman, Bennett A. "Children and Literature in Late Medieval England." *Children's Literature* 4 (1975):58–63.

———. "The Juvenile Audiences of Sir Orfeo." *Children's Literature Association Quarterly* 10, no. 1 (Spring 1985):18–20.

———. "Medieval Songs of Innocence and Experience." *Children's Literature* 2 (1973): 40–49.

———. "Robin Hood and the Invention of Children's Literature." *Children's Literature* 10 (1982):1–17.

Brüggemann, Theodor, with Otto Brunken. *Handbuch zur Kinder- und Jugendliteratur vom Beginn des Buchdrucks bis 1570.* Stuttgart: Metzler, 1987.

Butler, Francelia. "From the Editor's High Chair." *Children's Literature* 1 (1972): 7–8.

[Cato]. " 'Dicta Catonis': Introduction to *Disticha.* Text." In *Minor Latin Poets* vol. 2. Ed.

and trans. J. Wight Duff and Arnold M. Duff. 1934. Loeb Classical Library. 1982. Pp. 585–621.

Childs, Edmund. *William Caxton: A Portrait in a Background.* London: Northwood, 1976.

Comestor, Petrus. *Historia Scholastica Excellens Opus. Editio altera post Beneventam anni MDCIC. Accessit Index locupletissimus.* Venice: Antonius Bortolus, 1729.

Cunningham, Hugh. *Children and Childhood in Western Society Since 1500.* London and New York: Longman, 1995.

Curtius, Ernst Robert. *European Literature and the Latin Middle Ages.* 1948. Trans. Willard Trask. Bollingen Series no. 36. New York: Pantheon, 1953.

Darton, Harvey F. J. *Children's Books in England.* 1932. 3d rev. ed. Ed. Brian Alderson. Cambridge: Cambridge University Press, 1982.

Demers, Patricia. *Heaven upon Earth: The Form of Moral and Religious Children's Literature, to 1850.* Knoxville: University of Tennessee Press, 1993.

Demers, Patricia, and Gordon Moyles. *From Instruction to Delight: An Anthology of Children's Literature to 1850.* Toronto: Oxford University Press, 1982.

Dhuoda. *A Handbook for William: A Carolingian Woman's Counsel for Her Son.* Trans. Carol Neel. Regents Studies in Medieval Culture. Lincoln: University of Nebraska Press, 1991.

Dugdale, John. "Who's Afraid of *Beowulf*?" *The New Yorker,* 23 and 30 December 1996, 50–51.

Ecbasis Cuiusdam Captivi per Tropologiam (*Escape of a Certain Captive Told in a Figurative Manner: An Eleventh-Century Beast Epic*). Ed. and trans. Edwin H. Zeydel. University of North Carolina Studies in the Germanic Languages and Literatures 46. Chapel Hill: University of North Carolina Press, 1964.

Egbert of Liège. *Fecunda ratis Egberts von Lüttich.* Ed. Ernst Voigt. Halle: Max Niemeyer, 1889.

Gordon, E. V., ed. *Pearl.* 1953. Oxford: Clarendon, 1974.

Grimm, Jacob, and Wilhelm Grimm. *The Complete Fairy Tales of the Brothers Grimm.* 1812–1857. Trans. and with an introduction by Jack Zipes. New York: Bantam, 1987.

Hanawalt, Barbara A. *Growing up in Medieval London: The Experience of Childhood in History.* New York: Oxford University Press, 1993.

Hanks, D. Thomas, Jr. "Not for Adults Only: The English Corpus Christi Plays." *Children's Literature Association Quarterly* 10, no. 1 (Spring 1985):21–22.

Hildebrand, Ann M. "Jean de Brunhoff's Advice to Youth: The *Babar* Books as Books of Courtesy." *Children's Literature* 11 (1983):76–95.

Horace. *Satires, Epistles, and Ars Poetica,* with English trans. by H. Rushton Fairclough. Loeb Classical Library. 1926. Revised 1929.

Hrotswitha of Gandersheim. *The Plays of Hrotsvit of Gandersheim.* Trans. Katharina Wilson. Garland Library of Medieval Literature 62, Series B. New York: Garland, 1989.

———. *The Plays of Hrotswitha of Gandersheim.* Trans. Larissa Bonfante. New York: New York University Press, 1979.

Hunt, Peter. "Passing on the Past: The Problem of Books That Are for Children and That Were for Children." *Children's Literature Association Quarterly* 21, no. 4 (Winter 1996–97):200–202.

Hunt, Tony. *Teaching and Learning Latin in 13th-Century England.* Vol. 1, *Texts.* Cambridge, U.K.: Brewer, 1991.

Jambeck, Thomas J., and Karen K. Jambeck. "Chaucer's *Treatise on the Astrolabe:* A Handbook for the Medieval Child." *Children's Literature* 3 (1974):117–22.

Lontzen, Günter. "Das Gedicht 'De Puella A Lupellis Servata' von Egbert von Lüttich —eine Parabel zum Thema der Taufe." *Merveilles & Contes* 6, no. 1 (May 1992):20–44.

Marcus, Leah Sinanoglou. *Childhood and Cultural Despair: A Theme and Variation in Seventeenth-Century Literature.* Pittsburgh: University of Pittsburgh Press, 1978.

———. *Unediting the Renaissance: Shakespeare, Marlowe, Milton.* London and New York: Routledge, 1996.

McGillis, Roderick. *The Nimble Reader: Literary Theory and Children's Literature.* New York: Twayne, 1996.

McKitterick, Rosamond. *The Carolingians and the Written Word.* Cambridge: Cambridge University Press, 1989.

———. "A Ninth-Century Schoolbook from the Loire Valley: Phillipps MS 16308." In *Books, Scribes, and Learning in the Frankish Kingdoms, 6th–9th Centuries.* Aldershot: Variorum, 1994. Essay 9 (225–31).

———. "Nuns' Scriptoria in England and Francia in the Eighth Century." In *Books, Scribes, and Learning in the Frankish Kingdoms, 6th–9th Centuries.* Aldershot: Variorum, 1994. Essay 7 (1–35).

———, ed. *The Uses of Literacy in Early Medieval Europe.* Cambridge: Cambridge University Press, 1990.

McMunn, Meradith Tilbury. "Children and Literature in Medieval France." *Children's Literature* 4 (1975):51–58.

McMunn, Meradith Tilbury, and William Robert McMunn. "Children's Literature in the Middle Ages." *Children's Literature* 1 (1972):21–29.

McMunn, William Robert. "The Literacy of Medieval Children." *Children's Literature* 4 (1975):36–41.

Miner, Robert G., Jr. "Aesop as Litmus: The Acid Test of Children's Literature." *Children's Literature* 1 (1972):9–15.

Morris, Sidney. *Fons Perennis: An Anthology of Medieval Latin for Schools.* London: Harrap, 1962.

Myers, Mitzi. "Wise Child, Wise Peasant, Wise Guy: Geoffrey Summerfield's Case Against the Eighteenth Century." *Children's Literature Association Quarterly* 12, no. 2 (Summer 1987):107–10.

Nicholls, Jonathan. *The Matter of Courtesy: Medieval Courtesy Books and the Gawain-Poet.* Woodbridge, Suffolk: D. S. Brewer, 1985.

Nikolajeva, Maria, ed. *Aspects and Issues in the History of Children's Literature.* Contributions to the Study of World Literature 60. Westport, Conn. and London: Greenwood, 1995.

[Nivardus]. *Ysengrimus.* Ed. and trans. Jill Mann. Mittellateinische Studien und Texte 12. Leiden: Brill, 1987.

Nodelman, Perry. "The Other: Orientalism, Colonialism, and Children's Literature." *Children's Literature Association Quarterly* 17.1 (Spring 1992):29–35.

———. *The Pleasures of Children's Literature.* 1992. Rev. ed. White Plains, N.Y.: Longman, 1996.

———, ed. "Literary Theory and Children's Literature." *Children's Literature Association Quarterly* 18.1 (Spring 1993):36–46.

Perry, Ben Edwin. *Babrius and Phaedrus.* Newly Edited and Translated into English, Together with an Historical Introduction and a Comprehensive Survey of Greek and Latin Fables in the Aesopic Tradition. Loeb Classical Library. 1965.

Pollock, Linda A. *Forgotten Children: Parent-Child Relations from 1500 to 1900.* Cambridge: Cambridge University Press, 1983.

Reif, Stefan C. "Aspects of Medieval Jewish Literacy." In *The Uses of Literacy in the Early Medieval Period.* Cambridge: Cambridge University Press, 1990. Pp. 134–55.

Reynolds, Suzanne. *Medieval Reading: Grammar, Rhetoric and the Classical Text.* Cambridge: Cambridge University Press, 1996.

Riggio, Milla B. "The Schooling of the Poet: Christian Influences and Latin Rhetoric in the Early Middle Ages." *Children's Literature* 4 (1975):44–51.

Rouse, R. H., and M. A. Rouse. "The Vocabulary of Wax Tablets." *Harvard Library Bulletin* n.s., 1.3 (Fall 1990):2–19.

Schultz, James A. *The Knowledge of Childhood in the German Middle Ages, 1100–1350.* Philadelphia: University of Pennsylvania Press, 1995.

Shahar, Shulamith. *Childhood in the Middle Ages.* 1990. London and New York: Routledge, 1992.

Shaner, Mary. "Instruction and Delight: Medieval Romances as Children's Literature." *Poetics Today* 31 (1992):5–15.

Shavit, Zohar. "The Historical Model of the Development of Children's Literature." In *Aspects and Issues in the History of Children's Literature.* Contributions to the Study of World Literature 60. Westport, Conn. and London: Greenwood, 1995. Pp. 27–38.

Smith, Elva Sophronia. *The History of Children's Literature: A Syllabus with Selected Bibliographies.* 1937. Rev. ed. Ed. Margaret Hodges and Susan Stein. Chicago: American Library Association, 1980.

Spiegel, Harriet. "Instructing the Children: Advice from the Twelfth-Century *Fables* of Marie of France." *Children's Literature* 17 (1989):25–46.

Talbot, C. H. "Children in the Middle Ages." *Children's Literature* 6 (1977):17–33.

Victor, Claudius Marius. *Alethia.* Ed. C. Schenkl. *Corpus Scriptorum Ecclesiasticorum Latinorum* 16. Vienna, 1888.

Wright, Thomas, ed. *The Book of the Knight of La Tour-Landry: Compiled for the Instruction of His Daughters.* Early English Text Society orig. ser. 33, 1906. London: Kegan Paul, 1968.

Ziolkowski, Jan M. *Talking Animals: Medieval Latin Beast Poetry, 750–1150.* Philadelphia: University of Pennsylvania Press, 1993.

Coleridge's Poetry in the Hands of Schoolchildren

Jeanie Watson

Nineteenth-century England saw a proliferation of poetry written specifically for children. At the same time, "main line" poetry—that is, work written by poets acknowledged as the best in the language and written primarily for an adult audience—routinely was presented to children, under the assumption that the best English poets either had children in mind as a part of their general audience or wrote about subjects in which children would have some natural interest.[1]

School texts, in particular, sought to introduce children, from the youngest ages, to poetry that would prepare them for later, more mature appreciation and indeed for a life of moral self-reflection and right action. To this purpose, the poetry of Samuel Taylor Coleridge answered admirably. In his preface to *Lyra Heroica: A Book of Verse for Boys* (1892), which includes Coleridge's "Kubla Khan," along with works by Shakespeare, Milton, Dryden, Tennyson, and others, editor William Ernest Henley states: "My purpose has been to choose and sheave a certain number of those achievements in verse which, as expressing the simpler sentiments and the more elemental emotions, might fitly be addressed to such boys—and men, for that matter—as are privileged to use our noble English tongue." As the critic William Walsh implies, Coleridge would have agreed with Henley's approach:

> If education is to become what Coleridge thought it to be . . . it must become an inquiry, active and intimately personal, devoted to the interrogation of self, to all that is grounded in the self, and to that transformation of self hoped for in learning. In this inquiry only those questions should be posed which are pointed, revealing and important. And these will be found to be those which have excited and been framed by the best minds of any age. . . . To ask that education should aim at self-knowledge by the method of reflection is to require it to be . . . a mode of liberal education. . . . Throughout his writings Coleridge insists that an essential means of reflective self-knowledge—and an unsur-

Children's Literature 26, ed. Elizabeth Lennox Keyser (Yale University Press, © 1998 Hollins College).

passed educative agency—is an active analysis of language, and especially an interrogation of the texts of great writers. (172–73)

By the late nineteenth century, poetry school texts were easily distinguished from poetry anthologies meant for reading in the home.[2] Poems in school texts were chosen for their appropriateness to various grade levels, so series were divided into elementary, middle, and higher-level texts. A. Watson Bain, in his preface to *Poetry for the Young: A Graduated Collection in Four Parts* (1883), explains, "The childish delight in rhyme has to pass through many phases before it finally ripens into the mature love of poetry, and the verse which meets the requirements of one phase is either too simple or too difficult for another."[3]

Choosing poetry written by the best poets in the English language that is most appropriate for specific ages and grade levels is not necessarily an unambiguous task, and placement of particular poems could vary from editor to editor. One might favor progression from simple to complex poetry. For example, M. A. Woods, in his preface to *A First School Poetry Book* (1886), compiled for children aged seven through ten or eleven, states:

> My apology for adding another school poetry book to the many in existence must be the usual one, that I have found nothing quite suited to my purpose. The best are too ambitious, or, at least, contain too much that is difficult, to be really fitted for little children fresh from the nursery or kindergarten, craving food, but quite unable to assimilate strong meat. It may be a mistake to "write down" to them, but it is, I think, a still greater mistake to force good things upon them prematurely, and so create a disgust which it is difficult, in after years, to remove. Poetry intended for their use should appeal to their childish fancies, their fondness for flowers and animals, their delight in story, their mingled love of sentiment and fun. It should be simple in form, and simple in what I may call outward meaning. Some of it will unfold deeper meanings as the years go on.[4]

Other editors, however (for instance, Percival Chubb, discussed below), while agreeing to the progressive developmental understanding of children, also emphasized that the same poetry may be usefully presented several times to children, since their appreciation and understanding will grow as they mature. Complete comprehension is not necessary for enjoyment. The best poetry can be read at different levels by readers of different ages; therefore, repeated readings yield new insight and enriched pleasure. The mysterious fairy-tale quality or the sense of danger and adventure that appeals to youthful readers of "The Rime of the Ancient Mariner," for example, will continue to give pleasure but be augmented by moral and ethical considerations on the part of an adult reader. Thus, particular poems tended to move from one age classification to another or be included in more than one level, according to the view of the editor.

Another distinguishing feature of poetry school texts in the late nineteenth century is that they began to *look* like schoolbooks, that is, like material to be explained and studied. Additionally, since a child's attention tends to wander, school texts had to encourage sustained attention. Pictures not only focus attention and sustain interest, they also stimulate the imagination and invite response, so poems in school texts often were illustrated. Length and reading difficulty were also considerations. Shorter works that include narrative or concrete detail are more appealing to children than poems that are long or abstract or complex. Thus, texts for younger children often used only excerpts from longer poems. With the institutionalizing of poetry teaching came the now-familiar secondary apparatus of notes and other pedagogical materials. Student texts were accompanied by a "teacher's book"; and the poetry texts themselves included general introductory material, biographical introductions to authors, commentary on individual poems, notes, questions for study, and appendices.[5]

School texts gave children access to, and a sound understanding of, English poetry. They also helped to form children's attitudes about the function of poetry and about particular poets and their works. Coleridge is one of the poets represented in schoolbooks by a small number of works: simple prayers and moral examples, often excerpted from longer works, and a few great and immediately recognizable "mystery" poems, "Kubla Khan" and "The Rime of the Ancient Mariner," in particular. As the tide of opinion in the late nineteenth and early twentieth century gradually turned away from the overly didactic and moralistic toward works that instill a moral stance through the development of the imagination, Coleridge's poetry was thought to be an especially appropriate choice for children's reading and study. He continued to be one of the major poets most frequently included in the canon of poetry for children.

Appropriate Poems

Coleridge's mystery poems—"The Rime of the Ancient Mariner," "Kubla Khan," and "Christabel"—stand as the poet's crowning achievement. How, then, do they fare in school texts? The "Rime" and "Kubla Khan" prove to be particularly popular; "Christabel" is a more ambivalent case. Percival Chubb, principal of the high school department of the Ethical Culture Schools in New York and author of *The Teaching of English in the Elementary and Secondary School* (1902), writes that the book is "a plea for unity and continuity in the English course from its beginnings in the kindergarten up through the high school. All the leading principles governing the study of English are, in the author's view, present in the earliest stages of English teaching, emerging into greater definiteness as the pupil advances in intellectual power and practical skill" (vii). In his chapter "Reading in the Grammar Grades," Chubb notes that " 'The Ancient Mariner' . . . may be taken at any point between the fifth and the twelfth school year. It may be taken early and be repeated with advantage in the High School, to the delight of the maturer students, by whom its deeper meanings and richer music may now be appreciated" (147).

Although W. J. Alexander sees the "Rime" as especially appropriate for children, he does not find it as thematically complex as Chubb does. Instead, he confines the poem's significance to its aesthetic appeal and its place within the gothic tradition. In his preface to *Select Poems from Coleridge and Tennyson,* he writes:

> Now, the theme of *The Ancient Mariner* is like the theme of a fairy tale,—so remote in its incidents from reality, that it appeals but little to our sense of truth, and cannot intensely excite our emotional nature. Hence to those who lack the special ear for the essentially poetical, this poem is likely to seem trivial; whilst those, who [in] spite of the little value they are disposed consciously to put upon artistic charm, are yet captivated by the beauty of this poem, often seeking to justify their preference by alleging the existence of an allegorical meaning or a moral lesson. Such attempts to force a deeper significance upon *The Ancient Mariner,* are really destructive of its main strength, which is aesthetic, and lies in its artistic consistency and unity. . . . Fundamentally, then, this poem is a story addressed to the universal taste for the marvelous and weird, strongest in children and in

> the primitive stages of society, yet inherent, though it may be overlaid, in more mature minds and more enlightened ages. (vii)

Interestingly, Alexander also notes Coleridge's response to Mrs. Barbauld's complaint that the "Rime" has no moral—evidence contrary to his own position: "Mrs. Barbauld told me that the only faults she found with the Ancient Mariner were—that it was improbable, and had no moral. As for the probability—to be sure that might admit some question—but I told her that in my judgement the chief fault of the poem was that it had too much moral, and that too openly intruded on the reader" (*Table Talk,* 31 March 1832).[6]

Although Alexander remains more disinclined to advocate the study of deeper, perhaps allegorical, meanings than Chubb, they agree on the value of introducing poetry of superior artistic merit to children in the schools, and the appeal for children of a "mystery" poem such as the "Rime" is obvious to them both. The advantages of using poetry that has such immediate sensory and emotional appeal in order to stimulate creative thought in students are made explicit in the preface on Coleridge in *The Ancient Mariner, Kubla Khan, Christabel* (1898), edited by Tuley F. Huntington:

> By putting into this little volume the "Ancient Mariner," "Kubla Khan," and "Christabel," I have thought to make easily accessible to students of secondary schools the perfect flower of Coleridge's genius. The study of these three poems, if properly directed, should stir the imagination and foster the appreciation of poetic excellence. . . . Everywhere the aim has been to stimulate, rather than to supersede, thought. The numerous references given throughout the book are intended to aid the teacher in bringing to his class additional material; for there is every reason why such a poem as "The Ancient Mariner" should be carefully studied. Mere hasty reading, in fact, will reveal to the ordinary student very little of the wealth of imagination with which it is pervaded. (vii–viii)

Huntington's inclusion of both the "Rime" and "Kubla Khan" in the volume brings no surprise; "Christabel," however, deserves comment. "Christabel" is the least represented of the three mystery poems in both poetry anthologies and school texts. At one level, this seems curious. Like the "Rime"—and certainly more than "Kubla Khan"—the poem has immediate appeal by virtue of its narrative.

The central character, a young girl, is one with whom children can identify more readily than with a rather frightening ancient man or an Eastern potentate. And if the gothic elements—and more specifically, the fairy elements—are strong in the "Rime," they are at least as prominent in "Christabel."[7] Nonetheless, despite its unsurpassed "weird mystery," the poem (except for the excerpts on "broken friendship") has had a hard time securing a place in poetry books compiled explicitly for children. According to J. F. Macdonald, "*The Ancient Mariner* is unquestionably the greatest ballad in the language. *Christabel,* which rivals it in melody and picturesqueness and even surpasses it in weird mystery, was left unfinished. Only Coleridge, if even he, could have given it an ending that would not lower the effect of the two opening parts. *The Ancient Mariner* has no similar defect; it stands a rounded, perfect work of art" (113). Macdonald himself includes the "Rime" but not "Christabel." Part of the cause for "Christabel"'s exclusion may be length, part its unfinished state, part its initial ambivalent critical reception. I tend to think, however, that the primary factor is related to the psychological discomfort with which some adult readers respond to the sexual—and more specifically, lesbian—encounter at the center of the poem. An excerpt from "Christabel" on broken friendship may contain a moral appropriate for children's reading, but the entire poem seems quite another matter. The quality of the poetry is not at issue; the content is.

A letter held by the University of Toronto Coleridge Collection gives an interesting perspective, not only on the discomfort of some readers of "Christabel"—shown most effectively by their reluctance to be specific about the nature of their objection to the inclusion of "Christabel" in the school curriculum—but also on the careful, deliberate process by which particular poems made their way into the accepted educational canon of children's poetry. In 1885, Sir William Mulock, who evidently chaired the curriculum committee in Ontario that recommended "Christabel" for inclusion in the high-school curriculum, writes in response to the strong reservations raised by E. W. Ross about the inclusion of the poem:

> My Dear Ross
> I am in receipt of your letter of yesterday informing me that you understand that Christabel is objected to in certain quarters and suggesting that "Hymn" before Sunrise, In the Vale of Chamouni or some other of Coleridge's works should be substituted for

Christabel. I was a member of the committee that recommended Christabel which recommendation was made after most mature deliberation. The Marmion trouble was referred to and sought to be avoided. Accordingly the committee moved with very great care and before the decision was come I carefully read the poem to satisfy myself as to its unobjectionable character. Other members of the committee declared themselves as familiar with the work, and finally it was recommended unanimously, the committee being of opinion that it was not only unobjectionable but a most desirable subject for study and examination. The committee's report was presented to the Senate ordered to be printed and a copy sent to every high school master in Ontario with a request that he would kindly offer to the senate any suggestions that he thought would be of service and pointedly requesting that any features in the recommendation that appeared to him objectionable should be pointed out before the Senate adopted the report. All these directions were carried out, and ample time was allowed for criticism. How much I cannot say but the records will show. Speaking from recollection I think that about two weeks intervened between the distribution of the report and its adoption by the Senate. Well it came up for adoption; and it was then found that not one high school master in Ontario had raised one objection to Christabel or offered any suggestion as to any other subject being put on [*sic*] its stead. In fact the whole report was so satisfactory to the Masters that several pleasing letters approving of the report were the only replies to our circular inviting criticism, with the exception of a couple of letters I think from the same person objecting to the subject prescribed in French and one letter pointing out some verbal errors. Thereupon the report came up for consideration and when we came to the subject of Christabel, both of the High School representatives approved of it as they had in committee, only one member of senate had a suggestion to make in regard to it, and that objection was not to the suitability of the work but for some unexplained reason he would like some other subject in lieu thereof. He did outpress his view and finally after the exercise of the utmost care the report was unanimously adopted, and, I may add that in view of what I have above stated, it had the unanimous approval of every high school master in Ontario in all its details with the single exception above mentioned. So far as I can see, no mistake has been made but if even now, if any serious objection exists, I am open to consider it and to remove it if possible, but I think you will appreciate with me that without more information as to the objection than that contained in your letter I would not be justified in directing the attention of the senate to the matter. I shall be only too glad to discuss the matter, in the utmost confidence, with any one of the objectors, or with you and if a change appears desirable will endeavor to bring about that change. With the verdict of approval of the High School masters in favor of Christabel it will be well to see that in trying to satisfy someone else, we do not avoid Scylla to fall into Charybdis. In any event, "The Hymn" would be a wholly insufficient substitute. It is not the practice nor would it be worthy of the University, to prescribe for examination, an author's minor efforts. I have written you fully, not from any disinclination to re-open the question but to satisfy you as to the course pursued and the evident consensus of opinion on the point. If the objectors still press their objections let them be pointed out and I will most cheerfully yield to any well-taken objection and endeavor to bring about such a change as will overcome all difficulty.

Yours sincerely,
W. Mulock

Even without Ross's letter to set next to Mulock's, two conclusions can be drawn. First, Ross's letter evidently contained little or no specific information as to the nature of the objections being raised to "Christabel." At the same time, the length, content, and tone of Mulock's letter all indicate that he has some sense of the nature of Ross's objection.

Mulock's tone borders on the defensively belligerent. He clearly feels he must vindicate his own opinion regarding "Christabel," while simultaneously establishing that the decision to recommend it was not his alone. In a manner much more protracted than the occasion of the inclusion of one poem in a high-school curriculum would call for, Mulock carefully details the decision process. He notes that he himself "carefully read the poem to satisfy [himself] as to its unobjectionable character." In addition, his own evaluation was corroborated by the opinions of "other members of the committee [who] declared themselves as familiar with the work" and recommended it "unanimously, the committee being of the opinion that it was not only unobjectionable but a most desirable subject for study and examination." With continuing detail, Mulock points out that "every high school master in Ontario" has approved the committee's report—"not one high school master in Ontario has raised one objection to Christabel or offered any suggestions as to any other subject being put on its stead"—and that the Senate has also approved it. The long staccato march of words is at once a defense and an attack. The highly charged phrase "unobjectionable character" raises the question of what kind of poetic character would be "objectionable," as well as drawing attention to the fact that Mulock had already considered—though he subsequently dismissed—the question of whether there was indeed something objectionable about "Christabel."

Whether Ross's letter called forth a latent uneasiness on Mulock's part, or an issue of professional pride and integrity is at stake, one fact is clear: "Christabel" is a better, more substantial poem than "The Hymn." Thus the suggestion to substitute "The Hymn" for "Christabel" constitutes a "dodge" of some sort on Ross's part, and Mulock has the right of literary evaluation on his side in his rejection of the substitution. The students of Ontario are, therefore, given the opportunity to cope with one of Coleridge's superior poems.[8]

Appropriate Poet

After selection of the poems themselves, along with their accompanying introductory comments and notes, the second most important factor in controlling the presentation of a particular poet and his or her work to an audience of schoolchildren is the biographical sketch of the author that usually introduces the poetry. While the editor almost always is careful to make the biographical information convey an appropriate moral lesson, the sketches are often amazingly blunt, as well as entertaining. School text biographies in fact constitute a distinct, though "thumbnail," subcategory in the genre of children's biographies. They are especially significant because they provide what is often the only biographical information a reader will ever have about a particular writer. What is more, since these chosen details of the author's life—and the editor's reflected attitude toward these details—are absorbed in the impressionable years of childhood, they tend to become indelible parts of the reader's intellectual framework, difficult to abandon even in adulthood and even if fuller or more complex views of the writer may later come into play.

Coleridge's life presents some obvious challenges for school text editors. Standard attitudes about his life and work that find Coleridge to be less than exemplary—many of which he himself originated and perpetuated—find their way into the biographical sketches. These contrast awkwardly with Coleridge's acknowledged reputation as one of the stellar poets of the nineteenth century. In *Selected Poems from Coleridge and Tennyson* W. J. Alexander writes a full and detailed account of Coleridge in which the desire to be fair and balanced is apparent; yet he also emphasizes Coleridge's vagueness, his lack of will, and his misspent life. For his part, O. J. Stevenson places Coleridge in another poet's shadow, noting that "as a poet Coleridge produced most of his best work, during the years 1797–1798, while under the influence of Wordsworth" (89). The editors of *Coleridge's Ancient Mariner and Other Poems,* in the Chambers Classics Series (1872), comment succinctly, if somewhat evasively: "Being of an imaginative and irregular turn of mind [Coleridge] was ill adapted to the ordinary struggles of life, and in youth encountered various misfortunes" (18). George E. Woodberry gives the kinds of details that would surely appeal to children. For example, of the time at Clevedon when Coleridge was first married, Woodberry writes: "A sister-in-law and a male friend lived with the Coleridges. There was no servant; the men helped to do the work, and Coleridge continued to share the household labour more or less in his early married life" (17). Not surprisingly, Woodberry's sympathetic portrayal balances the poet's opium addiction with the love of his friends and his gift for eliciting admiration.

Coleridge's addiction is the one detail of the poet's life that students even today—though they likely know nothing else about the man—have managed to acquire. "Coleridge. He's the one who took drugs," they say. And, of course, he did—a fact especially laden with moral potential for children's biographers. Macdonald follows in Woodberry's vein with a generally favorable "Life" and straightforward account of the addiction, acknowledging the role of ill health in provoking the opium use, though he also deplores Coleridge's failure of will. He concludes:

> In 1816 [Coleridge] took the decisive step of putting himself under the care of Mr. James Gillman, a physician of Highgate. . . . Here he gradually overcame the craving of opium and regained something of his old power of working. . . . The closing years of Coleridge's life were brightened by frequent visits of his many

> friends and admirers, on whom his wonderful power of talk exercised a profound influence. The general verdict of those who heard him discourse was that his published work, great and influential as it has been, did not represent the amazing power of the man. It is idle to speculate on what he might have accomplished had his will been equal to his imagination and intellect. (107–108)

In contrast to the two accounts above, Guthkelch's rendering of the opium addiction and its consequences seems abrupt, rather like an objective listing of facts that, at the same time, manages to sound disapproving: "[Coleridge] had already taken opium to obtain relief from neuralgia and other troubles, which he attributed to having one day while at school, swum the New River, in his clothes; and now the habit grew upon him. The North did not suit him: his health became worse; and he took more and more opium daily, until at last he became a complete slave to it. The rest of his life is little more than the story of the ruin of what might have been a great career" (x). Guthkelch's own conflict over his feelings about Coleridge's life and his clear admiration of Coleridge's work emerge as he mentions Coleridge's criticism, calling it "some of the most subtle and sympathetic criticism of English poetry that has ever been written" and adding, "in philosophy the influence of Coleridge was hardly less far-reaching than in poetry or criticism" (xi).

The sketch that begins Blackie's School Classics' *The Rime of the Ancient Mariner* (1879) is unusual in presenting Coleridge as a model of moral rectitude: "Coleridge shortly afterwards visited Germany, where he wisely employed his time in learning the language and in studying the German literature. . . . During the last nineteen years of his life he lived with his friend Mr. Gillman, a physician, at Highgate Grove, London. Here he died, with calmness and Christian hope and resignation, on the twenty-fifth day of July, 1834." More standard is Tuley Huntington's gentle defense of Coleridge's "character as a man":

> Those who are unwilling to accept Carlyle's version of it, when he spoke of Coleridge's life as "the tragic story of a high endowment with an insufficient will," may apply to it a large part of what Coleridge said about Hamlet: "Hamlet's character is the prevalence of the abstracting and generalizing habit over the practical.

> He does not want courage, skill, will, or opportunity; but every incident sets him thinking; . . . I have a smack of Hamlet myself, if I may say so" [*Table Talk.* June 24, 1827]. But these words were his own condemnation, because many years before this he had said: "Action is the great end of all; no intellect, however grand, is valuable if it draw us from action, and lead us to think and think till the time of action is passed by and we can do nothing" [H. C. Robinson, *Diary,* vol. 1, ch. xv]. We should be careful, however, not to make too much of his defects. Some who have lived since his time have spoken of his "unlovely character," and have said that "he had no morals," but those who knew him in his habit as he lived loved and reverenced him. And whatever the judgment passed upon him, he was a man, take him for all in all, whose like we shall not look upon again. (xxxviii–xxxix)

The biographical sketch is thoughtful and fair without speaking condescendingly to student readers; rather, Huntington asks them to abandon a simplistic view of Coleridge in favor of a more comprehensive picture. With neither apology nor moralization, he encourages students to embrace a more complex understanding of human nature that will serve them well not only in reading poetry but also in living their lives.

The language of W. B. Henderson, editor of *The Ancient Mariner and Other Poems and Prose of S. T. Coleridge* (1920), is conversational, full of detail, and clearly aimed at a youthful audience. Almost half of the biography concentrates on Coleridge's early life—his boyhood, the Cambridge years, the Dragoons episode, and the Pantisocracy scheme—giving children a poet with whom they can identify and sympathize. Henderson—providing, perhaps, a background for some of the quirks of Coleridge's life—begins with stories of Coleridge's father that exemplify his eccentricity, for example: "Mr. Coleridge was also a very forgetful man. On one occasion he went away from home for a few days, and his wife after giving him a bag with several shirts bade him to be sure to put on a clean one every day. The vicar dutifully obeyed, but such was his absence of mind that he forgot to take off the dirty shirt before putting on the clean one, and he arrived home wearing all the shirts one on top of the other" (128). Humorous as the incident is (and appealing for its humor) still, children might well wonder what it would be like to have such a father. Reader identification with young Samuel would surely grow stronger as Henderson taps into the sympathy that both children and adults would feel for the nine-year-old boy, sent to Christ's Hospital in London, where he knew no one and where "on a holiday he had nothing to do but wander about the town by himself while the hours dragged slowly by until the time arrived when he might return to school and eat the modest supper that was provided for him" (129).

Henderson becomes a storyteller, relating a series of vignettes so that Coleridge, the hero of his own life, takes on the character of a hero of a novel. This approach—in addition to making Henderson in some degree the author of the poet's life and thus giving him the fiction writer's license to develop the hero's character as he deems fitting—allows Henderson to concentrate on story narration rather than biographical complexity. Henderson's sympathetic biography focuses on the positive, bringing to imaginative life first the boy and then the man. It is interesting, in this regard, to juxtapose Guthkelch's account of the New River bathing incident (quoted above) with Henderson's, which follows: "During the summer months he spent those holidays in bathing in the New River. Bathing and swimming were his constant delight, and his enjoyment of these helped to pass many weary days. Sometimes, when the weariness and monotony grew too strong for him, he was tempted to do rash and unwise things, and on one occasion he swam across the river with all his clothes on, and allowed them to dry on his back. This was the cause of a severe chill, and of an illness which occasioned him much suffering during the rest of his life" (129–30). The incident was foolish in itself, and it led, according to some, to illnesses that Coleridge relieved with opium. But Henderson, unlike Guthkelch, views the incident through a child's eyes. The long hours of childhood, which can be lonely and filled with "weariness and monotony," and the need for action of almost any sort makes young Samuel a comprehensible companion for young readers. Henderson, through anecdotal storytelling, shows very clearly that the boy's penchant for inhabiting imaginative worlds had deep roots in long stretches of lonely times as well as inherent temperament. The Mariner's despairing, "alone, alone, all, all alone" ("Rime" l. 232) takes on additional resonance in this context. Henderson continues his tale:

> In winter when bathing [in the river] was impossible, he used to wander about the streets of London, lost in fancy, knowing neither what he was doing nor where he was going. He used to

> imagine that he was some knight or hero, and the people whom he met took on the appearance of characters in a romance. On one occasion, while walking down the Strand he fancied himself to be Leander swimming across the Hellespont to visit his lover; he spread his arms in the air as if he were breasting some great wave: when, suddenly, he found his hand in the pocket of an old gentleman who was walking in front, and who, on feeling what he thought was a barefaced attempt of robbery, caught hold of the boy and exclaimed, "What! so young and so wicked!" Samuel, to excuse himself, had to tell the whole story, and the old man was so much interested that he took the boy to a neighboring circulating library and made him a member of it. This was a great boon, and Samuel spent many hours in reading, devouring books at the rate of two per day. (130)

What child has not felt the humiliation and distress of being wrongly accused? Young readers can share vicariously in Samuel's anxious response to the old man and his relief and delight, not only in being believed but also in having someone to talk to who takes an interest in him and tries in some way to alleviate the original, motivating isolation.

Henderson's sympathetic affection for the boy Samuel extends to his treatment of the adult. It is sometimes difficult to tell whether Henderson's passing over of certain events in Coleridge's life derives from his sense of appropriate fare for schoolchildren or his own reluctance to write about things that might put Coleridge in a bad light. He omits, for example, the quarrel between Wordsworth and Coleridge, and he fails to mention Sara Hutchinson. He treats the years of Coleridge's addiction reluctantly, stressing always the constant aid of Coleridge's friends: "The following three years form a period of Coleridge's life about which it is difficult to write. During this time a complete change took place. Coleridge fell into a state of gloom and despondency: his ill health, which up till then had only been occasional, became constant; worst of all, his poetical genius seems to have died. . . . For this change of mind and disposition two reasons may be given. Coleridge was not very happy in his home life, and he had become addicted to the taking of opium. Regarding the first reason nothing more need be said: regarding the second it is right that certain facts should be given" (143–44). It is interesting to note that in his rendering of the "facts," Henderson does not call Coleridge weak-willed or in possession of an "unlovely character"; nor does he moralize:

> Very early in his life Coleridge had begun to suffer from a form of acute rheumatism. His escapade in the New River while still at Christ's Hospital is thought by some to have been the origin of his trouble. In any case, the pain was at times very severe, and to deaden it Coleridge began to take small doses of opium. These gradually increased in size and in frequency, and before very long he found himself a slave to the opium habit. From that time onwards to the day of his death his life was one continuous struggle to get the better of it. He could not remain for long in any one place. From Greta Hall he tramped over the hills to Grasmere and back again, he made an excursion to South Wales; another to Bristol to visit Southey; another to Nether Stowey; another, in company with the Wordsworths to Scotland. (144–45)

In the course of Henderson's storytelling, Coleridge himself has become a beleaguered Ancient Mariner, forced by his own "woful agony" to "pass, like night, from land to land" ("Rime" ll. 579, 586).

Coleridge and the Creative Imagination

As the study of poetry progressively became institutionalized in the schools, a canon of poetry for children inevitably came into existence.[9] The poetry of Coleridge belonged to this canon—and rightfully so. Coleridge assumes an audience for his poetry ranging from the young child, through the adolescent youth, to the mature adult. And this is true whether he is writing a poem ostensibly for children, such as "The Raven," or one ostensibly for grown-ups, such as "Boccaccio's Garden." He never forgets that children will become adults and that adults were once children. Coleridge's poetic world is filled with babies and children ("Dejection: An Ode," "The Foster-Mother's Tale," and "On an Infant Which Died Before Baptism," for example); with parent-child relationships ("Christabel," "Frost at Midnight," "The Three Graves"); with fairies and elves and spirits ("Eolian Harp," "Songs of the Pixies," and the "Rime"); and with youthful love ("Love," "The Dark Ladie," and "Night-scene"). In addition, Coleridge uses genres and subject matter—ballads, fairy tales, travel stories, adventure tales, Bible stories, and legends—that appeal to children and adults alike. Finally, against this background, he uses simple language and natural description to describe a moral and ethical universe, sacramental in nature and unified by and through God's love. In Coleridge's view, God's Truth, Love, and Wholeness comprise a creative Reality in which each of God's creations, including children, participates and simultaneously makes manifest. The same profoundly religious world is present in the most childlike prayers and in the incredibly complex, yet ultimately simple, mystery poems.[10]

The broadly moral and religious character of Coleridge's poetry constitutes an important part of his acceptability to the editors of poetry school texts, since it embodies a view that adults wish to perpetuate.[11] A clear inference is that life and art are not entirely separable; rather, in fact, they are intimately related. A corollary inference suggests that the life of a poet can inform the reader's understanding of a poem, thus giving a rationale for the introduction of the poet's biography into school texts and making explicable the editorial ambivalence concerning the relation of Coleridge's life to his poetry. Especially in collections chosen for the youngest children, editors consider overtly religious poems—prayers, for example—obvious candidates for inclusion.[12] As the foregoing discussion shows, the most popular and most frequently anthologized of Coleridge's poems fall into two easily identifiable groups: (1) simple, childlike poems and prayers for children, typically "Answer to a Child's Question," "A Child's Evening Prayer," and "'If I had but two little wings'" and (2) the mystery poems, "The Rime of the Ancient Mariner," "Kubla Khan," and "Christabel." What unites these two seemingly disparate groups is their fundamental religious assertion: the world is One in Love. What is most full of mystery is also most simple.

If the overtly religious nature of much of his poetry made Coleridge's inclusion in poetry school texts acceptable, Coleridge's longest-lasting influence in children's poetry is attributable to his profound belief in the role of the creative imagination in developing the human soul, or spirit. In Coleridge's view, the human spirit participates in the Spirit that is God, and the creative power that characterizes God in the world also characterizes the creative imagination of the poet and the creative spirit of the child. Coleridge's poetry, from the simplest of prayers to the most complex and philosophical, presents this highly symbolic and thoroughly religious worldview: to value the imagination and the created works of the imagination is to value the Spirit of God. Henry Newbolt, in the introduction to *The Tide in Time in English Poetry,* illustrates rather dramatically the strength and pervasive influence of the Coleridgean belief in the primacy and fundamental value of the creative imagination, not so much through Newbolt's inclusion of "Fears in Solitude" and "The Knight's Tomb" as in the introduction's language, philosophical-religious assumptions, and allusions to Coleridge's poetry: "Our object, then, in noting or tracing out the resemblances and inheritances among the poets we read, is not in any way to accuse or to appraise them; it is to learn something of the movement of the human spirit when flowing at its fullest tide of power. It is a movement as mazy and mysterious as that of the sacred river Xanadu, and as impossible to state in direct terms; it can only be observed in glimpses, and only by long familiarity and reflection could we hope to form a coherent theory of it. But the theory can be left to wait, if only we can gain some idea of the secret forces at work, their power and their endless multiplicity, their depth and the depth of the source from which they are flung up momently and for ever."

Newbolt's statement does not refer explicitly to Coleridge; rather, the editor makes an implicit statement of belief that great poems in some way resemble each other because they are created when the human spirit of the poet is flowing "at its fullest tide" of imagination. In expanding on this idea, Newbolt puts into play language taken from Coleridge's writing, most specifically from the poems "Kubla Khan" and "Frost at Midnight." Newbolt is concerned to convey to children the power and the "movement of the human spirit," as well as the source of this imaginative power, a source associated—through Newbolt's use of Coleridge's poetic language—with the creative engendering of Kubla Khan's sacred river of Xanadu, as well as with the "secret" ministry of frost—symbolic of the act of imagination—in "Frost at Midnight." The creative power of the fountain in Kubla's garden is a symbolic analogue of God's creative energy, and the "secret forces at work" in nature cause the poet in "Frost at Midnight" to say a prayer of benediction over the baby sleeping next to him in a quiet cottage. Both the child referred to in that poem and, by implication, the child who reads Coleridge's poems in Newbolt's anthology are surrounded by and simultaneously partake of the mysterious power and force of life. That secret power—the creative force behind genius and innately, though unconsciously, present in the child—Newbolt implies, manifests itself in the multiplicity of great poems of imagination. Through "long familiarity and reflection" as the child grows to maturity, he or she may be able to "form a coherent theory of it." Thus the poetry of Samuel Taylor Coleridge contributes to the development of the human spirit in child after child.

Notes

1. Examples of the appropriateness of giving children the "best" poets abound. Ian Michael quotes editors over several centuries, e.g., paraphrasing Vicesimus Knox's admonition in *Liberal Education* (1781): "What then should the teacher do? He should read aloud to the boys and then give them Milton, Shakespeare, and Pope to read, keeping to the great poets until the boys' taste is formed" (189).

2. That school texts and anthologies for the home are overlapping categories earlier is not surprising, since England did not have a universal national system of education until 1870. See Richardson (77–103) and De Paolo (119–50) for an overview of Coleridge's relation to the national education movement.

3. Interestingly, the "Rime," included in part two, is deemed appropriate for fairly young readers, aged nine to thirteen, rather than being placed with "Hymn Before Sunrise in the Vale of Chamouni" and "Love," which are included in part four. Volume 1 of Yardley and Bright's *The Child's Book of Verse for Juniors,* compiled for children aged seven to eleven, contains "What the Birds Say." Similarly, *English Poetry for Schools. Book 1. Primary* (1899), "primarily and especially compiled for use in the Government schools of Egypt" (preface), contains "Answer to a Child's Question" and "Away from Home" ("If I had but two little wings"). Helps's *Poetry for Children. First Book* (1882), "the first of a series of three books compiled for use in the elementary schools . . . intended for children between the ages of seven and nine" (preface), contains "Evening Prayer" in a section on religious verse. There are no Coleridge poems in the second book, but the third book, for ages twelve to fifteen, uses "Sonnet to the Autumnal Moon."

4. In the *First School Poetry Book,* Woods includes "Answer to a Child's Question" and "Away from Home" ("If I had but two little wings"). In the *Second School Poetry Book* (1887), for ages eleven through fourteen or fifteen, Coleridge is represented by "The Knight's Tomb," "Kubla Khan," and "The Ancient Mariner." For the *Third School Poetry Book* (1889), for the upper forms of high school, Woods selects "Youth and Age," "Dejection," and "Christabel"—a clear progression in terms of the poems' demands on the reader's abilities and maturity.

5. Alexander's *Select Poems from Coleridge and Wordsworth Prescribed for Matriculation and Teachers' Examinations* (1906) is a good example. The text contains thirty-one Wordsworth poems and the "Rime." There are fairly full biographical notes for both poets, and the introduction to the "Rime" includes "The Characteristics of 'The Ancient Mariner.'" The appendix for Coleridge adds "Frost at Midnight," "Dejection: An Ode," "Sonnet, To The Autumnal Moon," and "Sonnet, La Fayette." In addition, a section titled "Selections for Comparison, Illustration, and 'Sight Reading'" includes two ballads, "Sir Patrick Spens" and "Sir Cauline"; Shakespeare's "Sonnet 29"; Milton's "On His Blindness"; Byron's "On the Castle of Chillon"; and "A Sonnet of Camoens," translated by Southey. Lake country photographs of Rydal Vale, Ullswater, Grasmere, and Kirkstone Pass serve as illustrations. Further examples abound.

6. Alexander would have known W. G. T. Shedd's edition of *The Table Talk,* in which the 30 May 1830 entry recounts the exchange between Coleridge and Mrs. Barbauld without Coleridge's direct attribution.

7. See Watson (159–200).

8. Mulock's letter and the Ontario committee's decision to include "Christabel" as "a most desirable subject for study and examination" make an interesting counterpoint to E. Davenport's *The Girl's Own Poetry Book* (1890). Despite sections titled "Heroines in Poetry" and "Tales in Poetry," the large anthology omits "Christabel," which would have been a rather obvious choice for a Coleridge poem in a girls' poetry book, in favor of "Homesick" and "Fancy in Nubibus." Davenport explains in the preface that this collection of poems "does not profess to give of necessity the best work of the writers represented, but that most suited to the interests and capacities of the juvenile

public whom it addresses; and an effort has been made to consult the wants of girls of various ages and all orders of intelligence. Hitherto, very little has been done by our poets in the way of celebrating matters of purely girlish interest; but, in the good time to come, it may be hoped that they, especially women-writers, may find occasion to sing of the new day dawning before English maidens." In addition to showing that not all editors have as a primary criterion that of giving the "best work of the writers represented," Davenport's preface raises a number of questions for exploration: How do selections in poetry anthologies for girls differ from those for boys, and are the distinctions preserved as the poems move from books to be read at home to books to be studied in school? What do the differences tell us about assumptions concerning gender? Do male and female editors make the same assumptions? How does gendered—or ungendered—poetry reading affect boys and girls and the assumptions they make about themselves? If Coleridge can serve as a representative example, Davenport's statement that the editor is not concerned to present "the best work of the writers represented" is abundantly true, so something else is at stake in the selection process. At the same time, in a sadly ironic fashion, the Coleridge selections are at odds with Davenport's implied hope for "English maidens" of the "new day."

9. Useful contemporary discussions of canonical and pedagogical issues in children's literature can be found in Sadler, *Teaching Children's Literature: Issues, Pedagogy, Resources.*

10. As Ian Michael notes: "Many [poetry anthology] compilers continue [in the nineteenth century] to express anxiety lest poetry should corrupt the young. Poetry, unless it is specifically religious, is felt to be potentially subversive of morality" (220).

11. Perry Nodelman, in his introduction to volume 1 of *Touchstones: Reflections on the Best in Children's Literature* (1985), raises, in a different time and context, the familiar central questions in canon formation—"How could the writers of [guides to children's literature] know what children like or need to learn? Who decides what children need to learn?"—as he recounts the Children's Literature Association's appointment of a Canon Committee in 1980 "to develop a 'canon'—a list of important children's books." His answer is not surprising: "Children's books, which are always written by adults for children, always proclaim adult values; while adults can hardly be faulted for wanting to teach children what it cost them much pain to find out themselves, the adult message to children is always conservative . . . for we *must* 'manipulate' children—or, to use a more positive term, to educate them. Should we choose to respect their individuality by refusing to manipulate them, by refusing, thus, to teach them our own values, we would have to give up, not just choosing touchstones, but also, writing books for children altogether" (4, 7, 10).

12. As Alan Richardson notes: "The questions of children's imaginative reading and their religious training were more closely related in the early nineteenth-century than is generally remarked" (59). This close relationship continues well into the next century.

Works Cited and Consulted

Alexander, W. J., ed. *Select Poems from Coleridge and Tennyson Prescribed for University and Normal School Entrance Examinations.* Toronto: Copp, Clark, 1915.

———. *Select Poems from Coleridge and Wordsworth Prescribed for Matriculation and Teachers' Examinations.* Toronto: Copp, Clark, 1905.

Bain, A. Watson, [ed.] *A Poetry Book for Boys and Girls.* Cambridge: Cambridge University Press, 1933.

———. *Poetry for the Young: A Graduated Collection in Four Parts.* Complete in one volume. London: Griffith and Farran; New York: E. P. Dutton, 1883.

Barker, Mrs. Lucy O. Sale, ed. *Illustrated Poems and Songs for Young People.* London: Routledge, 1885.
Bennett, Henry Garland, [ed.] *Trail Breaking.* New York: American Book, 1935.
Blishen, Edward, ed. *Oxford Book of Poetry for Children.* Illus. Brian Wildsmith. London: Oxford University Press, 1963.
The Book of a Thousand Poems. 1959. London: Evans Brothers, 1966.
Burt, Mary E., ed. *Poems That Every Child Should Know.* London: Doubleday, Page, 1904.
Cassell, [J.], [ed.] *Poetry for Children.* London: Cassell, 1898.
The Children's Poetry Book. Illus. Thomas Dalziel. London: Routledge, 1868.
Chubb, Percival. *The Teaching of English in the Elementary and Secondary School.* New York: Macmillan, 1902.
Clark, Leonard, ed. *Common Ground: An Anthology for the Young.* London: Faber and Faber, 1964.
———. *Drums and Trumpets. Poetry for the Youngest.* Illus. Heather Copley. London: Bodley Head, 1962.
Coleridge, Samuel Taylor. *The Poems of Coleridge.* Ed. E. H. Coleridge. London: Oxford University Press, 1912.
———. *The Table Talk.* Ed. W. G. T. Shedd. Vol. 6 of *The Complete Works of Samuel Taylor Coleridge.* New York: Harper, 1884.
———. *The Table Talk.* Ed. Carl Woodring. 2 vols. Vol. 14 of *The Collected Works of Samuel Taylor Coleridge.* Bollingen Series no. 75. Princeton, N.J.: Princeton University Press, 1990.
Coleridge's Ancient Mariner and Other Poems. Chambers English Classics. London: W. and R. Chambers, 1872.
Davenport, E., ed. *The Girl's Own Poetry Book.* London: Griffith Farran Okeden and Welsh, 1890.
de La Mare, Walter, ed. *Tom Tiddler's Ground: A Book of Poetry for the Junior and Middle School.* London: Collins Clear-Type, n.d.
De Paolo, Charles. *Coleridge's Philosophy of Social Reform.* New York: Peter Lang, 1987.
Easy Poetry for Children. London: John W. Parker, 1837.
Edgar, Pelham, ed. *Coleridge and Wordsworth: Select Poems Prescribed for the Matriculation and Departmental Examinations for 1903.* Morang's Education Series. Toronto: George N. Morang, 1902.
English Poetry for Schools. Book 1. Primary. Selected and arranged by George Cookson with preface and note by A. V. Houghton. London: Macmillan, 1899.
Gibson, J., and R. Wilson, [eds.] *Solo and Chorus Blue Book.* London: Macmillan, 1964.
Grahame, Kenneth, [ed.] *The Cambridge Book of Poetry for Children.* 1915. Illus. Gwen Raverat. Cambridge: Cambridge University Press, 1933.
Guthkelch, A., ed. *Coleridge's Ancient Mariner and Selected Old English Ballads.* Bell's English Texts for Secondary Schools. London: George Bell and Sons, 1907.
Helps, Edmund A., [ed.] *Poetry for Children: First Book.* London: George Bell and Sons, 1882.
Henderson, W. B., ed. *The Ancient Mariner and Other Poems and Prose of S. T. Coleridge.* The Kings Treasuries of Literature Series. London: Dent and Sons, New York: E. P. Dutton, 1920.
Hendrickson, Norejane J., and Nancy Taylor Coghill. "Nineteenth Century Children's Poetry: A Reflection of an Age." *Children's Literature Association Quarterly* 11 (1986): 72–77.
Henley, William Ernest, [ed.] *Lyra Heroica: A Book of Verse for Boys.* London: David Nutt, 1892.
Huntington, Tuley F., ed. *The Ancient Mariner, Kubla Khan, Christabel,* Justus C. Castleman, ed. *Sohram and Rustrum and Other Poems.* Rev. H. Y. Moffett with illus. by A. Gladys Peck and reprinted together. Boston: Macmillan, 1924.

Ingpen, Roger, ed. *One Thousand Poems for Children.* Illus. Sir Joshua Reynolds. London: Hutchinson, n.d.

Ireson, Barbara, ed. *Poet's Corner: An Anthology of Verse for Young People.* Illus. Elizabeth Corsellis. London: Nelson, 1969.

Jagger, J. H., ed. *A Book of English Poems Graded for Use in Schools.* 4 parts. Illus. Gladys M. Rees. London: University of London Press, 1925.

Jennings, J. G., ed. *English Poems.* 2 vols. London: Macmillan, 1903.

Lyttleton, Mary, [ed.] *A Girl's Book of Verse.* London: Philip Allan, 1925.

Macdonald, J. F., ed. *Selected Poems of Coleridge and Tennyson.* Toronto: Oxford University Press, 1918.

McIntire, W. R. S., [ed.] *Vigorous Verse.* Illus. Gilbert Dunlop. London: Macmillan, 1963; New York: St. Martin's, 1963.

Michael, Ian. *The Teaching of English.* Cambridge: Cambridge University Press, 1987.

Moorhouse, Reed, ed. *The Ring of Words: A Book of Verses for Children.* 3 vols. London: J. M. Dent and Sons, 1924.

Mulholland, Rosa, ed. *Gems for the Young from Favorite Poets.* Illus. Dublin: M. H. Gill and Son, 1884.

Mulock, William. "To E. W. Ross re the suitability of Christabel for the Ontario high school curriculum." University of Toronto Coleridge Collection (Misc. Ms. 8), 17 January 1885.

M'William, R. M., ed. *The Temple English Literature Series for Schools.* London: J. M. Dent, 1905.

Narrative Poetry for the Young. Illus. the Brothers Dalziel. London: George Routledge and Sons, 1877.

Newbolt, Henry, [ed.] *The Tide in Time in English Poetry.* London: Thomas Nelson and Sons, 1925.

Nodelman, Perry, ed. *Touchstones: Reflections on the Best in Children's Literature.* 3 vols. West Lafayette, Ind.: ChLA, 1985–1989.

O'Malley, Raymond, and Denys Thompson, [eds.] *The Tree in the Wood.* 4 vols. London: Chatto and Windus, 1966.

A Poetry Book for Children. Illus. London: George Bell, 1854.

A Poetry Book for National Schools. London: Bell and Daldy, 1856.

Pretty Poems for Young People. Illus. London: Cassell, Petter, and Galpin, 1877.

Richardson, Alan. *Literature, Education, and Romanticism.* Cambridge: Cambridge University Press, 1994.

The Rime of the Ancient Mariner. Blackie's School Classics. London: Blackie and Son, 1879.

'The Rime of the Ancient Mariner' and Other Poems. With Introduction and Notes. Collins School Classics. London: William Collins, Sons, 1873.

Sadler, Glenn Edward. *Teaching Children's Literature: Issues, Pedagogy, Resources.* New York: Modern Language Association, 1992.

Select Poetry for Children: A Book for School and Home Use. London: T. Wade, 1855.

Stevenson, O. J., ed. *Select Poems of Coleridge and Tennyson.* Toronto: McLeod and Allen, 1915.

Teasdale, Sara, [ed.] *Rainbow Gold: Poems Old and New Selected for Boys and Girls.* Illus. Dugald Walker. New York: Macmillan, 1922.

Walsh, William. *Coleridge: The Work and the Relevance.* New York: Harper and Row, 1973.

Warren, C. Henry, ed. *A Book of Verse for Boys.* London: Grant Richards, 1924.

Watson, Jeanie. *Risking Enchantment: Coleridge's Symbolic World of Faery.* Lincoln: University of Nebraska Press, 1990.

Wayne, Philip, ed. *A Child's Book of Lyrics.* London: Methuen, 1923.

Willcox, Louise Collier, ed. *The Torch: A Book of Poems for Boys.* Illus. Elizabeth Shippen Green. New York: Harper and Brothers, 1924.

Woodberry, George E., ed. *The Rime of the Ancient Mariner.* The Gateway Series. New York: American Book, 1904.
Woods, M. A., ed. *A First School Poetry Book.* London: Macmillan, 1886.
———. *A Second School Poetry Book.* London: Macmillan, 1887.
———. *Specimens of English Poetry.* London: Taylor and Francis, 1883.
———. *A Third School Poetry Book.* London: Macmillan, 1889.
Woodward, W. H., [ed.] *A Second Book of English Poetry for the Young.* Cambridge: Cambridge University Press, 1904.
Wright, Fowler, and Compton Rhodes, eds. *Poems Chosen by Boys and Girls.* Oxford: Basil Blackwell, 1925.
Yardley, M. D., and Elizabeth Bright, eds. *The Child's Book of Verse for Juniors.* London: Evans Brothers, n.d.

Edward Lear's Limericks: The Function of Children's Nonsense Poetry

John Rieder

Readers who seek to make sense of Edward Lear's nonsense limericks are in danger of putting themselves into the frustrating position of the people who question Lear's man of Sestri:

> There was an old person of Sestri,
> Who sate himself down in the vestry,
> When they said "You are wrong!"—he merely said "Bong!"
> That repulsive old person of Sestri. (192)

But if Lear's limericks defy critical interrogation, they do so with a good deal more charm than the repulsive old person of Sestri, because their resistance, unlike his, does not put an end to conversation. On the contrary, their inscrutability instead raises the crucial question of the difference between the meaning of Lear's nonsense and its function. The question I wish to raise here, then, is not what Lear's nonsense means but rather what it does.[1]

This important distinction appears, for instance, in a comment Lear made in 1871 regarding some of the reviews of his second volume of nonsense writings: "The critics are very silly to see politics in such bosh: not but that bosh requires a good deal of care, for it is a sine quâ non in writing for children to keep what they have to read perfectly clear & bright, & incapable of any meaning but one of sheer nonsense" (*Selected Letters* 228). Lear's point is that his nonsense's irrationality is the result of a painstaking, rational process. To attempt to see past the surface of such verse is to ignore precisely what is most important about it, so that such seeing is a way of being blind to its real artistic merit. Indeed, the tension produced by offering multiple invitations to interpretation within a piece of art that at the same time deliberately resists any attempt to make sense of it has been called the essential feature of literary or artistic nonsense in general (Tigges 27).

Yet Lear's emphasis here is not on the general character of nonsense so much as on its appropriateness to a certain audience. "Writ-

Children's Literature 26, ed. Elizabeth Lennox Keyser (Yale University Press, © 1998 Hollins College).

ing for children," he says, requires one to keep things "perfectly clear & bright." What purpose does this clarity and brilliance serve, and how is it specific to writing for children? One of the "clear & bright" things about Lear's limericks is his highly predictable handling of the form.[2] The first line usually uses the formula "There was an [old / young] [man / lady / person] of [place name]." Lear frequently echoes this formula in the final line: "That [adjective] old man of [place name]." The middle lines usually describe some sort of eccentric behavior on the part of the subject, often accompanied by a response to it by the people around him or her, as in the oft-repeated formula beginning the third line: "When they said." The "old man of Sestri" limerick is a good example of this basic structure. Sometimes the interaction between the eccentric and "the people" extends into the final line, yielding variations on the basic formula: "They [verb] that old man of [place name]" (e.g., "So they smashed that old man of Whitehaven" [39]) or "Which [verb] the people of [place name]" (e.g., "Which distressed all the people of Chertsey" [7]). Thus the rather chaotic interplay between Lear's eccentrics and "them" is tightly contained within the repetitive form, providing a combination of novelty and familiarity that, like much nonsense verse for children, provides the child with a strictly rule-bound, reliable, and therefore reassuring set of boundaries within which to experience the fantastically extravagant and sometimes threatening contents of the poems (Ede 58–60; Kennedy).

The most distinctive feature of Lear's poetic craft in the limericks is his handling of the final line. Here one often finds whatever frightening or violent material the limericks contain, such as the eccentric protagonist being smashed or killed or drowned or choked. The need to control such threatening possibilities may help to explain the curious restraint of Lear's formal handling of the final rhyme. Unlike most later composers of limericks, and in distinction even from the "sick man of Tobago," which Lear cited as the primary model for his limericks,[3] Lear almost never tries to deliver a witty or surprising rhyme at the end of a limerick. But this is not to say that the final lines contain no surprises. On the contrary, the adjectives that describe the eccentrics are fabulously various. Sometimes they deliver an appropriate description or judgment, but just as often the description or judgment is mildly or strikingly inappropriate, and on a good number of occasions it is entirely mysterious. For instance:

There was an Old Man of Peru,
Who never knew what he should do;
So he tore off his hair, and behaved like a bear,
That intrinsic Old Man of Peru. (12)

"Intrinsic" neither expresses a judgment nor plausibly describes any of the old man's qualities. It is quite as inscrutable as the man of Sestri's "Bong."

What the use of "intrinsic" achieves, in fact, is precisely the short-circuiting of interpretation that Lear describes as the "perfectly clear & bright" quality of his verse, that which makes it "incapable of any meaning but one of sheer nonsense." According to one eminent theorist of nonsense, "This is the beginning of nonsense: language lifted out of context, language turning on itself . . . language made hermetic, opaque" (Stewart 3). Nonsense, according to Stewart, is language that resists contextualization, so that it refers to "nothing" instead of to the word's commonsense designation. In this way Lear's wildly inappropriate adjectives are paradigmatic instances of one of the fundamental activities the limericks perform: the world of Lear's nonsense is a playground.[4] It separates itself from the "real" world, letting loose a number of possibilities, including dangerous and violent ones, and at the same time disconnecting those possibilities from the real world, that is, from what goes on after the game is over. Thus Lear's artistry is "repulsive," not quite in the unmannerly fashion of the man of Sestri, but in that, like him, it stakes out a territory where being "wrong" is only a way of rhyming with "Bong."

The insulation of the artistic event from its social context is hardly peculiar to children's nonsense verse, however. We enter similarly playful (and, Huizinga argues, quasi-sacred) spaces when we go into an art gallery or a theater. But the distance from the commonsense world achieved in Lear's limericks is not just that of aesthetic contemplation. Although the language of any verbal artifact can be said to play rather than to work insofar as its readers adopt an aesthetic disposition toward it, Lear's limericks direct themselves to a specific audience and function precisely by actively refusing to work as conventional communication. This is not to say that the language of the limericks falls out of referentiality altogether, but rather that the truncated or suspended referentiality of Lear's nonsense is what makes the limericks peculiarly appropriate for children. And to adapt

Lear's own critical vocabulary, the limericks' clear but restricted referentiality also makes them not just playful but festive in a full and complex way.

Lear declared both the limericks' intended audience and their festive character on the title page of his *Book of Nonsense* (1846) with this limerick and its illustration:

> There was an old Derry down Derry,
> Who loved to see little folks merry;
> So he made them a book, and with laughter they shook
> At the fun of that Derry down Derry.

The illustration (fig. 1) shows the dancing Derry down Derry handing his book to a group of frolicking children. Keeping in mind that most of Lear's limericks were not written with publication in mind, but rather as gifts for specific children, we might ask what relationship between the adult and the children the book is helping to create or mediate. Lear simply calls it "fun" in this limerick, but it is a special kind of fun. The adult dancing amidst the children may be in charge of the situation, since, after all, he wrote the book; or he may be giving up his authority, becoming one of "them," when he hands the book over to the children. The adult's size and dress clearly differentiate him from the children. What is not clear, however, is whether his dancing is a performance for them or an emulation of their excitement, and so, by implication, it remains unclear whether the book is primarily an entertainment for the children or a means of entrance into the children's fun for the adult. The point is not that it is one way or the other, but that both possibilities are offered. The adult's authority is neither protected nor abdicated, but rather suspended, at least for as long as the fun continues.

The suspended hierarchical relation between adult and child suggests social possibilities that move the limericks' fun beyond the formalistic aspects of play as understood by Huizinga and applied by critics such as Sewell and Ede. Instead, their engagement of social convention here resembles the highly charged mode of festivity that, according to Mikhail Bakhtin's classic book on Rabelais, was ritualized in the medieval carnival. Bakhtin argues that the carnival "celebrated temporary liberation from the prevailing truth and the established order; it marked the suspension of all hierarchical rank, privileges, norms, and prohibitions" (10). The relationship between Derry down Derry and the children is indeterminate, it seems to me, in much the

Figure 1. There was an old Derry down Derry (This illustration and all others in this chapter are from *A Book of Nonsense* by Edward Lear, Looking Glass Library Series.)

way that social rules and hierarchies were set topsy-turvy during carnival. That is, Lear's verses, like a carnival celebration, clear a space for nonsensical fun by creating a hiatus in social rules and hierarchies, so that for a while it may become hard to tell the difference between us and them, high and low, teacher and student, or even adult and child.

But there is also a crucial difference between the spirit of carnival and Lear's nonsense. If the carnival "offered a completely different, nonofficial, extraecclesiastical and extrapolitical aspect of the world" and so "built a second world and a second life outside officialdom" (Bakhtin 6), Lear's nonsense directs its parodic and liberating energies not against the state or the church but rather in less "official" directions. In keeping with the interests of his intended audience, it is the private, domestic realm rather than the public domain that most preoccupies Lear in the limericks. They consistently address some of the most basic social conventions with which children struggle, such as those governing eating, dressing, grooming, and talking. Lear's approach to these conventions is "meta-cultural," in that it manipulates and explores the limits of social codes (Bouissac). Consequently the limericks tend to expose the arbitrariness or artificiality of convention rather than laying down the law. The limericks on eating, for instance, include stories of starvation and of gluttony, of "old men" who sink into alcoholic depression and of others who enjoy pleasantly recuperative snacks, of accidental cannibalism but also of miraculous cures (such as the man who is cured of the plague by eating a bit of butter).

Within this festive frame it remains unclear whether the children receiving these limericks are supposed to identify with the eccentrics or with the people—or with neither. The people react to the protagonists' antics with delight, curiosity, embarrassment, perplexity, astonishment, solicitude, outrage, and sometimes violent retribution. In fact, the range of behaviors exhibited by the eccentrics is matched in its breadth and unpredictability by the range of attitudes expressed toward them by the other characters, and both the behaviors and the attitudes are as portable and transient as carnival masquerades. This similarity tends to undermine the notion, once popular among critics of Lear, that "they" represent an intolerant social normality and that the eccentrics stand for persecuted individualism, or that the limericks deliver a univocal polemic in favor of the eccentrics' freedom to be themselves or against the people, who often close ranks against Lear's oddballs (Hark, "Edward Lear").

If the boundaries and hierarchies put into play in Lear's carnival are not reliably congruent with the boundaries between the eccentrics and "them," nevertheless they surely refer to social conformity and the conventions that govern manners and private codes of behavior rather than sacrality or legitimacy. They quite often do this by way of a widely prevalent strategy in children's literature: that of inviting identification between humans and animals. For instance:

> There was an Old Man in a tree,
> Who was horribly bored by a Bee;
> When they said, "Does it buzz?" he replied, "Yes, it does!
> It's a regular brute of a Bee!" (7)

The old man, not the bee, is the one who is out of his proper place, perhaps invading the bee's territory, so that the word "brute" in the last line puns on the uncertain distinction the limerick sets up between a social animal and an unsociable human. The illustration (fig. 2) emphasizes the similarity between the old man and the bee in a more broadly comic way, since their faces are nearly mirror images of one another, right down to the pipes in their mouths. Perhaps this hints at some hypocrisy in the old man's attitude, and perhaps it also indicates the interchangeability of roles within the limerick's

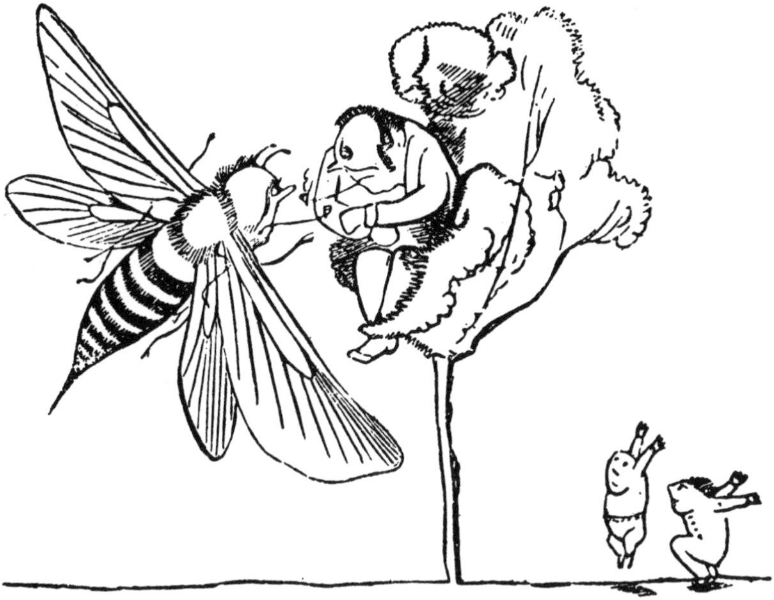

Figure 2. There was an Old Man in a tree

play space. At the very least, the limerick and the illustration cast serious doubt on whatever kind of authority the old man might have to pronounce the bee a "regular brute."

The social dynamics in this limerick involve a contest over who is occupying whose place and who has the right to say what is "regular." Although the limerick's general tenor is antiauthoritarian, the form of authority being satirized does not resemble that of general society toward the eccentric individual nearly as much as it looks like the interaction of an authoritative adult with a child. Or rather, the adult, like Derry down Derry, has been transformed into a comic entertainer, a clown, who mimics the irrationality and hypocrisy of adult authority in the face of the buzzing, childlike bee's own parodic imitation of him.

I am suggesting that the limericks consistently address themselves to the kind of authority adults exercise over children in general, and, more specifically, that the social institution toward which they are primarily directed is the Victorian family. The limericks offer a panoply of interactions between children and adults that refers, both mockingly and at times far more tenderly, to the family. For Lear himself, we can speculate, nonsense enacted an alternative to the parental relationship that some combination of muted homosexuality and serious health problems made psychologically, if not physically, impossible for him.[5] Lear's nonsense was for him a way of cementing a playful, avuncular relationship with the children he met in his travels. Lear's nonsense persona, Derry down Derry, gives way to "Uncle Arly" in Lear's last, most autobiographical poem; and the Lear of the nonsense in general is the one he called an "Adopty Duncle" on the drawings of an alphabet when he presented them, one by one, to a little girl at the hotel they were sharing (Noakes 243–44). The old man in the tree, I would argue, has no less entered into a fantasy of family life than the Lear in the self-portrait illustrating the following passage in a letter of 1871: "I think of marrying some domestic henbird & then of building a nest in one of my olive trees, whence I should only descend at remote intervals for the rest of my life" (*Selected Letters* 236).[6]

Whatever way the limericks may have functioned for Lear, they can be coherently understood as extending to the child reader an invitation to imaginative role-playing. The dramatistic game they open up refers predominantly to basic areas of socialization—eating, dressing, grooming, speaking, and so on—and to the kinds of tensions inherent in familial relationships, that is, ones involving obedience and authority, conformity and individuation, nurturance and independence. The limericks treat these relationships in a carnivalesque fashion, using parodic, grotesque, ridiculous, and subversive strategies of representation. Whether the limericks' overall effect is to rehearse rebellion or to provide a safety valve for antiauthoritarian energies seems to be precisely what the form of nonsense refuses to determine. Instead, the limericks' nonsensical resistance to commonsense interpretation draws a kind of magic circle around them, not only setting loose the extravagant energy and exuberant emotions of the nonsense world but also, at the same time, sealing off this world from "real" consequences. The limericks themselves often allude to and, indeed, theorize this magic circle in a quite detailed and often delightful way. Let me now, without presuming to make sense out of Lear's nonsense, try to trace this circle through a series of limericks.

We can begin with another man in a tree:

> There was an old man in a tree,
> Whose whiskers were lovely to see;

Figure 3. There was an old man in a tree

But the birds of the air, pluck'd them perfectly bare,
To make themselves nests in that tree. (191)

The old man in the tree appears to be another comic self-portrait of Lear, and the illustration (fig. 3) shows him smiling impishly on his branch while the little birds pluck him bare. Even more explicitly than in the bee limerick, the childlike animals have aggressively set on an adult invading their territory. But this is an unexpectedly tender poem, for it transforms the birds' attack on the old man's "lovely" whiskers into the benevolent activity of nest-building. Thus it rather pointedly reverses the plot of Humpty Dumpty, the nursery rhyme to which the illustration clearly alludes. This is not a cautionary tale about the irremediable consequences of a foolish action. Rather, this poem seems to encourage the child audience's aggressivity in the belief that such comic and aesthetic appropriation of the poem will ultimately have constructive results. The poem represents an adult attitude of optimistic tolerance toward the rambunctious and perhaps unruly children set free to play at nonsense.

At the opposite extreme from this old man's tolerance one finds a didactic adult being subjected to some of Lear's most clear-cut ridicule:

There was an old man of Dumbree,
Who taught little owls to drink tea;
For he said, "To eat mice, is not proper or nice,"
That amiable man of Dumbree. (184)

Figure 4. There was an old man of Dumbree

Here the illustration is particularly relevant (fig. 4). In it the old man of Dumbree has lined up the owls in front of him so that he can amiably instruct them to act in a way that goes against their nature. Lear presents this arrangement in such a way as to emphasize the uniformity being imposed on the owls, so that they turn into a faceless series of "proper" students of etiquette. The old man's authoritarian project is rendered thoroughly ludicrous by his own birdlike posture and beaklike nose. Thus this limerick renders quite explicit the antididactic element implied by the "Old Man in a Tree" reversal of Humpty Dumpty. At the same time, it may preserve some of that poem's tolerance by pronouncing the old man of Dumbree "amiable"; or perhaps this hint of tolerance enters the poem simply by way of the indeterminacy and playfulness enjoyed by the adjective in the final line. The fact that there is really no way of telling whether the limerick's sympathy for the man of Dumbree is congenial or nonsensical is, after all, precisely what keeps Lear's parodic strategy from breaking out of the circle of nonsense and turning into full-fledged, allegorical satire.

The emotional counterpart of the limericks' indeterminacy and tolerance is their strong ambivalence. For example:

> There was an old person of Crowle,
> Who lived in the nest of an owl;

Figure 5. There was an old person of Crowle

When they screamed in the nest, he sceamed out with the rest,
That depressing old person of Crowle. (195)

The person of Crowle seems to exemplify the quality of nonsense that Bakhtin, speaking of carnival laughter, would call its most egalitarian element, its holism: "It is directed at all and everyone, including the carnival's participants. . . . This laughter is ambivalent: it is gay, triumphant, and at the same time mocking, deriding." Unlike the laughter of satire, which places the satirist above and in opposition to the object of laughter, this kind of laughter "expresses the point of view of the whole world; he who is laughing also belongs to it" (Bakhtin 11–12). But this "depressing" old person's egalitarian laughter also has the appearance of an invasion. The price of its liberating effect on the "old person" may be that it threatens the stability of the social relationships inside the nest. The owls in the illustration (fig. 5) certainly seem to be of two minds about it. The largest ones, apparently assuming the role of parents, glare coldly at the demented-looking man in their midst, while the smallest ones look quite comfortable and secure in his presence. Thus a hierarchical reception of nonsense dictated by conventional familial roles uneasily resists the egalitarian possibility that nonsense might transform the nest of owls into a family made up entirely of children.

The art of Lear's nonsense is the art of sustaining its ambivalence and indeterminacy; but making the limericks "perfectly clear & bright" also involves providing some form of resolution or at least

Figure 6. There was an Old Man, on whose nose

security for the child audience. Thus Lear's success depends on his ability to balance the eruptive possibilities of the nonsense against a perhaps stronger, more imperative demand for closure. To say that the limericks ultimately satisfy this demand in a purely formal way is not to detract from them, but rather to epitomize much of my argument and bring it, so to speak, full circle. As an illustration let me offer this final limerick:

> There was an Old Man, on whose nose,
> Most birds of the air could repose;
> But they all flew away, at the closing of day,
> Which relieved that Old Man and his nose. (58)

Although the old man is said to be relieved by the birds' departure, the illustration (fig. 6) shows that he is quite happy in their presence. Yet the substitution of the old man's tremendous nose for the various nonsense perches, the trees or nests of the other limericks, confers some additional, strenuous responsibility on him. Even though it is the birds, not the man, who perch themselves on the nose, it is the old man who assumes the posture of a tightrope walker. The effort and the performance are ultimately his, and the birds enjoy it contentedly and seemingly without any awareness of the old man's artistry. Yet what relieves him and makes the balancing act possible is the knowledge that it will end and the birds will depart as surely as "the closing of day." Time is the partner of poetic form, and will bring about a kind of closure even where meaning remains open. Lear's artistry establishes an interlude where the children in his audience find themselves metaphorically suspended from the conventional world but still secure in the reassurance of the nonsense world's finitude, its balance of imaginative possibility and formal limits, and the certainty that the game always comes to an end.

Notes

1. Unless otherwise indicated, Lear's limericks are quoted from *The Complete Nonsense of Edward Lear.*
2. See Hark, *Edward Lear,* 24–29. The critical literature on Lear's limericks is very concisely and usefully surveyed by Colley, 1–31.
3. On the sources of the limericks and Lear's handling of them, see Hark, *Edward Lear,* 24–29; Byrom, 49–51; and Colley, 25–27.
4. On play in the limericks, see Ede, 58–60; on the marking-off of play space, see Huizinga, 9, 19–20.
5. Lear's most recent biographer states unequivocally that "there is no evidence whatever of homosexuality in [Lear's] life" (Levi 31); Lady Susan Chitty's 1989 biography, in contrast, takes Lear's love for Frank Lushington as the keynote of its interpretation of Lear's life. My argument adheres to the presentation of the problem of Lear's sexuality in Noakes's *Edward Lear: The Life of a Wanderer.*
6. See *Selected Letters,* 236, for the portrait as well, a charming sketch of an expressionless, bird-sized Lear sitting in a nest with his arm around a coyly smiling henbird.

Works Cited

Bakhtin, Mikhail. *Rabelais and His World.* Trans. Helene Iswolsky. Bloomington: Indiana University Press, 1984.

Bouissac, Paul. "The Meaning of Nonsense (Structural Analysis of Clown Performances and Limericks)." In *The Logic of Culture: Advances in Structural Theory and Methods,* ed. Ino Rossi. South Hadley, Mass.: J. F. Bergin, 1982. Pp. 199–213.

Byrom, Thomas. *Nonsense and Wonder: The Poems and Cartoons of Edward Lear.* New York: Dutton, 1977.

Chitty, Susan. *That Singular Person Called Lear: A Biography of Edward Lear, Artist, Traveller, and Prince of Nonsense.* New York: Atheneum, 1989.

Colley, Ann C. *Edward Lear and the Critics.* Columbia, S.C.: Camden House, 1993.

Ede, Lisa. "An Introduction to the Nonsense Literature of Edward Lear and Lewis Carroll." In *Explorations in the Field of Nonsense,* ed. Wim Tigges. Amsterdam: Rodopoi, 1987. Pp. 47–60.

Hark, Ina Rae. *Edward Lear.* Boston: Twayne, 1982.

———. "Edward Lear: Eccentricity and Victorian *Angst.*" *Victorian Poetry* 16 (1978): 112–22.

Huizinga, Johan. *Homo Ludens: A Study of the Play-Element in Culture.* 1950. Reprint. Boston: Beacon, 1955.

Kennedy, X. J. "Disorder and Security in Nonsense Verse for Children." *The Lion and the Unicorn* 13 (1990): 28–33.

Lear, Edward. *The Complete Nonsense of Edward Lear.* Ed. Holbrook Jackson. 1947. Reprint. New York: Dover, 1951.

———. *Selected Letters.* Ed. Vivien Noakes. Oxford: Clarendon, 1988.
Levi, Peter. *Edward Lear: A Biography.* New York: Scribner, 1995.
Noakes, Vivien. *Edward Lear: The Life of a Wanderer.* Boston: Houghton Mifflin, 1969.
Sewell, Elizabeth. *The Field of Nonsense.* London: Chatto and Windus, 1952.
Stewart, Susan. *Nonsense: Aspects of Intertextuality in Folklore and Literature.* Baltimore: Johns Hopkins University Press, 1979.
Tigges, Wim. "An Anatomy of Nonsense." In *Explorations in the Field of Nonsense,* ed. Wim Tigges. Amsterdam: Rodopoi, 1987. Pp. 23–46.

Gold Standards and Silver Subversions: Treasure Island *and the Romance of Money*

Naomi J. Wood

But there's no doubt but money is to the fore now. It is the romance, the poetry of our age. It's the thing that chiefly strikes the imagination.
—William Dean Howells, *The Rise of Silas Lapham*

Bromfield Corey's remark in *The Rise of Silas Lapham* has particular resonance for Robert Louis Stevenson's *Treasure Island.* After all, *Treasure Island* is first and foremost about a hunt for treasure, the pursuit of money—a fact often overlooked in critical discussions of the book.[1] Because *Treasure Island* is a historical adventure novel set in the eighteenth century, it has suggested to some readers a romantic distance from the factory and office work of industrial capitalism. Leslie Fiedler (1960) identifies the myths informing Stevenson's work as ones that defy the mundane and elude established systems of value: "There is an astonishing innocence about it all—a world without sex and without business—where the source of wealth is buried treasure, clean gold in sand, for which only murder has been done, but which implies no grimy sweat in offices, no manipulating of stock, none of the quiet betrayals of capitalist competition" (80–81). *Treasure Island* is, however, a romance about money, an excursion that, in its search for treasure, also defines the value of persons in monetary terms and provides an extensive commentary on the mechanisms of capitalist profit.

Fiedler's claim that *Treasure Island*'s appeal lies in its distance from the "quiet betrayals" of capitalism is belied by the structure of the book and by nineteenth-century critical responses to it. Edward Salmon, a children's literature critic and contemporary of Stevenson's, saw a tacit link between the novel and capitalism: "[*Treasure Island*]

I wish to thank the people who have so patiently read and reacted to the many drafts of this essay, including Dean Hall, Alison Wheatley, Carol Franko, Linda Brigham, Barry Milligan, Joe McLaughlin, Chris Cokinos, and Anne Phillips. I thank Kansas State University for supporting the research of this essay through its university small research grants.
Children's Literature 26, ed. Elizabeth Lennox Keyser (Yale University Press, © 1998 Hollins College).

is romance, pure and simple. There is little poetry, little humanity. It is desperately realistic, and desperately earnest; and regards nothing but the circumstances attending the strife for lucre and life" (107). Salmon's apparently contradictory assertions ("it is romance"; "it is desperately realistic") note a tension central to the problem of evaluation—economic and moral—not only in the book, but also in Stevenson's cultural milieu. *Treasure Island* thematizes questions about value and accurate representation, about romance and its debasement, and in so doing reveals that the bourgeois economic and moral systems, in the words of Marx and Engels, are actuated by "naked self-interest" rather than by "purer" devotion to God or country, thereby deconstructing the gold standard of value that they purport to uphold.[2]

My purposes here are twofold: I want to set *Treasure Island* accurately in one of its contemporary contexts, the economic debates over gold- and silver-based currencies and the ways they reflected cultural assumptions about value, and I want then to offer a fresh reading of the novel showing how it expresses the same concerns about surface and substance, signifier and signified, extrinsic and intrinsic value, what was gold and what was merely silver, that were being articulated by contemporary economists. Establishing the economic context of *Treasure Island* enables us to recognize Stevenson's ironic critique of essentialist evaluative modes. He demystifies value by revealing its binaries as constructed rather than essential; like money, value inheres not in the object but in its use. Furthermore, although Stevenson is often described as conservative and dualistic, a close reading of *Treasure Island* shows him resisting categories and actively deconstructing binaries in favor of a far more ambiguous aesthetic.

Gold, Silver, and Value

During the writing of *Treasure Island,* the merits of silver versus gold were being widely discussed in Europe and America; Robert Louis Stevenson lived both in the western United States and in the British Isles between 1879 and 1883, as gold was set against silver in public debates. These discussions are demonstrably reflected in the themes of the novel. Understood as representing competing socioeconomic interests and ideologies, the silver standard was associated with populist politics, whereas the gold standard was advocated by conservative establishment types. In England, silver was associated with counterfeit value and the commoner; gold-standard advocates justified their stance by making essentialist arguments about the transcendent value of gold, linked explicitly with claims for the transcendent value of the aristocratic classes and their virtues. *Treasure Island* breaks down the differences between "gentlemen born" and "gentlemen of fortune," thus breaking down the romance of "religious and political illusions"; by demonstrating the identical interests and strategies of the gentry and Long John Silver, the book reveals the profit motive to be "shameless, direct, brutal" (Marx and Engels 223). Money, whatever the surrounding ideology, has no moral core. Refracting the economic sphere, *Treasure Island* enacts the ideological struggle between gold and silver standards, demonstrating the fundamental similarities between the two but also accounting for gold's domination.

Between 1873 and 1896, international monetary policy was fomenting a "precious metals revolution": "Country after country was shifting from silver to gold as the basis for its currency. The associated oversupply of silver cut its price in half between 1872 and 1896. This was unprecedented in the history of the Western world and exceeds anything even hinted at in all other records" (Jastram 50). Although various countries had profitably maintained silver standards for years (among them France and India), the political and ideological climate of international finance now provoked gold and silver advocates to articulate their positions in value-laden terms, polarizing the metals as reflections of discrete populations and values. Historically on the silver standard, England had switched to a gold-based economy in the early days of the East India Company without fanfare.[3] Now, however, gold and silver had become more than bullion: they were political and moral stances. In the simplest terms, gold was perceived as being on the political right and silver on the left. Contemporary discussions acknowledged that currency decisions were being made on ideological rather than economic grounds. In 1886, Edward Sassoon submitted that Germany went to the gold standard not because it made economic sense but because it was imitating Britain as it began its own imperial mission at the end of the Franco-Prussian War in 1871. The gold standard was "the only fitting one for such proud victors" (Sassoon 884).

It was generally agreed that the gold standard benefited those who already had money to invest, those who had a stake in the economic status quo. During the early part of the nineteenth century, rampant inflation and the widespread use of inconvertible paper money[4] had created a volatile and risky economic climate by redistributing money away from the rentier classes to the mercantile classes. In England, the landowner-dominated parliament's drastic economic and political action during the first half of the nineteenth century—the Corn Laws and the Bank Charter Act of 1844—had stabilized the economy so that the gentry and the aristocracy could live confidently on their fixed incomes from rents and investments (Johnson 34–35). Unfortunately, these actions also brought widespread misery to the poor and stress to the manufacturing classes, resulting in widespread political protest throughout this period, expressed most notably in the Peterloo Massacre and the Chartist agitations. Toward mid-century, however, England's worldwide dominance as an industrial and export power ensured a favorable balance of trade so that the rentier and mercantile classes were able to combine forces, with some trickle-down advantages to the working classes. The gold-backed British pound sterling became the preferred currency for all who wanted conservative investment and reliable value.

The British gold standard, however, was not the only important force in the world market, and by the last quarter of the nineteenth century, other voices began to advocate a silver standard opposed to the values the gold standard represented. In contrast to gold, silver was considered a democratic force. Used by people with less ready money, silver was associated with commoners. As gold came to dominate the world market, currency was in shorter supply, which disproportionately hurt those areas already short on the metal: the result was a clamor for silver by groups negatively affected by the rule of the gold standard. In the United States, silver interests were associated with farmers in the Midwest and the South, whereas gold interests were associated with the old money and industrial power of the East. The conflict was between "agriculture versus industry; debtor versus creditor; West and South against the East" (Jastram 77).[5] Silver's greater availability encouraged inflation, which benefited those in debt, those who did not already possess wealth, whereas gold's comparative rarity benefited those whose wealth was already established, its rarity increasing its value. In England, British silver partisan Sassoon argued that American and British advocates of the gold standard must "submit to the inevitable" because the "awakened intelligence of the masses" would not permit the gold-standard establishment to continue working against their interests. Thus Sassoon argued that privileging gold would be "a source of the greatest disquietude to lovers of law and order" (887–88).[6] Stevenson clearly alludes to these politics of currency representation in pirate Long John Silver's name and persona, analyzing the division of social profit by means of money. It was clear that gold-standard policies benefited establishment persons and silver those on the margins of economic power; that gold was for investment and use as a hedge against inflation, whereas silver was for speculation and devaluation of money.

Undergirding discussions of gold and silver's political significance was the issue of accurate representation. Gold-standard advocates justified gold's centrality by making essentialist arguments about its inherent merit, merit that accrued also to those most interested in maintaining its predominance. To its advocates, gold was absolutely valuable; "solid gold . . . was associated with the substance of value" (Shell 6) because its physical qualities—its color and resistance to tarnishing—seemed to provide physical evidence of its "intrinsic" value. In this view, coining gold and inscribing value on its face simply affirmed what was already there, providing a virtuous connection between face and inherent value. By definition, the pound was worth a pound sterling of gold; thus there was no discontinuity between surface inscription and substance. In economic discourse, "sound" money—especially gold—was identified with moral as well as monetary integrity.[7] England's gold sovereign represented established worth; as the master-signifier of the culture, gold appeared to rationalize this signifying system as denoting an absolute, essential, and natural value in those who possessed it. Gold served as a touchstone for the relative value of all other currency. Against gold's absolute and positive value, all other substances were defined by their lack of that quality, a binarism that neatly reflected other social dichotomies, to the gold standard's advantage.

By contrast, silver connoted debasement, both literal and figurative. Unlike sovereigns, shillings were not worth the metal on which their value was stamped. British policy makers had determined that "silver coins should be considered as *representative* coins and should be legal tender not in excess of two guineas" (Jastram 24, italics mine). As writing without substance—a mere "promise to pay" (Trotter 24)—the shilling seemed inherently dishonest. Robert Lowe, Viscount Sherbrooke, a gold-standard advocate, argued that the character of silver coinage was morally suspect: "The only advantage which can be got out of the second metal [silver] is by a cheat—that is, by mixing an inferior with a superior article and palming them off on the customer as of equal worth, a practice well known to dishonest pedlars, but, I venture to submit, scarcely fit to be adopted into the finance of an honest nation" (Sherbrooke 508).[8] The debased connotations of silver coin carried over into British slang—silver implied deception and counterfeit identity; a "silver-beggar" or "silver-lurker" was "a tramp with forged papers showing he had suffered great losses through shipwreck."[9] Iconographically, then, money conveyed publicly sanctioned messages about social position and substance. Associations about the relative status of silver and gold and the coins into which they were made had become a matter of public discussion and everyday speech. That people readily associated the character and integrity of coin with the character and integrity of people is evidenced by the slide from "a pound sterling" to the "sterling qualities" of a gentleman.[10]

Treasure Island*: An Economic Reading*

Refracting the economic sphere, *Treasure Island* enacts the struggle between gentlemen born and gentlemen of fortune as a struggle between gold and silver standards. The category of "gentleman born" suggests an inherent quality, one having little to do with the fluctuations of chance. Gentlemen born understand the gold-standard advantages accruing to those who invest and save; they discipline themselves according to the conservative morals of capitalist religion. Because they are born to gold, they can forego current pleasure for future profit.[11] Gentlemen born appear to have inherent value, validated by land and law-based authority. They are what they appear to be, and they are marked accurately. The marooned pirate, Ben Gunn, trusts the word of gentlemen born as true coin because he understands that there will be no misleading difference between words and deeds: "He puts a precious sight more confidence . . . in a gen'leman born than in these gen'lemen of fortune, having been one hisself" (*TI* 98).

In contrast, the Silver-led gentlemen of fortune gain their identity not from blood but from the turns of fortune's wheel: rather than maintaining a static position, gentlemen of fortune fluctuate in value, deriving their significance from contextual rather than inborn traits. Driven by luck's vagaries, gentlemen of fortune live wholly for the moment, gaining or spending as the opportunity presents itself. As Long John Silver himself describes the situation: "Here it is about gentlemen of fortune. They lives rough, and they risk swinging, but they eat and drink like fighting-cocks, and when a cruise is done, why, it's hundreds of pounds instead of hundreds of farthings in their pockets. Now, the most goes for rum and a good fling, and to sea again in their shirts" (*TI* 67). To the pirates, the money is a means to an end, a way to fuel and temporarily satisfy their desires. Their disdain for delayed gratification, their refusal to act like canny Protestants, is precisely what costs them the treasure. Although Jim tries to contain the term "gentleman of fortune" by isolating its meaning as "neither more nor less than a common pirate," the euphemism subversively perpetuates linguistic inflation. By juxtaposing "gentlemen born" with "gentlemen of fortune," Stevenson suggests other connections that become clearer during the course of the book. Thus, comparing people to coins might also suggest that value itself can be misread. As David Trotter writes, "People resemble coins in that they may derive their identity from the stuff they are made of, or from the marks which social orderings have impressed upon them" (28). *Treasure Island* refracts this value-imbued economic sphere by dramatizing the ideological struggle between gentlemen born and gentlemen of fortune as one between gold and silver standards and then deconstructing that struggle by allowing Long John Silver to have the last word.

In *Treasure Island* we see Stevenson extensively examining value and the discontinuities between socially sanctioned marks, moral substance, and survival. At the beginning of the novel, the young narrator, Jim Hawkins, believes that personal value is to be measured in relation to gentlemen born. As master signifiers, gentlemen born, like gold sovereigns, are thought to embody the qualities that their marks of social rank and status simply corroborate. Working-class people—servants, sailors "before the mast," and, in this novel, pirates—are deliberately compared with gentlemen born and almost invariably found wanting. Frequently compared to children or animals, conspicuously less valued by the social economy, nongentlemen seem to be shadowed negations of real value.[12]

At first, such binary oppositions contrast the "positive" values of the establishment with the "negative" values of the antiestablishment: gentlemen born versus gentlemen of fortune; law-abiding versus lawless; clean versus dirty; adult versus child; good versus bad; notions of duty versus a corrupted "dooty." Stevenson clearly intends for readers to root for the former against the latter, and, indeed, the narration traces a child's transition from one to the other as the poor, lower-class "pirate" narrator, Jim Hawkins, is transformed into a wealthy, law-abiding gentleman. Jim's transmutation from Other into establishment man, however, is effected by the debasing influence of Long John Silver, whose adulteration of moral bullion and deceptive face value throw into question the standard of the establishment figures. In the end, all the establishment figures have become gentlemen of fortune.

Initially Jim Hawkins believes that the difference between gentlemen born and gentlemen of fortune can be determined by their face value. A dutiful social animal, Jim thinks that moral value corresponds to marks of social status. Gold-standard men are clean, well-dressed, and whole; they occupy prominent positions in society admirably; they use their money well. Pirates are recognized by their deformities and filthiness. Billy Bones, Black Dog, and Pew are all dirty, unkempt, and maimed. The contrast between the two sides is tendered almost immediately: Dr. Livesey, physician and magistrate for the district, stops by to tend Jim's ailing father. He is waiting for his horse, and Jim notes "the contrast the neat, bright doctor, with his powder as white as snow and his bright, black eyes and pleasant manners, made with the coltish country folk, and above all, with that filthy, heavy, bleared scarecrow of a pirate of ours" (*TI* 7). There seems to be no question about where value resides, as evidenced by a contest of wills in which the doctor prevails by reminding the pirate of his legally inscribed power, a power validating his own face value (powder "white as snow" and "pleasant manners"): "I'm not a doctor only; I'm a magistrate; and if I catch a breath of complaint against you . . . I'll take effectual means to have you hunted down and routed out of this [district]" (*TI* 8). Billy Bones submits, and the doctor's superiority, a pure expression of his face value, would seem to have had the last word.

These simple binaries break down quickly, however; the gentlemen of fortune do embody their own values and are admired for it. At the beginning of the novel, we are told that the English take a perverse pride in the ferocity of their pirates because it reflects well on the English spirit: the squire says even of Captain Flint, "the Spaniards were so prodigiously afraid of him, that, I tell you, sir, I was sometimes proud he was an Englishman" (*TI* 36). And although the countryfolk are terrorized by the "captain," as Billy Bones calls himself, and Jim's father "was always saying the inn would be ruined, for people would soon cease coming there to be tyrannised over and put down, and sent shivering to their beds," Jim asserts his belief that "his presence did us good. People were frightened at the time, but on looking back they rather liked it; it was a fine excitement in a quiet place" (*TI* 6). Even at this stage, the benefits of piracy begin to accrue indirectly to Jim's account. Though Billy Bones is dirty, he is also commanding and grotesquely attractive: "a party of the younger men . . . pretended to admire him, calling him a 'true sea-dog,' and a 'real old salt,' and such-like names, and saying there was the sort of man that made England terrible at sea" (*TI* 6).

Judging only by their competition for the treasure, the pirates and the official representatives of English society are difficult to distinguish. Any qualitative differences surface chiefly in their relation to the law, through their social positions. When Dr. Livesey, realizing that Jim has found the map to Flint's buried treasure, asks if Captain Flint had money, the squire responds: "What were these villains after but money? What do they care for but money? For what would they risk their rascal carcasses but money?" (*TI* 36). Only a few pages later, however, the squire exclaims: "We'll have favourable winds, a quick passage, and not the least difficulty in finding the spot, and money to eat, to roll in, to play duck and drake with ever after" (*TI* 39). The reactions of gentlemen born and gentlemen of fortune to the idea of seven hundred thousand pounds of buried treasure is strikingly uniform. Moreover, if the "work" the pirates do can be seen as their "earning" Captain Flint's treasure, the crew who scuttle the ships and loot the towns to accumulate the wealth might be considered to have more title to it. These blurrings of the divide between the establishment and the antiestablishment make some argue that *Treasure Island* itself is a celebration of lawlessness.[13] Certainly the interconnections between piracy and legitimate profit demonstrate the continuities between the gold-standard values of moral goodness, social standing, and legal privilege and the debasing silver-standard values of expediency and contingence.

In practical terms, the strict honesty recommended by the gold standard is demonstrated in the book to be incautious, even obtuse. After Billy Bones's death, Jim's mother rifles his sea chest for the money he owed the inn. In trying to "show these rogues that I'm an honest woman . . . . I'll have my dues and not a farthing over" (*TI* 25), Mrs. Hawkins's too-fastidious concern nearly gets them killed: "It was a long, difficult business, for the coins were of all countries and sizes—doubloons, and louis-d'ors, and guineas, and pieces of eight, and I know not what besides, all shaken together at random. . . . But my mother, frightened as she was, would not consent to take a fraction more than was due to her, and was obstinately unwilling to be content with less" (*TI* 26). Because Jim's mother will not simply take all the booty and run, they are almost caught by the returning pirates. When the pirates' whistle is heard, indicating imminent disaster, Jim's mother takes what she has, resolved to save her life at the expense of abstract fairness. Jim, on the other hand, has fewer compunctions: "I'll take this to square the count," said I, picking up the oilskin packet" (*TI* 26). Later, as they tremble in a ditch hoping the pirates won't find them in the moonlight, Jim "blame[s his] poor mother for her honesty and her greed" (*TI* 27).

Jim's *dis*honesty, his casual theft of the oilskin packet and utter disregard for correct ledger balances, pays off in a vast fortune, later described as a larger version of Billy Bones's hoard:

> I think I never had more pleasure than in sorting them. English, French, Spanish, Portuguese, Georges, and Louises, doubloons and double guineas and moidores and sequins, the pictures of all the kings of Europe for the last hundred years, strange Oriental pieces stamped with what looked like wisps of string or bits of spider's web, round pieces and square pieces, and pieces bored through the middle, as if to wear them round your neck—nearly every variety of money in the world must, I think, have found a place in that collection; and for number, I am sure they were like autumn leaves. (*TI* 215)

Here, the key to successful accumulation of money is a lack of discrimination about what is owed and to whom. Initially gathered by the illegal and bloodthirsty acts of Captain Flint's crew, the gold itself appears to be unsullied. This list of coins reads like a prose poem of money. Categorized by nation and king, organized simply by sound similarities and exoticism, the words blend with one another in a surplus of meaning, just as their materiality provides a surplus of value: "*doubl*oons and *double* guineas and moidores and sequins" call up all the romance of fabulous wealth and faraway places, the words suggesting not only buccaneering but also the hoards in the Arabian Nights. The oriental coins with holes "bored through the middle" might be suitable for personal ornament, recalling gold-bug theorization of gold's inherent aesthetic qualities.[14] Rather than frustrating accuracy in their multiplicity, the gold coins delight by their proliferating representations of value, setting their own standard of pleasure.

Long John Silver's ability to change sides and his destabilizing effect on the gold standard of institutionally established authority, although not strictly allegorical, play the role that contemporary economists saw silver playing in the drama of global economics. Long John Silver subverts claims that natural value resides in gold by demonstrating that gold too is only money and not virtue. Silver changes roles as easily as shillings change hands, thereby challenging establishment determinations of value; he is informed by self-interest rather than the gentry's moral code. When Silver reveals himself to be one of the most feared pirates of the age, the gentry's belief in face value is shaken; Silver, by ingratiating himself into the gentry's trust, has demonstrated that the difference between gentry and pirates is primarily one of presumption, only a matter of social inscription. Though society affirms the truth-value of face value, in motivating both gentry and pirates by their desire for wealth *Treasure Island* debases that notion. Even as Great Britain dominated the world with a gold monopoly, disquieting incursions of silver—metaphoric and actual—around the world disrupted claims about solid and unchanging value. Money is disloyal; as the most convenient mode of exchange, it benefits first one owner, then another, without regard to moral status. In the economy of *Treasure Island,* Long John Silver threatens the gold standard not simply by his brutality but because he is persuasive, practical, useful.

On what grounds, therefore, do the gentlemen born deserve the gold? Ultimately, the gentlemen of fortune disqualify themselves as proper guardians of treasure because they do not manage it properly. Stevenson shows the money gravitating to its "proper" owners, those who will most nurture it in investment, rather than those who would squander it in a grand spree. In the "Apple Barrel" chapter, Jim overhears Silver planning the mutiny. Although Silver promotes delayed gratification—he would like to wait to mutiny until the treasure is safely on board and they are returning to England—he acknowledges that he would have no followers with such a plan: "I know the sort you are. I'll finish with 'em at the island, as soon's the blunt's on board, and a pity it is. But you're never happy till you're drunk. . . . If you would on'y lay your course, and a p'int to windward, you would ride in carriages, you would. But not you! I know you. You'll have your mouthful of rum tomorrow, and go hang" (*TI* 69–70). In this speech Silver predicts how the pirates' plot will go awry. As Jim Hawkins confirms, "I never in my life saw men so careless of the morrow; hand to mouth is the only word that can describe their way of doing" (*TI* 196).

Gentlemen of fortune, living by fortune's largesse, will never have lasting wealth; gentlemen born understand investment and know how to keep and enlarge treasure when they come upon it. Read only from this perspective, the book would seem to be a capitalist tract on the virtues of the gentlemen born: discipline and hard work, delayed gratification, and solid loyalty to establishment firms. The gentlemen of fortune, by contrast, demonstrate the corollary lesson about what happens to those who live, as children and animals do, for the moment.

Silver bridges this binary, however. He is a gentleman of fortune in both senses of the phrase: luck and funds. Silver undermines the gold standard by demonstrating that what appears to be absolute value is in fact an empty signifier. Silver mingles the categories "gold" and "dross": so genteel that Captain Flint himself was intimidated by him, he still can kill efficiently and ruthlessly when necessary. Because Silver runs a different course from the rest of the pirates, he confutes the "face" value of the gold standard. Initially, informed by his expectation that face value denotes true worth, Jim worries that Silver is the "seafaring man with one leg" Billy Bones has warned against. But Silver looks nothing like Jim's idea of a pirate—"I thought I knew what a buccaneer was like—a very different creature, according to me, from this clean and pleasant-tempered landlord" (*TI* 49)—and his suspicions are allayed. Silver appears to be as solidly worthy, in gold-standard terms, as Smollett: as the doctor declares to Trelawney, "Contrary to all my notions, I believe you have managed to get two honest men on board with you—[Captain Smollett] and John Silver" (*TI* 57). As we have seen, however, silver money was associated with popular rule, convenience, secondary value, and even counterfeiting. Moreover, Silver's bank account, "which has never been overdrawn," marks him as "a man of substance" to fellow property owner Squire Trelawney (*TI* 45).

Long John Silver's name aptly conveys his connections with currency and exchange. Like the silver bars that ultimately remain on the island, Silver bears no stamp. These connotations are abundantly realized in Long John Silver's characterization. Like the shilling, which did not contain the value of the metal it represented, and in contrast with the golden guinea, Long John Silver's value is only superficially related to his interior. Silver's "honesty," remarked on by his superiors, is a function of his silver tongue and his quicksilver fungibility. Silver easily counterfeits the gold standard's value. Equal to any circumstance, Silver pleases by his obsequiousness while simultaneously cowing unruly buccaneers; Silver's value reflects whatever position he takes. His changeable surface may finally prevent identifying him as "pure gold," but it fittingly displays the situational contingency of all value.

Pressed by repetition into Stevenson's "silver" coin is Long John Silver's tautological slogan, "dooty is dooty." Its corrupted orthography corrodes the gold standard's definition of duty even as it reveals its status as an empty signifier. Captain Smollett provides the gold-standard definition of duty as he assures the guilt-stricken Squire Trelawney concerning his faithful servant Tom Redruth (who dies of a wound inflicted by the pirates): "All's well with him; no fear for a hand that's been shot down in his duty to captain and owner. It mayn't be good divinity, but it's a fact" (*TI* 113). In Smollett's eyes, true value lies in duty rather than dereliction, and a dutiful death, though recognized as perhaps questionable religion, is sound balancing in eternity's ledger—"all's well."

Silver's corrupt echo of the concept at first signifies a submissiveness pleasing to the capitalist owners; however, we learn during the course of the novel that Silver's only true "dooty" is to himself. Silver first uses the expression when he reports to his employers that Jim has seen a known pirate, Black Dog, at Silver's own tavern (*TI* 52). When Jim recognizes the man, Silver acts as though he has never seen him before and then promptly reports the incident to Squire Trelawney. In deceiving Jim about his own connections with Flint's crew, Silver accrues credit for his own honesty while deceiving all but his own cohorts (thereby accruing credit in the pirates' eyes as well). During the first part of the voyage, Silver's genial competence inspires approval in his superiors and loyalty in his inferiors. The obverse of Silver's "dooty" coin is revealed, however, in the "Apple Barrel" chapter as his loyalty to himself, a good capitalistic value, oversteps conventional morality and he votes for murder: "I'm an easy man—I'm quite the gentleman, says you; but this time it's serious. Dooty is dooty, mates. I give my vote—death. When I'm in Parlyment and riding in my coach, I don't want none of these sea-lawyers in the cabin a-coming home, unlooked for, like the devil at prayers" (*TI* 70). When the mutiny fails and Long John's best interests once again lie alongside the establishment's, back he comes to the camp, ready to be "the same bland, polite, obsequious seaman of the voyage out," saying only: "Come back to my dooty, sir," by way of explanation (*TI* 214). Silver's triumph is complete as we recognize that he has debased even the gentlemen's gold standard—the squire declares it "a gross dereliction of [his] duty" that he is forced to accept Silver's return (*TI* 213).

Long John Silver reveals duty to be something paid, exchanged, dependent on the grammar of circumstance, not something that defines the value of a man's life, as Captain Smollett would have it. Silver's creed, and his own definition of duty, are summed up in his rhyme: "Here's to ourselves, and hold your luff, plenty of prizes and plenty of duff" (*TI* 71). Silver's success, such as it is, depends on his sensitivity to situational changes and his quick adaptability to those changes. When the pirates, led by Silver, discover that the treasure has already been "found and rifled," Silver recovers from the blow almost immediately: "Every thought of his soul had been set full-stretch, like a racer, on that money; well, he was brought up, in a single second, dead; and he kept his head, found his temper, and changed his plan before the others had time to realize the disappointment" (*TI* 209). Although Jim tells us that he is "revolted at these constant changes," he plays by the same rules because his life too is at stake. Adopting Silver's standard, he cannot rigidly hold to the gold standard of Captain Smollett, who refuses to bargain with the pirates. And although Smollett tells Jim that he will not again sail with such a "born favorite," it is Jim's luck and duplicity that saves them, as Jim repeatedly reminds us. Jim eavesdrops, deserts his post, "takes French leave," and bargains his life against justice, telling Silver that if he is protected he will try to save Silver from his deserved end on the gallows. Certainly Smollett, a consistent though rigidly virtuous man, would never stoop to such negotiations. But it is equally certain that, if Smollett's orders had been followed to the letter, the gentlemen born would have perished.[15] Even practitioners of gold-standard values are subject to Silver's debasing influence—and ultimately are saved by it.

Silver's ultimate failure in the mutiny is a result of his inability finally to consolidate his corporation; although he has all the requisite gifts for success, his accomplices do not. This flaw in his infrastructure is tellingly demonstrated in the obsessive tally the gentlemen born keep of the numbers on each side. When they first discover the plot, Jim writes: "There were only seven out of the twenty-six on whom we knew we could rely; and out of these seven one was a boy, so that the grown men on our side were six to their nineteen" (*TI* 77). Things look grim. Because of the pirates' reckless, spendthrift attitudes toward life as well as money, however, the scales begin to balance. After the first exchange of fire, Dr. Livesey reports, "From nineteen they were already reduced to fifteen, two others were wounded, and one at least—the man shot beside the gun—severely wounded. . . . we had two able allies—rum and the climate" (*TI* 120). Because the gentlemen born control their natural desires (or are led to by Smollett), natural forces are their allies. Even though they have lost all three of the squire's servants by the next skirmish, the captain can declare triumphantly: "Five against three leaves us four to nine. That's better odds than we had at starting. We were seven to nineteen then" (*TI* 133). By the end, only four of the original mutineers are alive, whereas five of the gentlemen born and their allies survive to enjoy their share of the treasure. Such profit vindicates the risky but sound speculation of the gentlemen born.

As the ultimate owner of the treasure, Stevenson parcels it out to demonstrate the relative value of the survivors of the hunt. Gunn, though deserving of a large enough stake to make something of himself, cannot overcome his piratical predilection for dissipation: he spends his thousand pounds "in three weeks, or to be more exact, in nineteen days, for he was back begging on the twentieth" (*TI* 219). Significantly, Gray, the *honest* seaman, is smitten with a desire to "rise," buys into the traditional schemata for success, and is eventually rewarded (and here Stevenson stretches the time frame to allow a more polite and ordinary and definitely unpiratical rags-to-riches story) with ownership and family. Though we learn no more of Silver, he does escape from conventional justice and Smollett's promise to hang the mutineers. Jim envisions, almost as a reward for Silver, a comfortable end, hoping that "he met his old Negress, and perhaps still lives in comfort with her and Captain Flint [the parrot]" (*TI* 219). Even while the virtue of the gold standard would seem to have triumphed, Silver has nevertheless escaped and presumably prospers.

Though we are never told exactly how much of the money reverts to Jim, his own treasure is debased by bad dreams: "The bar silver and the arms still lie, for all that I know, where Flint buried them; and certainly they shall lie there for me. Oxen and wain-ropes would not bring me back to that accursed island; and the worst dreams that ever I have are when I hear the surf booming about its coasts and start upright in bed with the sharp voice of Captain Flint still ringing in my ears: "Pieces of eight! Pieces of eight!" (*TI* 219–20). With these last words[16] echoing in his nightmares, Jim's aversion to the island is understandable. Silver has debased the romance of adventure in *Treasure Island;* not only has Silver committed murder and mutiny, Jim's mutable imitations of Silver's survival techniques have debased his values as well (he too mutinies against authority and is responsible for lost life). Jim's loss of "favorite son" status is akin to the dereliction of duty the gentlemen born feel when they reaccept (of necessity) Silver into their group.

Jim's nightmare should be expected, given the reality checks Stevenson provides throughout the course of the historical romance. When the crew of the *Hispaniola* arrive at their destination, Jim is disappointed. Beginning with the first discovery of the map, Jim has dreamed of lurid adventure straight out of the blood-and-thunder boys' papers of the late nineteenth century: "Sitting by the fire in the housekeeper's room, I approached that island in my fancy from every possible direction; I explored every acre of its surface; I climbed a thousand times to that hill they call the Spy-glass, and from the top enjoyed the most wonderful and changing prospects. Sometimes the isle was thick with savages, with whom we fought, sometimes full of dangerous animals that hunted us" (*TI* 43). With such a build-up, particularly in a boy's adventure story, one would expect the island to live up to Jim's fancies. His first sight of it, however, is curiously anticlimactic and even glum: "grey" and "uniform," with "naked rocks" and "grey, melancholy woods," and with a feverishly hot sun, Jim's long-anticipated island seems curiously dull, like a black and white print in a book. Just as Stevenson had described "the whole ship [as] creaking, groaning, and jumping like a *manufactory*" (*TI* 81, emphasis mine), the island brings us out of preindustrial, eighteenth-century romance and into the thick of the late-nineteenth-century realistic novel; it is no wonder, then, that Jim writes, "My heart sank, as the saying is, into my boots; and from the first look onward, I hated the very thought of Treasure Island" (*TI* 82). Even though the island portion of the tale is just beginning, Jim already begins to realize that there is no escaping industry, that ships are to "make" money, and that romance is inevitably debased by the overwhelming reality of the market.

Raising the question of the relative value of romance and realism, however, forces us to confront the fact that although the ending of *Treasure Island* appears to support a simplistic duality of value—the good and the bad, the true gold and the false silver—a continuing subtext about writing and representation forces us to reconsider our conclusion. Even if Stevenson appears to debase his currency, he still plays with inscription and text as representatives of value that may or may not be trustworthy. Alongside the debates about gold and silver currency was the concurrent issue of paper money and its representational value. Paper was similar to silver in that it was legal tender but was only a "promise to pay," rather than the substance of payment. In a prosperous economy, paper money issued in excess of the bank's holdings could stimulate commerce, but if anything went wrong, investors stood to lose everything. Paper money, as Michael O'Malley points out, was associated with "speculative optimism" and "could serve perfectly well if everyone believed in future prosperity: eventually, the local economy would catch up with the dreams of its boosters, and the value of paper money would stabilize as gold filled the bank's vaults" (373).

In strikingly similar fashion, *Treasure Island* begins as a map, and the map within its narrative provides the best example of the perils of paper exchange, of money as rhetoric. The gentlemen born and the gentlemen of fortune both rejoice in the map as they would in the treasure itself: on the basis of the map's discovery, Squire Trelawney and Doctor Livesey instantly give up their everyday life to pursue it. When the map is traded to the pirates, they finger the map as if it were the treasure itself: "You would have thought not only were they fingering the very gold, but were at sea with it besides, in safety" (*TI* 187). Although the map represents the treasure and thus is "worth" the fortune to which it points, the narrative also demonstrates the way in which paper creates an illusion of value without necessarily backing it with cash. When the pirates follow the map to the treasure site, it has already been rifled and its contents placed somewhere else; thus, Silver himself has bargained for a counterfeit, and the gentlemen born have caught him with his own tricks.

Notwithstanding this questioning of the value of paper and writing within the text of *Treasure Island,* the situation of its writing and the presence of an intriguing coda to the action—"A Fable: The Persons of the Tale"—suggest that Stevenson's thoughts on value cannot be understood as a simple dualism of the kind we have studied here. Significantly, it is paper and rhetoric that become the source of value and of income. That Robert Louis Stevenson was concerned about the competing claims of truth value and represented value in literature as well as money is clear when one studies his writing for references to the use and exchange value of literary products. Immediately apparent is a series of oppositions denoting the positive and negative poles of literary and economic value: the novel is opposed to the short essay; the adult novel to children's romance; seriousness to pleasure.

In 1881 Stevenson had been praised as a promising writer, but he had not yet written a full-length novel. He had published travelogues, occasional essays, and short stories, but nothing that commanded a living wage. Stevenson's inability to support himself by his own labors had gnawed at him for some time: "I passed my days in toil, the futility of which would sometimes make my cheek to burn,—that I should spend a man's energy upon this business, and yet could not earn a livelihood" ("My First Book" xxiv). No wonder, then, that he figured the writing of his first novel as the discovery of a "lucky vein" of precious metal.[17] As he wrote to W. E. Henley, "I'll make this boy's business pay. . . . I feel pretty sure the 'Sea Cook' [the working title of *Treasure Island*] will do to reprint, and bring something decent at that."[18]

Stevenson delighted in the boyish pleasures of his topic and in the prospect of a "hundred jingling, tingling, golden, minted quid";[19] however, at the same time he was battling the opinions of his friends and critics that he ought to be doing something of more substance: "John Addington Symonds . . . looked on me askance. He was at that time very eager I should write on the *Characters* of Theophrastus" ("My First Book" xxix)—an indubitably adult project. An anonymous reviewer suggested that it was time for Stevenson to grow up: "It is clear that fiction is a field in which Mr. Stevenson is even stronger than in essay and in humorous and sentimental journeying. After this romance for boys he must give us a novel for men and women."[20] And even more emphatically, George Moore, who often criticized Stevenson for superficiality, assumed that Stevenson confirmed his second-rate status with his choice of genre:

> I will state frankly that Mr. R. L. Stevenson never wrote a line that failed to delight me; but he never wrote a book. You arrive at a strangely just estimate of a writer's worth by the mere question: "What is he the author of?" For every writer whose work is destined to live is the author of one book that outshines the other, and, in popular imagination, epitomises his talent and position. What is Shakespeare the author of? What is Milton the author of? What is Fielding the author of? What is Byron the author of? What is Zola the author of? What is Mr. Swinburne the

author of? Mr. Stevenson is the author of shall I say, "Treasure Island," or what?[21]

Indeed, Stevenson's posthumous status as a writer suffered precisely because of this kind of attack. Following Matthew Arnold's metaphor of literary value as pure gold, to be determined by the touchstones of pure literary artifact, the new gold standard of literary evaluation, as articulated by George Moore and others, became its "adult" qualities. Noteworthy, however, is the fact that Stevenson's romances continue to be far more widely known than any of Moore's novels.

Felicity Hughes has argued that the aesthetic stock of the novel genre rose in the 1880s because of the concerted effort that critics such as George Moore and Henry James made to distinguish literature (which educated men read) from mere fiction (which women, children, and the working classes read).[22] By making the novel serious, novelists could claim for themselves the status of artist, safe from the connotations of dissipation and pleasure the novel had for some scholars and critics.[23] Stevenson himself was aware of the déclassé status of his first book, but he, like his heroes, argued for the contingent value of circumstance rather than the absolute value of allegiance to a certain position. In the critical marketplace, the gold standard of evaluation was identified with the substance of seriousness—merely childlike antics would gain no admittance here. Stevenson appreciated the lucrative aspect of writing popular fiction—a regular income. In a climate in which substance was attributed to the weighty realistic novels being produced by George Moore and others, whereas romance, and particularly children's books, were seen as comparatively valueless, Robert Louis Stevenson subversively argued for the surface pleasures of romance, demonstrating in *Treasure Island* that value is a matter of context rather than of absolute qualities. Even more subversively, in his letters and commentary from this period, Stevenson located the value of a text in its ability to furnish a living wage, countering any romantic notion of the nobility of the starving artist.

If *Treasure Island* romanticizes the pursuit of money, it also demonstrates the extent to which the value of money and morality is ungrounded, a nexus of continual struggle, compromise, and betrayal. Although value can be a matter of life and death—certainly the number of deaths in *Treasure Island* would testify to this—it is also socially defined and politically established. But even more crucially the book thematizes and demonstrates the doubleness so often remarked on by Stevenson's commentators, in particular the attractiveness of the "bad" and the repulsiveness of the "good." To understand this theme only in terms of Stevenson's bohemian struggle against his Scottish Presbyterian roots overlooks a significant aspect of the conflict between gold and silver standards. In exploring the pleasures of piracy alongside the rigors of capitalist virtue—or indeed the pleasures of mixing and debasing each with each—Stevenson was exploring expediency and its correlates as an endlessly fluctuating system. He was reproducing the mechanism of valuation itself.

Treasure Island, Stevenson's boy's romance, is underpinned by the reality-based principles of delayed gratification and self-discipline. While teasing his readers with the possibility of escape from capitalist modes, *Treasure Island* closes it off, most notably in Jim Hawkins, the child's stand-in and the victim-hero of the economic process. Jim, after all, tells of no personal gain except nightmare. Long John Silver, the eighteenth-century pirate, points from the preindustrial past to the finance-informed future. In his quicksilver adaptability and "dooty" first and foremost to himself, Silver defines the capitalist mold; his successful counterfeit of the gold standard exposes its contingency.

Finally, value inheres in what "works," a decisive blow to the secondhand pieties tendered by various characters during the course of *Treasure Island.* Silver's splendid villainy is much more appealing than Smollett's virtue, a fact with which Silver taunts him in "A Fable: The Persons of the Tale": "After the 32nd chapter of *Treasure Island,* two of the puppets strolled out to have a pipe before business should begin again." Silver and Smollett, true to their characters, begin to argue about value. Smollett tells Silver that he's "in a bad way" and calls him a "damned rogue." Silver responds, "There's no call to be angry with me in earnest. I'm on'y a chara'ter in a sea story. I don't really exist" ("Fable" 223). Excusing himself on the grounds that he is mere paper and not "real," Silver questions Smollett's assumptions. When the captain asserts that his worth is valued by a supposed author, Silver counters: "If there is sich a thing as a Author, I'm his favourite chara'ter. He does me fathoms better'n he does you—fathoms, he does. And he likes doing me. He keeps me on deck mostly all the time, crutch and all; and he leaves you measling in the hold, where nobody can't see you, nor wants to, and you may lay to that!" ("Fable" 224). Refusing simplistic judgments based on naturalized, gold-standard norms of virtue, Silver questions the very grounds of virtue, egged on by his author: "What is this good? I made a mutiny, and I been a gentleman o' fortune; well, but by all stories you [Captain Smollett] ain't no such saint. I'm a man that keeps company very easy; even by your own account, you ain't, and to my certain knowledge, you're a devil to haze. Which is which? Which is good, and which bad?" ("Fable" 225). In this postscript Silver confidently assumes the value of pleasurable rhetoric, romance, and contingency, dismissing any foundational notions of virtue or value. In all the texts in which he appears, Silver reveals that social, economic, and moral value are manufactured, artificial; that success is a matter of context and expedience. In depicting this new definition of heroism, Stevenson acknowledges the beguiling potentiality of the new world order, the romance of money.

Notes

1. Leslie Fiedler reads *Treasure Island* as an example of the myth of "Beloved Scoundrel or the Devil as Angel" (79) and as a struggle with the desire to escape adulthood. Robert Kiely echoes this position with his thesis that *Treasure Island* allows us an "exhilarating sense of casting off . . . in the nautical sense of leaving port and in the conventional sense of throwing off encumbrances" (68–69). He denies the book any complexity: the characters, according to Kiely, are no more than fancy-dress pirates (70). David Daiches denies the importance of the goal: "The immediate interest lies in the quest, not in the nature and significance of what is sought after" (56). Jenni Calder (*Life Study*) asserts that *Treasure Island* was important not as a children's book but because "Stevenson was more concerned with writing out of his system certain elemental fantasies" (173). She does not link Stevenson's desire to make money with the themes of the book. Sam Pickering reads the novel as a celebration of fancy, in the Wordsworthian sense. Mann and Hardesty ("Stevenson's Method") focus on the ways in which Stevenson altered the plot devices of earlier adventure novels; they also note the importance of Stevenson's revisions of the text, which make the adult authority figures less parodic and more dignified ("Stevenson's Revisions" and, with Patricia Hardesty, "Doctoring"). Jacqueline Rose cites *Treasure Island* as an example of the way children's literature "conceals the slide between nature study and suspense" (80) to mystify language itself as an absolute and concrete entity. David H. Jackson argues that *Treasure Island* is important as a "Late-Victorian Adults' Novel" because of its conservative ethos. The argument of Joseph Bristow bears interesting parallels to my own in that he treats the economic aspects of Stevenson's production of *Treasure Island* but finally argues that the book is about story-telling. Jean Perrot links *Treasure Island* with a resurgence of interest in Pan and in pagan aestheticism. Griffith and Frey do argue that "treasure, to find and to hold, is the goal in Stevenson's tale" (148–49), but their psychoanalytic framework does not allow for the materiality of money. Although *Treasure Island* will certainly bear a psychoanalytic reading, it needs to be balanced with history; Griffith and Frey rely on easy psychoanalytic equivalences without addressing Stevenson's context.

2. I take my quotation here from the grand passage in *The Communist Manifesto:* "The bourgeoisie, wherever it has got the upper hand, has put an end to all feudal, patriarchal, idyllic relations. It has pitilessly torn asunder the motley feudal ties that bound man to his natural superiors, and has left remaining no other nexus between

man and man than naked self-interest, than callous cash payment. It has drowned the most heavenly ecstasies of religious fervour, of chivalrous enthusiasm, of philistine sentimentalism, in the icy water of egotistical calculation. It has resolved personal worth into exchange value, and in place of the numberless indefeasible chartered freedoms, has set up that single, unconscionable freedom—Free Trade. In one word, for exploitation, veiled by religious and political illusions, it has substituted naked, shameless, direct, brutal exploitation" (*Communist Manifesto* 223).

3. Up until the late seventeenth century, England had been on the silver standard; however, the huge outlay of silver to pay for Indian trade forced England to adopt the gold standard.

4. This was currency that could not be converted into gold on request.

5. Richard Hofstadter quotes William Hope "Coin" Harvey: "If one tries to salvage whatever there may be of fact in Harvey's attempt to claim primacy for silver, it must be simply that gold, being too valuable to serve as common coin, was coined only in units ranging from $2.50 up to the $10 gold eagle, and that the coinage handled by the common man was of silver. ('Gold was considered the money of the rich . . . the poor people seldom handled it, and the very poor people seldom ever saw any of it')" (273). "Coin" Harvey was a propagandist for free silver in the United States. His widely read pamphlet *Coin's Financial School,* published in June 1894, influenced the pro-silver stance of William Jennings Bryan and countless others (Hofstadter 242).

6. The point is corroborated by later economic historians (see Hawtrey). Gold tripled in value in relation to silver (Hawtrey 82). "It was Germany's sudden demand for £50,000,000 in gold that drove her neighbours to suspend the free coinage of silver" (Hawtrey 81).

7. The twentieth-century economist George Winder argued that the gold standard was essentially a moral standard as well: "Like all other sound forms of modern money, the Bill on London was the product of honour, integrity, and freedom" (32–33). According to Winder, abandoning the gold standard not only caused inflation (something hurtful to the owners, but not to the debtors) but also compromised the moral character of the British economy—the action cost Britain its substance.

8. Sherbrooke's position is particularly interesting in that he demystifies the notion of money = value and anticipates the widespread use of paper money as a good solution to currency shortages but still comes down conservatively when it comes to discussing the actual metals.

9. *Dictionary of the Vulgar Tongue.* I am indebted to Bruce Rosen for this citation.

10. The history of the term *sterling* is an example of fluctuating value. Originally referring to silver, the term came to mean "conforming to the highest standard," although silver money was debased and therefore ineligible to be considered sterling. And although a "pound sterling" originally referred to a pound's weight of silver pennies, by the nineteenth century it had come to mean a unit of money that was represented chiefly by gold.

11. As economic historian Robert Johnson points out, the gold standard was thought to act like a moral yardstick, a standard that demanded the capitalist virtue of saving rather than extravagance: "Gold was to act like a kind of censor which expressed, in Sir Robert Kindersley's phrase, 'the sins or virtues as the case may be, of all the inhabitants of a country,' its departure creating 'that anxiety which brings home to them that they are being extravagant' " (Johnson 42).

12. Such metaphors have led some critics to oversimplify the conflict of the book. David Jackson calls Silver an "imitation adult" who mimics the gentlemen born and thus gains power through language (30); his adult-child dichotomy falsifies the issues even as he raises important questions about literary value. Sam Pickering, in emphasizing imagination, actually calls Billy Bones an "old wife" who nurtures Jim's fancy and enables him to enact it (100). Claudia Nelson argues that Smollett is the only "true"

adult in the book (129), basing this judgment on the idea that "true" adults don't care for treasure but only for duty. By this argument, the squire's servant Redruth also counts, but I don't believe that the argument that adults don't care for treasure would really hold if one were to compare the attitudes of adults in almost any nineteenth-century realist novel toward inheritance and income.

13. See Fiedler and Kiely in particular.

14. "A man, walking in a ravine one day, picked up a small bright mass of shining metal. . . . This little mass of metal, which afterward came to be designated as gold, the man carried home to his wife, who in turn was so much pleased with it that she hung it by a string about her neck as an ornament. Its attractiveness of course excited the desire of every other woman to have the same" (Wells 38).

15. Recall Jim's mother's similar rigid honesty and its peril.

16. The last words of the book, "Pieces of eight," provide an apt metonym for Silver during the course of the narrative. Silver coins from South America, pieces of eight are associated with piracy but also with Silver himself through the parrot. And Silver eludes his shipmates in a South American port.

17. In order for a novice to prevail and actually write the novel, Stevenson claimed, "there must be something for hope to feed upon. The beginner must have a slant of wind, a lucky vein must be running, he must be in one of those hours when the words come and the phrases balance of themselves—*even to begin*" ("My First Book" xxiv).

18. Letter to W. E. Henley, September 1881 (*Robert Louis Stevenson: The Critical Heritage,* 125).

19. Letter of 5 May 1883, *Letters* 2:238.

20. Anonymous review of *Treasure Island,* 15 December 1883, *Pall Mall Gazette* 38, 4–5. Possibly by Andrew Lang. *Robert Louis Stevenson: The Critical Heritage,* 139.

21. George Moore, *Confessions of a Young Man* (1888) 284, reprinted in *Robert Louis Stevenson: The Critical Heritage,* 329.

22. Felicity Hughes 542–61. I highly recommend this discussion of the ideology informing separation of the novel into "realism" and mere romance. Compare her quotations from James and Moore: "The high prosperity of our fiction has marched very directly, with another 'sign of the times,' the demoralisation, the vulgarisation of literature in general, the increasing familiarity of all such methods of communication, the making itself supremely felt, as it were, of the presence of the ladies and children—by whom I mean, in other words, the reader irreflective and uncritical" (Henry James, "The Future of the Novel"); "Let us renounce the effort to reconcile these two irreconcilable things—art and young girls" (George Moore, *Literature at Nurse, Or, Circulating Morals*) (Hughes 547).

23. This was the period in which the study of English literature as an academic discipline was being established in English schools other than the Oxbridge establishment (Eagleton 27). "English literature might be a suitable subject for 'women . . . and the second- and third-rate men who [will] become schoolmasters' " (Gossman 341–42). As I have already noted, Felicity Hughes has shown how this attitude grouped not just working-class men and women but also children. Certainly, James in "The Art of Fiction" argues passionately for its seriousness and for the need to distinguish good from bad novels. In response to Besant, who argues that a novel without adventure is an "impossible thing," James writes of adventure as expendable and even detrimental to the genre: "Why without adventure, more than without matrimony, or celibacy, or parturition, or cholera, or hydropathy, or Jansenism? This seems to me to bring the novel back to the hapless little role of being an artificial, ingenious thing—bring it down from its large, free character of an immense and exquisite correspondence with life" (61).

Works Cited

Bristow, Joseph. *Empire Boys: Adventures in a Man's World.* Reading Popular Fiction. London: HarperCollins*Academic,* 1991.

Calder, Jenni. *Robert Louis Stevenson: A Life Study.* New York: Oxford University Press, 1980.

———, ed. *Stevenson and Victorian Scotland.* Edinburgh: Edinburgh University Press, 1981.

Coleman, Elizabeth. "Henry James Criticism: A Case Study for Critical Inquiry." *Nineteenth-Century Fiction* 40 (1985): 327–44.

Daiches, David. *Robert Louis Stevenson and His World.* London: Thames and Hudson, 1973.

Dictionary of the Vulgar Tongue. Northfield, Ill.: Digest, 1971.

Eagleton, Terry. *Literary Theory: An Introduction.* Minneapolis: University of Minnesota Press, 1983.

Fiedler, Leslie, "RLS Revisited." In *No! in Thunder: Essays on Myth and Literature.* Boston: Beacon, 1960. Pp. 77–91.

Gossman, Lionel. "Literature and Education." *New Literary History* 13, no. 2 (Winter 1982): 341–71.

Graham, Kenneth. *English Criticism of the Novel, 1865–1900.* Oxford English Monographs. Oxford: Clarendon, 1965.

Griffith, John W., and Charles H. Frey. *The Literary Heritage of Childhood.* New York: Greenwood, 1987.

Hardesty, Patricia Whaley, William H. Hardesty, and David Mann. "Doctoring the Doctor: How Stevenson Altered the Second Narrator of *Treasure Island.*" *Studies in Scottish Literature* 21 (1986):1–22.

Harvie, Christopher. "The Politics of Stevenson." In *Stevenson and Victorian Scotland,* ed. Jenni Calder. Edinburgh: Edinburgh University Press, 1981. Pp. 107–25.

Hawtrey, R. G. *The Gold Standard in Theory and Practice.* 5th ed. London: Longmans, Green, 1947.

Hofstadter, Richard. "Free Silver and the Mind of 'Coin' Harvey." In *The Paranoid Style in American Politics and Other Essays.* New York: Alfred A. Knopf, 1966. Pp. 238–315.

Hughes, Felicity. "Children's Literature: Theory and Practice." *ELH* 45 (1978):542–61.

Jackson, David H. "*Treasure Island* as a Late-Victorian Adults' Novel." *Victorian Newsletter* (Fall 1987):28–32.

James, Henry. "The Art of Fiction." In *Literary Criticism: Essays on Literature, American Writers, English Writers,* ed. Leon Edel. Vol. 1. New York: Library of America, 1984. Pp. 44–65.

Jastram, Roy W. *Silver: The Restless Metal.* New York: John Wiley and Sons, 1981.

Johnson, Brian. *The Politics of Money.* London: John Murray, 1970.

Kiely, Robert. *Robert Louis Stevenson and the Fiction of Adventure.* Cambridge: Harvard University Press, 1964.

Mann, David D., and William H. Hardesty. "Stevenson's Revisions of *Treasure Island:* 'Writing Down the Whole Particulars.'" *Text: Transactions of the Society for Textual Scholarship* 3 (1987):377–92.

———. "Stevenson's Method in *Treasure Island:* 'The Old Romance, Retold.'" *Essays in Literature* 9 (1982): 180–93.

Marx, Karl, and Friedrich Engels, "The Communist Manifesto." In *Karl Marx: Selected Writings,* ed. David McLellan. Oxford: Oxford University Press, 1977. Pp. 221–47.

Michaels, Walter Benn. *The Gold Standard and the Logic of Naturalism.* Berkeley: University of California Press, 1987.

Nelson, Claudia. *Boys Will Be Girls.* Athens: University of Georgia Press, 1991.

O'Malley, Michael. "Specie and Species: Race and the Money Question in Nineteenth-Century America." *American Historical Review* 99, no. 2 (1994):369–95.

Perrot, Jean. "Pan and *Puer Aeternus:* Aestheticism and the Spirit of the Age." *Poetics Today* 13 (1992):155–67.

Pickering, Sam. "Stevenson's 'Elementary Novel of Adventure.'" *Research Studies* 49, no. 2 (June 1981):99–106.

Robert Louis Stevenson: The Critical Heritage. Ed. Paul Maixner. London: Routledge and Kegan Paul, 1981.

Rose, Jacqueline. *The Case of Peter Pan, Or, The Impossibility of Children's Fiction.* London: Macmillan, 1984.

Salmon, Edward. *Juvenile Literature as It Is.* London: Henry J. Drane, 1888.

Sassoon, Edward. "The Crusade Against Silver." *The Nineteenth Century* 19 (1886):882–95.

Shell, Marc. *Money, Language, and Thought: Literary and Philosophical Economies from the Medieval to the Modern Era.* Berkeley: University of California Press, 1982.

Sherbrooke, Viscount (Robert Lowe). "What Is Money?" *The Nineteenth Century* 11 (1882):501–9.

Stevenson, Robert Louis. "A Fable: The Persons of the Tale." 1894. Vol. 2 of *The Works of Robert Louis Stevenson.* Tusitala Edition. London: Heinemann, 1923. Pp. 223–26.

———. *The Letters of Robert Louis Stevenson, Volume 2.* Ed. Sidney Colvin. Vol. 32 of *The Works of Robert Louis Stevenson.* Tusitala Edition. London: Heinemann, 1924.

———. "My First Book: *Treasure Island.*" 1894. Vol. 2 of *The Works of Robert Louis Stevenson.* Tusitala Edition. London: Heinemann, 1923. Pp. xxiii–xxxi.

———. *The Silverado Squatters.* 1883. Vol. 18 of *The Works of Robert Louis Stevenson.* Tusitala Edition. London: Heinemann, 1924. Pp. 155–247.

———. *Treasure Island.* 1881–82; 1883. Vol. 2 of *The Works of Robert Louis Stevenson.* Tusitala Edition. London: Heinemann, 1923. Pp. 3–220.

Swearingen, Roger G. *The Prose Writings of Robert Louis Stevenson: A Guide.* Hamden, Conn.: Archon, 1980.

Trotter, David. "Gold Standards: Money in Edwardian Fiction." *Critical Quarterly* 30, no. 1 (1988): 22–35.

Wells, David A. *Robinson Crusoe's Money; or, the Remarkable Financial Fortunes and Misfortunes of a Remote Island Community.* New York: Peter Smith, 1931.

Winder, George. *A Short History of Money.* London: Newman Neame, 1959.

A Change in the Family: The Image of the Family in Contemporary Chinese Children's Literature, 1949–1993

Jane Parish Yang

For the past two months, a most unforgettable event has been coursing through my brain. At nights before I sleep or in mornings when I have just awakened, this event clearly unfolds before my eyes like a scroll painting. It seems as if I can still feel the crisp air in my nostrils, so cold and sharp, and the moonlight flooding over my head, still so radiant and luminous. My hand, which Father had grasped tightly, still surges with warmth; my face still benumbed by Mother's icy tears! I have often told them both: "I will never forget that night." Mother then hugs me closely: "My child, I hope you will remember this forever."

And what was it? That night two months ago, on the night of January thirteenth, when Father and Mother took me to Tiananmen Square to mourn our beloved Premier Zhou in front of the Monument to the People's Heroes.

—Bing Xin, "Ji Yijian Zui Nanwang de Shiqing [Recalling a Most Memorable Event]" (1977)

The quotation in the epigraph, from one of China's most famous modern writers, depicts a warm family relationship between parents and child connected to a larger political cause: the then-dangerous expression of support for moderation during the Cultural Revolution (1966–1976). From the thirteenth century on, how family and state relate to each other had been a central concern of Neo-Confucian philosophical and political teachings. Writings from the time of Confucius and Mencius, *The Four Books,* were annotated and explicated by the Neo-Confucian Chu Hsi (1130–1200), and were made the state-sanctioned texts for education in all of China. It was not the Neo-Confucians who first spoke of the family-state relationship, how-

I would like to thank Gervais Reed, Frank Doeringer, and Daniel Taylor, Lawrence University, for their helpful comments and careful editing. I would also like to thank Suzanne Gay and Paula Richman, Oberlin College, for their comments on an earlier version of this chapter, as well as its three anonymous reviewers.

Children's Literature 26, ed. Elizabeth Lennox Keyser (Yale University Press, © 1998 Hollins College).

ever, as noted historian Donald Munro states: "To consider the government an extension of family relationships was a policy of Chou [1122–256 B.C.] feudalism" (46). Munro asserts that Chu Hsi and the Neo-Confucians merely tried to reconcile the "potential incompatibility between family-centered role fulfillment and duty to the public" (113).[1]

Proper relations among family members and between the family and the state were a central concern in these ethical teachings of Confucius: an individual was first and foremost a member of a family group, with duties and obligations to that group. Familial roles, especially the duties of the male side—father, elder brother, son—were specifically a part of these teachings. Only after one's duty to the family was fulfilled was one capable of serving the larger entity beyond the family: the state. The two roles were interconnected in Neo-Confucian thought, with reciprocal obligations for each, but serving the family was seen as a prerequisite to serving the state. In fact, service to the state could be a means of empowering and enriching a family, and so service to the state often was subverted to the particular interests of the family.

Neo-Confucians taught that one who was filial, that is, who carried out the proper role of a son, would not offend a superior. Likewise, it was thought that one who was fraternal, that is, who carried out the proper role of a brother, would know his correct role in regard to superiors. It was assumed that having learned proper behavior at home, one would know how to relate to superiors and inferiors in the wider realm outside the family. Yet even so, one's primary loyalty and interest lay with the family. The collective good of society was a secondary consideration in this family-centered ethical system.

A change in values came with the advent of communist ideology, which influenced Chinese writings from the first part of the twentieth century. In the communist view, the interests of the individual, as well as of the family unit, were subsumed by the interests of society as a whole. The literary expression of communist ideology, socialist realism, allowed for no negative or vacillating characters in fact or fiction—only positive, exemplary ones, who would carry the Revolution to its inevitable victory. Such a didactic approach in which literature serves larger social and political goals is common in children's literature and dates to the beginning of Chinese literary writings.[2] But some writers of the pre-Revolutionary period, obviously struggling with the dictates of socialist realism, tended more toward naturalism and included negative, individualistic, or vacillating characters who did not support collective goals. After the communist victory in 1949, fiction of this latter type all but disappeared for perhaps forty years. Only in more recent times has depiction of negative, uncooperative individuals (and families) been allowed.

Since the family-state relationship is political, depiction of the family in contemporary Chinese literature has not been static but has changed according to political needs. The change in the image of the family in contemporary Chinese children's literature, the focus of this study, can be divided into four distinct phases: the post-revolutionary period up to the Cultural Revolution (1949–1966), the ten-year-long Cultural Revolution period (1966–76), the immediate post–Cultural Revolution period (1976–1985), and the contemporary period (late 1985–1993).[3]

Post-Revolutionary Period (1949–1966)

Early post–1949 fiction attributed family support for the new collective system to the concrete benefits of socialism. This fiction showed how families adapted to and accepted socialism. Socialist values were shown to bolster the family, not conflict with its interests. Indeed, it was the older generation's individualistic and feudalistic ideas that were shown to have hindered family progress. For example, in the 1957 story by Miao Ge "Jin Yin Dong," new ways of treating peasants in the socialist society allow the family to flourish. A grandfather, able to borrow money from the cooperative credit union for his grandson's marriage, is won over to the new socialist state and ceases to believe in the old superstitious ways of getting wealthy.

Similarly, in a 1964 story, Sun Jibin's "Jiejie," state and family purposes blend in joint hatred of the "imperialists." At the end of the story even the meaning of family has been blurred. When the elder sister is killed by imperialists, a substitute sister, orphaned in the same attack, is welcomed into the family. It is she who states the new creed: "Your mother is my mother; your sister is my sister" (31).[4] The meaning of family has thus widened to include those who have undergone similar experiences and who share hatred of the same enemy.

Proper social behavior in the new society, less selfish and more cooperative, was stressed in another 1957 story, Yang Meiqing's "Women Sange." When a young man decides to mend his ways and work with, not against, a classmate, his first thought is to have this newfound friend and helper over for dinner. He will ask his mother to fry some eggs, probably an expensive dish in China at that time. The family unit is depicted as celebrating his newfound devotion to the wider community. Indeed, in contrast with some later stories discussed below, it is often the mother in these stories who cooperates with the schoolteacher, the usual agent of social change, to alter a child's behavior.

In summary, then, fiction for children in the period from 1949 through 1966 did not posit a conflict of interest between the family and the state; it tried to encourage the family to support the new social system by pointing out real benefits for the family and the individual under socialism.

Cultural Revolution Period (1966–1976)

During the second stage, the Cultural Revolution (a period known in China as the ten years of chaos), children's literature was virtually destroyed. Publication of storybooks ceased between 1967 and 1970.[5] What was published after 1970 came from the radical Shanghai People's Publishing House and consisted of picture books, most of which showed children as diligent supporters of Red Guard initiatives and Mao's thought. Children's publications from this state-run publishing house rarely depicted family life, paralleling the absence of the family in school textbooks.[6] Roberta Martin makes the following observation after reviewing textbooks from the period: "It appears that the Chinese Government has attempted to weaken the image (and ultimately the role) of the family in an effort to diminish its socializing influence, while simultaneously enhancing the image of certain peer group units in an effort to shape the norms and values which the groups project and thereby to regulate their socializing influence" (253). In place of the family readers saw peer groups at school or in the state-run day care centers where the young spent the majority of their waking hours. The child is shown as interacting with peers and teachers and taking her values from the peer group. Her primary duty is service to the state, not the family. Children are self-conscious little ideologists fighting against social injustice, exposing public enemies of socialism, upholding the thoughts of Chairman Mao, and placing the state above all other loyalties.

Almost all role models in literature published during the Cultural Revolution were positive, exemplary ones. Children exercise not just for their own pleasure but in order to be soldiers in the revolutionary struggles on behalf of the proletariat. This theme of self-strengthening for a higher purpose, common in nineteenth- and early-twentieth-century children's literature in the West, predominated in China in the twentieth century, reflecting the nationalist sentiment that future generations must be prepared for the rigors of protecting the nation. Even preschoolers on a playground slide supposedly are exercising in order to improve their bodies on behalf of the Revolution. Little children bouncing balls and counting the number of bounces similarly are not motivated by personal amusement or ambition: they are practicing "revolutionary will."[7]

This notion of the child existing for a cause beyond herself is not new, nor is it peculiar to communist ideology. The child-socialization process in general can be seen as a way to wrest control of the child's body away from the child herself and enlist it in a higher cause—for the family, clan, community, or state. But in this epoch control of the child was so pervasive and rigid that it goes well beyond any previous attempts at socialization, which typically built on family relationships, rather than trying to destroy them. There is no mention in this literature of family relationships or connections, nor any depiction of the child in a relationship other than with peers. The child is depicted as directly linked to the state and in tune with its revolutionary goals.

Not surprisingly, symbols of the Cultural Revolution era abound in these stories. For example, in *San Jian Maoxianyi* a little girl praises the talents of classmates who can build models of Tiananmen (the Gate of Heavenly Peace, where Mao stood to review parades) or draw a red star (the symbol of the Red Army). Her unselfish behavior toward these classmates is commended as being in the spirit of Lei Feng, the paragon of virtue praised during the Cultural Revolution (and recently resurrected). The children are thus praised to the extent that they identify with state symbols and ideals.

The most graphic depiction of children transferring their loyalties from the family to the state comes in *Hong Xiaobing Nupi Shentong Shi.* A group of children probably no older than seven or eight meets in periodic study sessions on Marxist-Leninist thought, where they try to devise concrete ways to carry out class struggle. When the grandfather of a classmate orders his grandson to copy some reactionary verse, the grandson's classmates encourage him to disobey.[8] The grandson talks back to him, tattles on him to his teacher, and humiliates him in an open session convened to expose and criticize public enemies. The child stands solidly against his family when family values are closely scrutinized and found to be in conflict with values taught in the schools.

Literature from the Cultural Revolution period shows young children in a state-controlled setting interacting with peers, not family. They are shown as caring and concerned when members of their peer group are in need, but self-righteously vindictive and unmerciful against opponents of the revolutionary ideology they profess—including family members who represent the old ways and the old ideology. They do not have to wrestle with the moral dilemma of turning against their families; for them there is no dilemma. The moral authority of elders is eroded if not completely gone, and the family hierarchy has been turned on its head. It is now the young who lecture their elders on proper conduct in this new age. Privy to the new wisdom, the young have a duty to see that their elders follow the correct path. Children, with their new peer groups, uphold state ideology against the parochial interests of the family.

Fiction for older children in this period was less simplistic and more nuanced. It often continued in the same vein as pre–Cultural Revolution stories to show the family as supporting collective work and goals and opposing individual, selfish gain at group expense. For example, in Xin Le's "Cai Luo" (1973), the culprit is an obstinate individual who cannot see beyond his own personal benefit to the benefit of the whole group. Two young children whose father and brother are party cadres take the lead in upholding the collective's rules against individuals' netting fish during spawning time. One child says dramatically: "We've held a family meeting. Dad and Elder Brother have both given their opinions. Cadre must be the first to uphold revolutionary regulations. Family members must also guarantee impartiality. All of us can do this, including my sister and me. We can even guarantee that our dog Spottie won't ever harm the government's interest. Give me the muzzle" (82). The child proceeds to muzzle the family dog to make sure it doesn't steal food from the collective.

During the Cultural Revolution period, if an individual family was portrayed at all, it demonstrated firm support for collective goals as against the opportunism of those who did not heed the call of socialism. Interestingly, the traditional power holders of the patriarchal family, the father and the eldest brother, are still shown as exercising power in the family during the Cultural Revolution.

Immediate Post–Cultural Revolution Period (1976–1985)

In the third period, the immediate post–Cultural Revolution era of the late 1970s to the mid-1980s, less militaristic and dogmatic stories were offered to the young reading public. In contrast to the lack of family scenes and interactions in the Cultural Revolution period, the stories of this period again brought the family back to the center of concern. The suffering of the family as a unit during that ten-year period (unnamed but very obvious) is often depicted, as in Kang Fukun's "Xiao Xiang Nunu," a 1978 fable exposing the hardships families faced, including separation of family members or death at the hands of evildoers.[9] Perhaps in recognition of hardships suffered, authors of this period treat the family in quite a favorable light. As the government's standing suffers, the reputation of families seems to rebound.

Along with this graphic depiction of past suffering the stories display a recognition that the family must support collective goals in order to survive and prosper. The enticement of becoming wealthier begins to figure prominently in such stories as Yang Xiao's 1980 "Yeye Dangxuanle Fuye Duizhang." The grandmother in this story, whose family had suffered hardship during the Cultural Revolution because of her husband's "capitalist road" policies, becomes convinced that her own village can now prosper like a neighboring village, and she comes to see that active political involvement in the community can bring prosperity, not ruin, to the family.

Yang's story, part of the "Scar Literature" that detailed the sufferings of the people during the Cultural Revolution, attempts to reconcile the conflicting demands of family and community, as well as to erase doubt about the future direction of the country.[10] The grandmother also gives voice to a persistent fear during this period: that government policy will change once again and the family will be punished for being on the wrong side politically. She is assured that this is not possible in the new political climate. The very fact that such a sensitive issue could be discussed in this fiction shows the great change in government policy of this era.

Niaore Ertu's "Qicha Jijiao de Gonglu," remarkable for its Faulkneresque setting in the wilderness, seems to dismiss the conflict between family and state as irrelevant. Instead, it places the individual in the wider context of the natural world, where human beings are but small and rather insignificant players. A rare example of minority literature in a Han Chinese–dominated literary world, this story from the Evenki (Solon) nationality in Heilongjiang Province depicts a young man's confrontation with his stepfather as he grows into manhood in the primitive hunting culture of the northern steppes. The older man compares his stepson to a lazy domesticated animal: "You're like a cat, staying inside the tent all day, letting me take care of you" (333).

Though he has three chances to shoot a seven-point buck that he had promised to bring back to his stepfather, the young man has come to admire the buck's courage in fighting for its survival against its natural enemies and thus refuses to kill it. For this he is beaten. In the end, the stepfather, having watched his stepson's attempts to free the buck from wolves and from a trap, recognizes that allowing the buck to live was the right decision.

Both men subordinate their own survival and that of their "family" to preservation of this symbol of freedom and courage. The stepfather recognizes, as the young man earlier learned, that there is some higher value beyond the individual, something unnamed but obviously not simply the community or state: nature itself. The buck comes to symbolize beauty, strength, and the stubborn will to survive in an often harsh environment. Through his observation of his stepson's struggle to save the buck, the stepfather, an alcoholic, also comes to acknowledge his obligation to care for his stepson.

The stepson's three encounters with the buck alternate with recurring dreams of deer and wild swans, which seem to serve as symbols of freedom to the young man caught in an unhappy family situation. He is also haunted by a dream of the buck being butchered. His fear of his stepfather gradually disappears as he discovers freedom, ease, and a sense of belonging in the woods while tracking the deer. The beauty of the landscape is described in loving detail whenever the buck is encountered: the tall mountain peak covered with pine and birch, the golden leaves shimmering in the sunlight against the white birchbark. He likens the mountain peak to a proud giant with pine woods and sheer cliffs clinging to its shoulders. He feels no fear or strangeness in the wilderness, since it is the source of everything on which his tribe depends. In the protective embrace of the forest, he states: "I forgot I was an orphan who had lost my parents" (335).

The raw primitivism of the story and the stark depiction of a dysfunctional family are an anomaly among the Han Chinese stories of functional family relationships in densely populated urban settings. The story's careful attention to lyrical detail, and its evocation of the wilderness's beauty and its hidden terrors, stands in stark contrast to the neglect of nuance, shade, and craft common in other stories written in this period. Yet a comic structure is maintained in this story, as in others of this period, in that the individual is reintegrated into the family or community at the end of the narrative.

Family support of legitimate state ideals is highlighted in many of these stories. Families are emotionally involved with the fate of the state and even willing to take a political stand in public. The family's willingness to act in this manner indicates that family and state ideals need not always conflict. For example, in Bing Xin's story "Ji Yijian Zui Nanwang de Shiqing" a family is shown reacting emotionally to the news of Zhou Enlai's death in January 1976. Family members are willing to brave both the harsh winter weather and the wrath of the Gang of Four regime to gather in Tiananmen Square for a memorial tribute to Chou. The contrast between the warmth of the people's response to Zhou's death and the indifferent official state is especially acute. This story by the venerable modern writer Bing Xin pointedly was placed first in Jin Jin's 1986 *Anthology of New Chinese Literature, 1976–1982: Collection of Children's Literature,* as if to underscore the idea that the family can be a morally responsive entity in the state.

In fact, in literature of the late 1970s support for the state or the community was often depicted as derived from the positive values of the family. When one reached beyond the family unit to help a stranger, it was the image of the welcoming warmth of home that led one to recognize the needs of the wider social group. In "Yilu Lihua" by Peng Jingfeng, a laborer returning from a hard day's work in the mountains is motivated to rebuild and refurbish a mountain hut for others to use after he himself has gratefully used it as a way station on a trip home. In detailing the laborer's pleasant images of the hut as a place like home, providing food and warm shelter from the harsh weather, the story shows his increasing awareness that each person has an obligation to others to make "way stations" for their journeys through life.

A 1979 story, "Chi Tuolaji de Gushi" by Luo Chensheng, shows a young child sacrificing his family's newly bought fish to cover up for the greed of an officious visiting party cadre in the hope that the village will benefit from this relationship. The deed is exposed by an impetuous young child who can't tolerate the injustice and corruption he sees. Naturally, it is his appeal to an evenhanded and fair higher-level cadre that saves the day. The story is remarkable for showing the family as willing to make sacrifices in order to benefit the larger group.

In a third story, Wang Anyi's "Shei Shi Weilaide Zhongdui Zhang," father and son vent their hatred of "squealers" in the factory and at school—those who toady to authorities by reporting on the minor transgressions of others. The father and son vow to get even in the next election of officers. Thus the family is shown in a positive light, taking action against those who abuse power and position or whose judgment is faulty.[11] This is also one of the few children's stories that show a father interacting with his child.

In these stories the family is depicted as supportive of true socialism and courageous enough to fight against corrupt party cadres and leftist extremists. At the time when leftists were discredited in post–Cultural Revolution fiction, the family regained favor as a morally legitimate unit. This is perhaps because other institutions in Chinese society—the state and entities representing the state—were too closely tied to discredited policies. Only the family emerged relatively unscathed.

The Contemporary Period (1985–1993)

Post–Cultural Revolution publications continued to depict some children as the catalysts for socialist change in society, although without the self-righteous fervor of the Cultural Revolution period. Writers praised children who strove toward independence and personal autonomy. Some were depicted as goal-oriented self-starters whose curiosity and intelligence propelled them to pursue interests outside the family circle. Family members (often the mother) who tried to prevent this independence were described in unflattering terms. Children were also depicted as trying to be independent in order to lessen the burden on hard-working parents. The authors of these stories clearly differentiated between selfish behavior beneficial only to the child and independent behavior meant to help the family or some larger social unit.

At the same time, children in stories of this period were not depicted as overly good. The editors of an early 1980s collection stated opposition to fictional perfect children who resembled model "little adults."[12] Although some children in the late-1970s stories did display heroism—protecting family friends from leftist extremists, or protecting the interest of the collective against selfish individuals, or showing a teacher the error of her ways in dealing with her students—other stories showed average children mending their ways, changing into self-disciplined, more cooperative students.[13] As the reputation of the government was restored after the Cultural Revolution, authors were once again able to focus on the contemporary family and its faults. In the period immediately after the Cultural Revolution, the focus had been on government shortcomings and the people's "scars." Now family scars could be exposed once again.

In publications appearing at the end of the 1980s, the contemporary family is overwhelmingly portrayed as a one-child urban family, in contrast to the prevalence of rural settings during the Cultural Revolution. There was a shift from lauding peasants with revolutionary values to promoting population control in urban centers. In picture books, a family portrait usually shows at most four members: two parents, one child, and one grandmother. In a few stories both grandparents are present; in others both are absent. Only in animal fables or stories set in premodern China are there siblings. Although the terms for older and younger brother and sister are introduced in a widely disseminated elementary picture book for teaching simple Chinese characters,[14] in only two instances in the picture books I have collected are these terms actually used in stories set in contemporary times.[15] Depiction of politically correct one-child families may go hand in hand with a general trend during this period to deemphasize the importance of the family.

The only child is depicted as a lonely child, often shown home alone with a mountain of toys bought by her indulgent, but absent, parents. Without other relatives or siblings at home, social interaction comes only with peers. In "Lanlan Zhao Pengyou" a little girl unwilling to attend preschool is shown home alone with her inanimate toys or silent pets. She finally decides school is preferable to this loneliness and goes off to the preschool to find playmates. It is clear from the story that the child has made a good choice. That her parents have spoiled her, while unstated, is obvious as well.

The suspicion that most people only look out for their family members is gently emphasized in a 1986 story found in the People's Educational Publishing House's text for elementary school students, *Yuwen*. In the story "Ta shi shei?" a passerby is amazed to see a young lad rushing to help an old lady who had just taken a spill. The passerby reveals an assumption that one only responds when a family member needs help as he asks the boy, "Is she your paternal granny?"

"No." "Is she your maternal granny?" "No." "Who is she then?" "I don't know." The passerby's values are challenged by the unselfish behavior of the young child who is schooled in communal values. In Zhan Dai'er's "Ma Jia de Mama," the story is told from the point of view of a classmate who takes the teacher's seemingly indifferent attitude toward Ma Jia's helpfulness at school as an indication that the teacher dislikes her friend. "Not so," says Ma Jia. "She's my mother!" The classmate is astounded to learn that the mother has deliberately avoided favoring her own child.

Many picture books show spoiled, boorish children unable to perform even the simplest tasks, such as peeling a hard-boiled egg (this is the topic of many jokes), tying their own shoes, holding a spoon by themselves, or using a broom. For example, in "Da Lan Chong Lixian Ji," a little boy, Fatty, will put on his clothes only with Granny's help and needs his father to help him wash his face. In "Wo Pa" a grandmother intervenes to keep her granddaughter from having to help clean up the school grounds by telling the teacher the girl is sick. When the teacher had asked the children to return to the school to do this work, the girl had whined to her granny: "Adults do all the work at home, why do we kids have to do work at school?" The family here thwarts the teacher's attempt to foster social responsibility.

Not surprisingly, celebrations of work, the work ethic, and self-discipline occur often in this literature, usually in cautionary tales in which the wavering, undisciplined child sees the correctness of mending his ways. Because a whole generation of young children has grown up not performing chores at home, due to their elevated status as indulged only children, it is little wonder that another form of literature has appeared: how-to manuals that teach these children basic living skills. Among the useful tasks taught are how to boil rice, buy food in the market, adjust the television, mop the floor, sew a button on, wash a handkerchief, fold clothes, select a watermelon, and mail a letter. The tasks are narrated in such excruciating detail that one is led to believe that the child has had no prior experience in dealing with them.[16]

Despite the many stories showing lazy, helpless, and overly demanding children ordering their parents about, in some stories the children are depicted sympathetically and as trying to learn to be independent. In one story a little girl, observing that her mother is busy hanging up the laundry, tries to dress herself. When her little friends laugh at her mismatched buttons, she retorts: "I put it on all by myself!"[17] Others are portrayed as captives of overly doting mothers or grandmothers (or, rarely, a grandfather) who anticipate the child's every need and whim and do not allow the child to act independently. In the collection of stories *Xiao Tao Qir,* there are numerous examples of this vigilance. In one clever story, "Wo Xuehuile Zuo Shenme?," a little boy is unable to write a school theme about something he has learned to do at home because his mother does not allow him to do chores. In the end, frustrated in his attempt to boil rice for lunch, he hands the task of writing the theme over to his mother as well.

Two novels for the intermediate primary level written in the mid- to late 1980s show young people striving toward independence and self-autonomy. Kuang Bangyu and Wen Lianghua's *Hui Fei de Xiao Pengyou* (1986) shows a teacher and a sympathetic outsider who encourage several students to pursue their beekeeping interests, despite objections and obstruction from home. These people outside the family circle intervene at critical times to counter the family's objection, voiced by the mother, that raising bees takes away valuable study time. They offer advice and resources to enable the youths to carry out their plans. Contrast this assistance with what one of the mothers offers: constant nagging about her child's primary duty to study, in the very narrow sense of reading books, which does not include carrying out such real-life experiments as raising bees (21).

Since children are rarely shown interacting with their fathers, it is usually the female characters in these stories who discourage social responsibility and independence. Although women work outside the home, they still tend to prohibit the child's integration into a larger social unit beyond the family. If family members help the child become independent, it is usually the male characters (cousins, uncles, grandfathers) who offer assistance, perhaps because males have always been involved in the wider sphere outside the household.

In the above story, for example, male teachers at school and male government bureaucrats offer help to the young boys who are interested in raising bees. Although the boys voice their support for the state goal of becoming more scientific, the main thrust of the story is their single-minded devotion to the activity despite family (mother's) opposition. The mother figure has changed from a transmitter of positive values, as she was in the Scar Literature, into someone extraneous to the lives of her children. Lacking a positive (male) force to propel him outside the home, the child remains in limbo, captive of the family and unable to make the necessary break.

A 1988 picaresque novel, *Heimao Jingzhang Xinzhuan* by Chu Zhixiang, details the adventures of an entrepreneur in post–Cultural Revolution China. The author purports to present the heretofore-unknown past of Black Cat before he became the well-known star of pulp cops-and-robbers comic books. His life as a trickster in the service industry who succeeds for a time in fooling the unsuspecting public seems to be the perfect metaphor for the new society in the 1980s: one succeeds by cleverness, staying one step ahead of the masses. Youth need not choose between family and state, since they are devoted to neither, only looking out for themselves.

The tale of Black Cat's early life begins with his school days, omitting any account of his family background. This con artist, after studying a little bit of every sort of trade, sets up a succession of shops —TV Repair, Tailor Shop, Appliance Shop, Photography Studio, Cloud-seeding Service to Farmers—and then becomes a rock star. In each line of work his failures become more colossal and more bizarre until finally he succeeds as a restaurant manager selling rat meat. Despite these earlier setbacks, in the second half of the novel he inexplicably turns into an officer in the Animal Public Security Bureau, aiding the public in ferreting out criminals and con artists not unlike his former self.

In most late-1980s stories, the state is mentioned not at all or only in remarks tacked on at the end of a story. School is the place where social values are taught, and there is great effort to depict the teacher-student relationship in positive terms. With the shift in the late 1980s to depicting parents and the family as obstacles to independent, socially responsible youth, the positive image of the teacher has been resurrected. It is still questionable, however, whether the social values transmitted to the student are acted on outside of school.[18] In many stories the family and the child are concerned with immediate, individual goals: study hard and win a place in an institution of higher education, or work hard as an individual on the make and concrete benefits will accrue. For example, in the children's poem by Lou Feifu "Gege Ji," the granny's sideline of raising chickens in the small courtyard and selling their eggs brings immediate material benefit to the family. The poem extols the new television set and air conditioner, all bought with funds from granny's new occupation. Her enjoyment comes from hearing the hens cluck each time they lay an egg: "They cluck so much that Granny chuckles" (1).

Literature for children in postwar China has always reflected adult concerns and public policy issues, and the past two decades are no exception. In the 1970s the focus was on the state concern of forwarding the revolution toward socialism. Thus the individual was depicted in positive terms to the extent that he or she supported the new social system. The explicit revolutionary ideology prevalent in those times has all but disappeared, replaced ten or more years later with issues of personal conduct, such as being unselfish and socially responsible to one's family and community. These ideas are not completely incompatible with the 1970s slogan "Serve the people"; the difference is one of emphasis and degree. What writers attacked in the 1980s was not explicit reactionary ideology but the selfish individualism exhibited by some children and at times encouraged by their families.[19]

In many stories, examples of undesirable or negative behavior outnumber examples of desirable, positive behavior. The Chinese family is presented as an entity lacking in moral authority, incapable of truly carrying out national goals such as the Four Modernizations, which in the 1980s aimed to propel China into the forefront of the industrialized nations by upgrading agricultural and industrial infrastructure. In these stories the family is criticized, if not undermined. The family is shown in general as undisciplined in the training of its young, who are largely irresponsible in the social sphere. Thus in many cases children must look for assistance to parent substitutes outside the family. These role models, usually found in educational institutions, are not tied to the parochial concerns of the family. This, then, may be the ultimate legacy of the Cultural Revolution: the family, discredited during those ten years, has once again been discounted as a dependable institution for working toward the larger goals of the state.

Notes

1. See Munro's "Two Polarities and Their Modern Legacy: The Moral Sense and Its Content," 192–232, especially "Family" (221–27) and "Public Love" (227–30).

2. See James J. Y. Liu, *Chinese Theories of Literature*, 106–16. Liu terms this approach "pragmatic" rather than didactic.

3. My collection of literature concentrates on preschool through upper primary grades, approximately age one through ten or eleven. I have examined around two hundred examples of picture books and about fifty short stories published in China from the 1950s through 1993. I include in this broad category preschool texts for learning to count and to do other practical skills; mother-child texts for ages one to six; etiquette handbooks; how-to texts for elementary schoolchildren; translations of Western fairy tales; one-minute bedtime storybooks; Chinese legends; modern age-appropriate picture books; character-learning texts; and two anthologies of intermediate-level fiction. Publishing houses in the following areas are represented with one or more books:

the cities of Beijing, Shanghai, and Tianjin; and the provinces of Heilongjiang, Hebei, Henan, Jiangsu, Guangxi, Sichuan, Yunnan, and Zhejiang. Note that until the early 1990s there were no legal private publishing houses in China since all publishing was state-run, whether in national publishing houses as in Beijing and Shanghai or in provincial publishing houses as in virtually every province. Some major cities, such as Tianjin, have their own publishing houses as well. The content of the published material seems to be a state-sanctioned view of what society is or ought to be like.

4. See Zhong Kuanhong, "Luo Na de Ming Zhu (Luo Na's bright jewel)," *Yunnan Ertong Wenxue Xuan,* 14–23. In this story a lonely little girl away from home in a summer camp, seeing a portrait of Chairman Mao on the wall, calls out, "Chairman Mao, our close relative!" as she clutches the clothes her mother made for her.

5. Parris H. Chang, "Children's Literature and Political Socialization," 243.

6. For information on textbooks in China, see Roberta Martin, "The Socialization of Children in China and Taiwan, 243–50.

7. *Da Jia Lai Duan Lian* (Everybody come exercise).

8. Only twelve years earlier, a 1964–66 science series had presented the grandfather as a "proverbial figure of wisdom." See Frank Swetz, "Children's Picture Books in the People's Republic of China," 11.

9. See also Lu Fei (1979), "Ding Ning."

10. In 1985 the Scar Literature (or Wounded Literature) of the late 1970s and early 1980s was officially accepted by the Fourth Writers Congress. See Gayle Feldman, "The Organization of Publishing in China," 524. For more examples of this literature, see Perry Link (ed.), *Stubborn Weeds* (Bloomington: Indiana University Press, 1983); Lee Yee (ed.), *The New Realism* (New York: Hippocrene, 1983); and Michael Duke, *Blooming and Contending: Chinese Literature in the Post-Mao Era* (Bloomington: Indiana University Press, 1985).

11. For another story depicting a teacher's erroneous judgment, see Qiu Xun, "Sanse Yuanzhubi."

12. Jin Jin, "Introduction," *Zhongguo Xin Wenyi Da Xi,* 3.

13. Cui Ping, "Bai Yan" (44–49); Luo Chensheng, "Chi Tuolaji de Gushi" (59–64); Liu Houming, "Hong Ye Shuqian" (10–14); Hu Qi, "Lao Yumi" (24–27); Liu Xinwu, "Kanbujian de Pengyou" (27–31); and Luo Chensheng, "Bai Bozi" (82–88); all in Jin Jin, ed., *Zhongguo Xin Wenyi Da Xi.*

14. *Kantu Shizi* (Look at the picture, recognize the character), 1:21.

15. Both are in *Jiao Baobao* (Teaching Precious), 1:22.

16. See *Xiao Xuesheng Shenghuo Zili Changshi Zhidao* (Guide to everyday knowledge of daily living for primary school students).

17. *Jiao Baobao* (Teaching Precious), 3:3–4.

18. Attitudes toward teachers have changed over the past forty years. During the Cultural Revolution, teachers were often criticized as being upholders of the discredited traditional culture. In the literature, see, e.g., Lu Fei, in Jin Jin, ed., *Zhongguo Xin Wenyi Da Xi,* 78–82. For further analysis, see Richard Solomon, "Educational Themes in China's Changing Culture."

19. An interesting example of making the past learn from the present is in the way the legend of Kua Fu was presented in the 1986 collection *Zhongguo Shenhua, Tonghua Gushi Xuan* (19–21). The original legend presents the individual exploits of Kua Fu in his quest to race the sun. As it is presented in this new version, Kua Fu's goal is not individual glory but rather the well-being of the community: he seeks to capture the warmth of the sun after being encouraged by the elders of the community.

Works Cited and Consulted

Ai Qingjie, Jiang Weisheng (Love cleanliness and support sanitation). Shanghai: Shanghai People's Publishing House, 1975.

Arai, Kuniko. "Political Education in China: A Study of Socialization Through Children's Textbooks." *Journal of Northeast Asian Studies* (Fall 1984):30–47.

Bing Xin. "Ji Yijian Zui Nanwang de Shiqing (Recalling a most memorable event)." Jin 3–8.

Chang, Parris H. "Children's Literature and Political Socialization." In *Moving a Mountain: Cultural Change in China,* ed. Godwin Chu and Francis Hsu. Honolulu: East-West Center, 1979. Pp. 137–56.

Chu Zhixiang. *Heimao Jingzhang Xinzhuan* (New biography of Police Officer Black Cat). Kunming: Yunnan Juvenile and Children's Publishing House, 1988.

Cui Ping. "Bai Yan (Bai Yan)." Jin 44–49.

Da Jia Lai Duan Lian (Everybody come exercise). Shanghai: Shanghai People's Publishing House, 1974.

"Da Lan Chong Lixian Ji (The adventures of the big lazy bug)." *Zhongguo Shenhua Tonghua Gushi Xuan.* 1:54–55.

Ebrey, Patricia. "The Family in the Classical Tradition." In *Family and Property in Sung China: Yuan Ts'ai's Precepts for a Social Life.* Princeton: Princeton University Press, 1984. Pp. 30–60.

Ertong Wenxue Lunwen Xuan (Anthology of essays on children's literature). Kunming: Yunnan Juvenile and Children's Publishing House, 1987.

Eutsler, Nellvena Duncan. "Journey to the East: Impressions of Children's Literature and Instructional Media in Contemporary China." *Children's Literature* 9 (1981):73–91.

Farquhar, M. "Through the Looking Glass: Children's Stories and Social Change in China (1918–1976)." In *Society and the Writer: Essays on Literature in Modern Asia (1981),* ed. Gungwu Wang. Canberra: Research School of Pacific Studies, The Australian National University, 1981. Pp. 173–98.

Feldman, Gayle. "The Organization of Publishing in China." *China Quarterly* 107 (1986): 519–29.

Hong Xiaobing Nupi Shentong Shi (The Little red guards angrily attack the poem of the venerable child). Shanghai: Shanghai People's Publishing House, n.d.

Hu Qi. "Lao Yumi (Old corn)." Jin 24–27.

Hu Wa (Tiger baby). Shanghai: Juvenile and Children's Publishing House, 1989.

Jiao Baobao (Teaching Precious). Vols. 1–4. Shanghai: Juvenile and Children's Publishing House, 1985.

Jin Jin, ed. *Zhongguo Xin Wenyi Da Xi (1976–1982): Ertong Wenxue Ji* (Anthology of new Chinese literature, 1976–1982: Collection of Children's Literature). Beijing: Zhongguo Wenlian, 1986.

Kang Fukun. "Xiao Xiang Nunu (Little Elephant Nunu)." Jin 118–31.

Kantu Shizi (Look at the picture, recognize the character). Henan: Haiyan, n.d.

Kuang Bangyu and Wen Lianghua. *Hui Fei de Xiao Pengyou* (Little friends who can fly). Kunming: Yunnan Juvenile and Children's Publishing House, 1986.

"Lanlan Zhao Pengyou (Lanlan finds a friend)." *Jiao Baobao* 1:7–8.

Liu Houming. "Hong Ye Shuqian (Red leaf bookmark)." Jin 10–14.

Liu, James J. Y. *Chinese Theories of Literature.* Chicago: University of Chicago Press, 1975.

Liu Xinwu. "Kanbujian de Pengyou (Invisible friend)." Jin 27–31.

Lou Feifu, "Gege Ji (Clucking Hen)," Xiaoxue Yuwen Bao (Diyouban) (Elementary School Literary Newspaper [Lower Grades Issue]), vol. 4 (Jan. 1, 1993), 1.

Lu Fei. "Ding Ning (Ding Ning)." Jin 78–82.

Luo Chensheng. "Bai Bozi (White neck). Jin 82–89.

———. "Chi Tuolaji de Gushi (The story of eating the tractor)." Jin 59–64.
Lystad, Mary. "A Contemporary Note on Early American, Modern Russian, and Chinese Books for Children." In *A Child's World.* Rockville, Md.: National Institute of Mental Health, 1974. Pp. 119–24.
Martin, Roberta. "The Socialization of Children in China and Taiwan: An Analysis of the Elementary Textbooks." *China Quarterly* 62 (June 1975):242–62.
Miao Ge. "Jin Yin Dong (Gold and silver cave)." *Yunnan Ertong Wenxue Xuan* 1–6.
Mitchell, Edna. "Children's Books from the People's Republic of China." *Language Arts* 57, no. 1 (January 1980):30–37.
Munro, Donald. *Images of Human Nature: A Sung Portrait.* Princeton: Princeton University Press, 1988.
Niaore Ertu. "Qicha Jijiao de Gonglu (Seven-point buck)." Jin 333–41.
O'Dell, Felicity Ann. *Socialisation Through Children's Literature: The Soviet Example.* Cambridge: Cambridge University Press, 1978.
Peng Jingfeng. "Yilu Lihua (Waystation plum blossoms)." *Yunnan Ertong Wenxue Xuan* 95–102.
Price, F. "Chinese Textbooks: Fourteen Years On." *China Quarterly* 83 (September 1980):550–62.
———. *What Chinese Children Read About: Serial Picture Books and Foreigners.* Victoria, Australia: Centre for Comparative and International Studies in Education, School of Education, 1976.
Qiu Xun, "Sanse Yuanzhubi (Three-colored pen)." Jin 125–32.
Sanjian Maoxianyi (Three sweaters). Shanghai: People's Publishing House, 1974.
Solomon, Richard. "Educational Themes in China's Changing Culture." *China Quarterly* 22 (April–June 1965):154–70.
Sun Jibin. "Jiejie (Elder sister)." *Yunnan Ertong Wenxue Xuan* 24–31.
Swetz, Frank. "Children's Picture Books in the People's Republic of China." *Science and Children* (December 1971):11–13.
"Ta Shi Shei (Who is she)?" *Yuwen* 2:47–48.
Wang Anyi. "Shei Shi Weilaide Zhongdui Zhang (Who will be our future monitor)?" Jin 39–44.
"Wo Pa (I am afraid)." *Xiao Tao Qir* 19–20.
"Wo Xuehuile Zuo Shenme [What have I learned to do]?" *Xiao Tao Qir* 1–3.
Xiao Tao Qir (Little mischief-maker). Tianjin: Tianjin People's Publishing House, 1989.
Xiao Xuesheng Limao Xuzhi (Essential knowledge of etiquette for elementary school students). Shanghai: Shanghai Educational Publishing House, 1982.
Xiao Xuesheng Shenghuo Zili Changshi Zhidao (Guide to everyday knowledge of daily living for primary school students). Kunming: Yunnan Juvenile and Children's Publishing House, 1989.
Xiao Zhu Nuni (Little pig nuni). Shanghai: Juvenile and Children's Publishing House, 1989.
Xin Le. "Cai Luo (Cai Luo)." *Yunnan Ertong Wenxue Xuan* 79–87.
Yang Meiqing. "Women Sange (We Three)." *Yunnan Ertong Wenxue Xuan* 60–73.
Yang Xiao. "Yeye Dangxuanle Fuye Duizhang (Grandfather was chosen head of the subsidiary production unit)." Jin 119–25.
Yunnan Ertong Wenxue Xuan (Yunnan children's literature anthology). Kunming: Yunnan People's Publishing House, 1983.
Yuwen (Language). Harbin: Heilongjiang People's Educational Publishing House, 1986.
Zaniello, Thomas. "Flowers in Full Bloom: The Variety of Chinese Children's Literature." *Children's Literature* 7 (1978):181–90.
———. "Heroic Quintuplets: A Look at Some Chinese Children's Literature." *Children's Literature* 3 (1974):36–42.
Zhan Dai'er. "Chinese Literature for Children." *Children's Literature* 10 (1982):183–85.

———. "Ma Jia de Mama (Ma Jia's Mother)." *Xiao Tao Qir* 26–27.

Zhang, Meifang, and W. Gale Breedlove. "The Changing Role of Imagination in Chinese Children's Books." *The Reading Teacher* (February 1989):406–12.

Zhongguo Shenhua, Tonghua Gushi Xuan (Selections of Chinese legends and children's stories). 2 vols. Jiangsu: Jiangsu Juvenile and Children's Publishing House, 1986.

The Quest for Masculinity in The Chocolate War*: Changing Conceptions of Masculinity in the 1970s*

Yoshida Junko

The first paragraph of Robert Cormier's *The Chocolate War* (1974) is metaphorical: "They murdered him. As he turned to take the ball, a dam burst against the side of his head and a hand grenade shattered his stomach" (7). We are immediately exposed to this violent scene without any knowledge of who "he" is, who "they" are, or what this scene is about. As the story unfolds, we learn that Jerry Renault, the protagonist, is involved in a conflict called the "chocolate war." But what is Jerry fighting against? And who or what is the enemy? On one hand, Patricia J. Campbell places the story in a moral context: "What he is opposing is not Brother Leon, not Archie, not Emile, but the monstrous force that moves them . . . evil" (46). Anne Scott MacLeod, on the other hand, maintains that Cormier's novels are "political novels" because he "is far more interested in the systems by which a society operates than he is in individuals" (74). I prefer to place *The Chocolate War* in a social and cultural context, reading it as a novel about changing conceptions of masculinity during the turbulent 1960s and early 1970s.

Many sociologists view masculinity as a set of behaviors and attitudes that are constructed and maintained by a complex system of rewards and punishments. According to Arlene Skolnick, the sociocultural changes of the '60s were rooted in the unexpressed discontents of the '50s. In the mid-'70s, stimulated by the second wave of feminism, various men's movements began to develop. The First National Conference on the Masculine Mystique and the first Men and Masculinity conference were held in 1974 and 1975, respectively. In 1974 Marc Feigen Fasteau's *The Male Machine* was published, followed in 1975 by Warren Farrell's *The Liberated Man.* The year 1976 saw the publication of Richard Doyle's *The Rape of the Male* and Herb Goldberg's *The Hazards of Being Male.* The various men's movements argued over conflicting ideals of masculinity. In fact, sociologist Kenneth

I am greatly indebted to Roberta Trites for helpful comments throughout.
Children's Literature 26, ed. Elizabeth Lennox Keyser (Yale University Press, © 1998 Hollins College).

Clatterbaugh identifies eight perspectives ranging from the "conservative" to the evangelical Christian" (9–14). Nonetheless, America's cultural anxiety about masculinity was based on a narrow image of the white middle-class heterosexual male. As in the film *Rebel Without a Cause* (1955), this image often caused a "masculinity crisis" (Griswold 185; Skolnick 111), for such men were expected to conceal their vulnerabilities, suppress their emotions, provide for their families, control their women, and, at the same time, be democratic and affectionate husbands and fathers. In other words, "the ideology of the strong male was at odds with the ideology of togetherness" (Skolnick 71).

This masculinity crisis is deeply connected to unease about the feminine side of masculinity. As the sociologist E. Anthony Rotundo shows in his book *American Manhood,* the concept of masculinity is defined by the notion of a "separate sphere," which has become the norm for American society. This sphere excludes any attributes that are thought to be feminine, such as the nurturing, the caring, the intimate, and the emotional. As though to reflect the omission of the feminine from this conventional notion of masculinity, Cormier's *The Chocolate War* lacks major female characters except for Jerry's dead mother. The story unfolds in the all-male world of Trinity School. This unnatural absence of females in the novel emphasizes a masculinity that has excluded the feminine. Cormier is daring enough to portray the all-male world as bleak, to find fault with traditional gender roles, and to depict his protagonist, Jerry, as seeking a new male identity.

I would first like to examine the novel as a mythological quest story in which a young man seeks a masculine identity. Percival's quest in Arthurian legend is one of the most representative stories in which a fatherless young man leaves his mother and sets out to seek adventure. Because of his upbringing in the depths of the forest, Percival is ignorant of the outside world and, especially, of the power politics in the men's world. His encounter with the wounded Fisher King, whose kingdom is barren, is a crucial incident in his quest. When Percival witnesses a procession of Grail objects at a banquet, he misses a chance to ask specific questions, one of which is "Whom does the Grail serve?" Later Percival learns from his cousin of a legend predicting that an innocent fool would wander into the castle and ask questions by means of which he would heal the Fisher King. After wandering many years, Percival meets the Hideous Damsel, who reminds him of his failure to ask questions, thus prompting him to resume his Grail quest. Finally, he encounters an old hermit who reminds him a third time of his failure and its relation to his abandoned mother's death. Although Chrétien de Troyes's *Le Roman de Perceval ou le conte du graal,* one of the oldest stories of Percival, ends at this point, many scholars presume that he returns to the Fisher King and questions him. As a result the wounded king is miraculously healed and the Waste Land becomes fertile again.[1]

Among the many Jungian interpretations of this story as a boy's quest for masculinity,[2] Robert A. Johnson's is especially insightful. From a feminist point of view, however, Johnson's focus on Percival's "homespun garment," a gift from his mother, is problematical. Johnson regards the garment as a metaphor for the mother complex in relation to Percival's failure to ask the questions (48). Instead, I see a connection between this failure of Percival's and the death of his abandoned mother, a connection made by two different characters: the cousin and the old hermit. From a feminist perspective, the healing of the wounded Fisher King is closely connected with Percival's reconciliation with his dead mother. In other words, reconciling with the feminine is essential for the rebirth of masculinity. We shall return to this point later in the analysis of the novel.

The Percival archetype can be found in several books contemporaneous with *The Chocolate War.* Isabelle Holland's *The Man Without a Face* (1972) and Laurence Yep's *Dragonwings* (1975) can be read as mythological quest stories, for both depict "fatherless" boys who seek their "fathers" after leaving home. In *The Man Without a Face,* a virtually fatherless boy, Charles Nostad, encounters Justin McLeod, the man without a face, in his isolated house on top of a cliff. The encounter takes place away from Charles's home, where his mother tries to tame and domesticate both Charles and his male cat (21). Likewise, in *Dragonwings,* Moon Shadow, who has been brought up without a father, departs from China, where his mother and grandmother live, and sets out for the United States to live with his father, Windrider. In both stories "fathers" are overwhelmed by suffering: Justin, who takes on the role of surrogate father, has a facial disfigurement and has secluded himself from society; Windrider is spiritually lost and entrapped within Chinese-American society.

The Chocolate War, in the same vein, unfolds as a boy's quest for a masculine identity. Jerry Renault, who lost his mother half a year before, is now being initiated into an all-male world, Trinity School, and is on his way to establishing his masculinity. Jerry's problem derives from the fact that his father is devastated by the loss of his wife and therefore cannot give adequate attention and care to his son. In other words, Jerry is a psychically fatherless son at a significant point in his development. Commenting on such situations, the psychoanalyst Guy Corneau maintains that the "lack of attention from the father results in the son's inability to identify with his father as a means of establishing his own masculine identity" (13). Such fatherless sons "tend either to idealize the father or to seek an ideal father-substitute" (19). To make matters worse, Jerry, who is portrayed as a "skinny kid," cannot find an ideal model of masculinity even in his all-male world. Janza and Carter, his macho peers, are too physically tough to be adequate role models, nor can Jerry conform to the conventional model of masculinity represented by Archie and Brother Leon.

While Jerry is suffering from the trauma caused by his mother's death, he is thrown into "the chocolate war" by vice principal Brother Leon, who compels the students to sell chocolates as part of their annual fund-raising effort. Archie Costello, the leader of the students' secret society, "The Vigils," gives Jerry an "assignment" to refuse to sell the chocolates. By giving assignments to his peers, Archie forces them to rebel against school authority, especially Brother Leon. Jerry's ultimate refusal to sell the chocolates drives him into isolation at school, especially in Brother Leon's class. Jerry knows that his rebellion is not against the chocolate sales but against the conformity underlying this activity. He says to himself, "It would be so easy, really, to yell 'Yes.' To say, 'Give me the chocolates to sell, Brother Leon.' So easy like the others, not to have to confront those terrible eyes every morning" (98).

Jerry at first obeys Archie's order and continues to say no, but he gradually comes to realize that the Vigils' rebellion is not an ultimate threat to the school. The Vigils are tacitly allowed to exist because of their behind-the-scenes cooperation with Leon. As is shown in their later cooperation in the chocolate sale, the Vigils' members are merely conforming to Leon's expectations. Archie and Leon are in an interdependent relationship, as Archie admits: "Officially, The Vigils did not exist. How could a school condone an organization like The Vigils? The school allowed it to function by ignoring it completely, pretending it wasn't there. But it was there, all right. . . . The Vigils kept things under control. Without The Vigils, Trinity might have been torn apart like other schools had been, by demonstrations, protests, all that crap" (25).

Aaron Esman sheds light on the relationship between Brother Leon and the Vigils when he argues that adolescent rebellion during the tumultuous '60s did not derive from a "generation gap" but rather from efforts to live up to their elders' expectations. According to Esman, "the 'young radicals' . . . were, in most cases, expressing in an intensified form the liberal, antiauthoritarian view of their parents, who in many cases supported and encouraged their children's supposed 'rebellion.' . . . Most adolescents in most cultures conform rather quietly to the expectations of their elders" (29). Jerry learns from three illuminating encounters or observations that his assigned role is not to rebel at all but to conform to his peer group. To begin with, a hippie who meets him only once at a bus stop criticizes him for his passive conformity, saying he is "middle-aged at fourteen, fifteen. Already caught in a routine" (20). In fact, Jerry is afraid to become like his middle-aged father, who after his wife's death lives in a "gray drabness" (52). Jerry cannot help but ask, "*Was this all there was to life, after all?*" (52, emphasis added), and we are told that "now he [can] see his father's face reflected in his own features" (53). Next the quotation on a poster, "*Do I dare disturb the universe?*" (emphasis added) from T. S. Eliot's "The Love Song of J. Alfred Prufrock," urges Jerry to rebel against the whole school and "disturb the universe." Finally, when he sees his best friend Goober exploited by Archie, Jerry recognizes that the assignment, despite its rebellious appearance, requires nothing but conformity to the Vigils.

Both Jerry's and Prufrock's questions are radical ones, posed by males who need to grow emotionally in order to escape their bleak situations. And, just as Percival is rebuked for his failure to ask the right questions, Jerry is challenged by the hippie and the poster to ask the right questions in the face of the suffering man and the Waste Land. When Jerry finally says no of his own will, however, his question takes the form of rebellion against the conventional masculinity embodied in both Brother Leon and Archie. On the eleventh day of his assignment, when he is supposed to say yes, Jerry declares, " 'No. I'm not going to sell the chocolates.' Cities fell. Earth opened. Planets tilted. Stars plummeted. And the awful silence" (89). At last Jerry has disturbed the universe. The only way Jerry has been able to establish his gender identity has been by arming himself with stubbornness and by fighting against conformity. Thus, even though Jerry has no positive role models at home or at school, he inaugurates his quest for masculinity by staging his own rebellion. So great is the difficulty of challenging the status quo in total isolation that Jerry's quest virtually becomes a war.

As *The Chocolate War* unfolds, it becomes clear that the type of conventional masculinity embodied in Leon and Archie is power-oriented. As their status as vice principal and vice president of their respective groups suggests, both of them are ambitious. Thus, despite their external differences, they are quite similar in their attempts to pursue power. Perry Nodelman points out that all the characters are "obsessively concerned with the chocolate sale" (24) because that is "the showcase" where power is exercised and displayed. In Leon's daily roll call, for example, students are not allowed to respond to their names without accepting the chocolates and reporting their sales. In the students' eyes, Leon is a tyrant who stands on top of the hierarchy: "Everyone could see that Brother Leon was enjoying himself. This is what he liked—to be in command and everything going smoothly, the students responding to their names smartly, accepting the chocolates, showing school spirit" (63). Archie is no different from Leon in his orientation to power. As Campbell points out, "arch" means "principal or chief" (45); he is another tyrant in his realm, that of the Vigils, who, Cormier writes, "*were* the school. And he, Archie Costello, was The Vigils" (26, emphasis in original). And when Archie sells all the chocolates, he is "on top again, . . . in charge once more, the entire school in the palm of his hand" (170). It is to this power-hungry masculinity that Jerry says no, starting the war.

Such power as Archie and Brother Leon wield, which has particular features and patterns, warrants a closer look. First, their power is exercised through controlling information. Archie has Obie record personal information on all the students at the school. "His notebook was more complete than the school's files. It contained information, carefully coded, about everyone at Trinity" (15). Archie thus manipulates information instead of threatening others by physical power and avoids using violence as much as possible. Archie explains, "I usually lay off the strong-arm stuff in the assignments. The brothers would close us down in no time and the kids would really start sabotaging if we started hurting people" (134). He is afraid that violence might reveal his manipulation of power. And visibility might threaten the existence of the Vigils at Trinity.

Archie's manipulation of psychology and information demonstrates his awareness of a principle that Michel Foucault identifies in *Discipline and Punish:* "The power exercised on the body is conceived not as a property, but as a strategy, that its effects of domination are attributed not to 'appropriation,' but to dispositions, maneuvers, tactics, techniques, functionings; . . . In short this power is exercised rather than possessed; it is not the 'privilege,' acquired or preserved, of the dominant class, but the overall effect of its strategic position" (26). To put it another way, power is something manipulated in a political relationship; it cannot be obtained or possessed. Thus Foucault illustrates how "docile bodies" were constructed in the process of Western civilization by rulers' exercise of power within the institutionalized panopticism[3] of discipline and punishment, where a watchful eye is unceasingly vigilant for social deviates. The same was true of American society during the '50s, when there was a sort of McCarthyism with respect to gender roles (Skolnick 65). Griswold maintains that in the postwar era there was "conformity, a plague that infected middle-class men. . . . Men had become slaves to conformity" (199). Conformity in the '50s, no doubt, worked as a shaper of conventional manhood. And there was no more perfect place to socialize white middle-class adolescent boys into conformity than prep schools such as Trinity.

Archie, as the leader of the Vigils, is aware of the principle of discipline and punishment in every detail of school life and manipulates people best by only hinting at the possibility of force. That is why he hates to see Janza and Carter exercise physical power, although he relies on them as a threat of violence. In this way, Archie meticulously distances himself from such a macho image. For example, he hates "the secretions of the human body, pee or perspiration" (106) and "betraying an emotion" (130) such as anger. The ideal image of masculinity for Archie is an isolated man "in harness," "cool" and "in command," with a poker face, who uses his brain instead of his body. Leon exercises power in a similar way, using his eyes and his pointer to manipulate his subjects, "watch[ing] the class like a hawk, suspicious, searching out cheaters or daydreamers, probing for weaknesses in the students and then exploiting those weaknesses" (23–24). Leon is consistently portrayed as one who gazes from the top of the hierarchical power structure. Like Archie, Leon avoids intimacy with the students, insisting that a "line must be drawn between teachers and students . . . that line of separation must remain" (35). Leon's exercise of power, represented by his hawklike, ever-vigilant eyes and his isolation from students, resembles the Vigils' panopticism.

The type of masculinity described above—one that manipulates power and, at the same time, is manipulated and constructed by power—has several problems. First, a man who adopts such a masculinity consciously or unconsciously suppresses his emotions and is therefore dehumanized and disindividualized. Just as Archie is portrayed as an impassive man who tries to erase the proof of his human body (urine or perspiration), Leon's existence is often reduced to his most prominent physical feature, his moist and hawklike eyes, thus obliterating his personality. He epitomizes what Fasteau calls "the male machine," whose "armor plating . . . is virtually impregnable. His circuits are never scrambled or overrun by irrelevant personal signals. . . . His relationship with other male machines is one of respect but not intimacy" (1). Brother Leon has taken the conventions of masculinity so far that he seems at times an automaton. In *The Hazard of Being Male* the psychologist Herb Goldberg issues a warning to "men who live in harness." From the standpoint of the men's liberation movement, he stresses men's oppression more than women's: "They have lost touch with, or are running away from, their feelings and awareness of themselves as people. They have confused their social masks for their essence and they are destroying themselves while fulfilling the traditional definitions of masculine-appropriate behavior. . . . Their reality is always approached through these veils of gender expectations" (3). This passage seems an accurate description of Brother Leon.

A second problem with conventional masculinity is its tendencies toward isolation and dominance over others. As demonstrated by Archie and Leon, a man with this type of masculinity is isolated from others by his position at the top of the hierarchy. As the feminist psychologist Carol Gilligan points out in her *In a Different Voice,* males tend to form hierarchical relationships, separating themselves from other males in order to gain power, whereas females tend to form weblike interdependent networks (62, 160, 170). As a result, the masculinity constructed through the exercise of power began to acquire stereotypical images: it was seen as aggressive, emotionless, dehumanized, disindividualized, isolated, and incapable of intimacy. Consequently, by the time *The Chocolate War* was published, the various men's movement groups were trying to dispel this myth of masculinity.

It was in this social climate that several noteworthy adolescent novels dealing with masculine identity issues were published, including, as already mentioned, *Dragonwings* (the Chinese Windrider) and

The Man Without a Face (the homosexual Justin). In *A Wizard of Earthsea* (1968), published only slightly earlier, Ursula K. Le Guin portrays an adolescent boy, Ged, who seeks his male identity as an immature young wizard. Two things are worth noting in this novel. First is Ged's act of naming the gebbeth, the nameless shadow, which has been conjured up by the power-hungry Ged himself. Interestingly, the shadow reminds us of the cultural anxiety about gender exhibited during the 1950s, when adolescent boys rebelled "without a cause." By confronting the suppressed side of his conventional masculinity, Ged finally identifies his shadow. Second, Le Guin presents readers with an unconventional dark-skinned hero. Le Guin writes in *Earthsea Revisioned,* "I meant this as a strike against racial bigotry" (8). Similarly, Virginia Hamilton's *The Planet of Junior Brown* (1971) also deals with the identity crisis of a fatherless boy, Junior Brown. In place of his absent father are two black surrogate fathers, Buddy Clark and Mr. Pool. Whereas conventional American masculinity had been based on the image of the white middle-class heterosexual male, these writers suggest the new types of masculinity evolving from the changing social environment.

This social environment, however, was not necessarily a favorable one for adolescents attempting to establish a masculine identity. In the case of *The Chocolate War,* refusing to conform, that is, choosing to disturb the universe, means that Jerry himself is thrown into chaos. When he opens his locker to find it vandalized and is attacked by his peers, he finally understands the meaning of disturbing the universe: he has disturbed the norm for manhood in his society. The disturbed locker is a metaphor for both Jerry's inner disturbance and the disturbed norm of manhood at the school. This confusion is further reflected in Jerry's bewildered response to a violent attack by the school bullies, Janza and his buddies. Overwhelmed by the desire for revenge, Jerry identifies himself with the macho image of violent manhood. What is worse, he goes on to confront Janza physically in the boxing ring and temporarily becomes intoxicated with the thrill of physical violence. But then, a "new sickness invaded Jerry, the sickness of knowing what he had become, *another animal, another beast, another violent person* in a violent world, inflicting damage, not disturbing the universe but damaging it" (183, emphasis added). Cormier thus successfully demonstrates the violent and dark side of masculinity and provides readers with a powerful indictment of conventional manhood.

Jerry's violent response expresses his understanding of power and masculinity. He mistakenly believes that he can gain power and manliness if he physically confronts Janza, that power is some entity of which he can be robbed, and that gaining hierarchical power is masculine. Jerry eventually realizes that this masculine identity is self-defeating. Note that a similar motif can be found in the story of Percival when he encounters and kills the Red Knight. According to Johnson, "The Red Knight is the shadow side of masculinity, the negative, potentially destructive power. To truly become a man the shadow personality must be struggled with, but it cannot be repressed" (24). This passage is also reminiscent of the vital scene in *A Wizard of Earthsea* in which Ged confronts the shadow. He names and accepts it as part of himself, just as Jerry later recognizes and calls himself "another beast, another violent person."

Jerry calls his recognition of his deep psychological wound "knowledge." It is the knowledge that he should not have disturbed the universe, that he should have conformed, that he should have continued to play aggressive masculine sports such as football. Thus the novel ends with Jerry's despairing warning to Goober, "Don't disturb the universe" (187), which is also a spiritual death sentence pronounced on himself. In other words, Jerry is "murdered" by other males on the all-male "field," as is metaphorically depicted in the opening scene. In this sense, Jerry seems to be an "American Adam," R. W. B. Lewis's term for the innocent, isolated, nonconformist hero so common in American literature, especially the one in "the party of Irony" (7), who suffers a "Fortunate Fall" on his way to maturation. *The Chocolate War* ends at the very nadir of the hero's fall, however; there is no happy ending, no rebirth of the hero. As MacLeod writes, "Cormier has abandoned an enduring American myth" (76). Even in *The Catcher in the Rye*,[4] which also ends unhappily, Holden Caufield is not "murdered." Although psychologically weakened and wounded, Caufield escapes into a world of innocence, allowing Edgar Branch to say with some justification that Caufield embodies the "myth of American youth" (207). Similarly, Rebecca Lukens criticizes *The Chocolate War* in comparison with *The Catcher in the Rye:* "Holden finds that he is his own best hope for the phoniness of adult life. Cormier's characters come to no such faith. They are left *without hope.* The world grew darker between 1951 and 1974. Both writers skillfully create a realistic picture of the adolescent world, but unlike Salinger[,] who offers discovery, Cormier offers only *despair*" (13, emphasis added).

From a feminist perspective on changing masculinity, however, I do not share this opinion. We cannot simply charge that Cormier offers us only despair or a hopeless world but instead must ask: Why does Caufield survive as an American Adam, while Jerry is "murdered"? An answer lies in the fate of the "Earth Mother," described by Goldberg in *The Hazards of Being Male* as "fragile, helpless, and dependent . . . modest, pure, sexless, and unworldly" (14). The Earth Mother—the externalized and institutionalized feminine nature—was alive and well in the 1950s because, during the postwar marriage rush and baby boom, "the gender-based division of labor at the heart of male breadwinning remained more or less unquestioned" (Griswold 6–7), even if some, like Caufield, suspected the phoniness of such manhood. While Caufield complains of his "damn lonesome" feeling, he often seeks warmth, compassion, and affection in female characters such as Phoebe and Jane Gallagher. As long as women assumed the institutionalized role of the Earth Mother, men could safely escape into the realm of childhood, a metaphor of innocence, and remain American Adams.

But by the time *The Chocolate War* was published, the social climate had changed drastically. The Earth Mother was already dead to many of those who had believed in her. As Goldberg declared, "Earth mother is dead and now macho can die as well. The man can come alive as a full person" (20). Many women questioned the gender-based division of labor and rejected the role of Earth Mother. But since many men excluded feminine nature from their construction of masculinity, death of the Earth Mother was even more critical. This crisis for manhood is implied in *The Chocolate War* by the death of Jerry's mother and by the description of the power-hungry hierarchical men's world as "rotten" (87, 116), consisting, in Archie's words, "of two kinds of people—those who [are] victims and those who [victimize]" (80), or those who are "greedy and [those who are] cruel" (175).

It should be noted that in 1973, a year before the publication of *The Chocolate War,* the Vietnam War ended, and rumors of Watergate spread. According to the historian Peter N. Carroll, America was suffering a "raw, painful, unhealing wound" or "a gaping crack in the American identity" (*It Seemed Like Nothing Happened* 20) inflicted by the "dishonesty of the Vietnam War" and the Watergate scandal (159). Symptomatic of this "gaping crack," films of the period reflect the ongoing dispute over a new male image. According to the Japanese scholar of American culture Kamei Shunsuke, "So-called 'New

Cinemas' without any conventional heroes were in vogue. There were no heroes who would fight for the country, society, and its citizens, or for the righteousness and peace, but those who indulge in sex and violence, or those who roam around without any explicit purpose. What were there were anti-heroes" (10). Kamei[5] further points out that, around the same period, the American hero was resurrected in the character of Rocky, played by Sylvester Stallone (12–13). As the popularity of Stallone's sequels and Rambo films show, this new hero was accepted by American society in general. Thus in the 1970s and 1980s two competing types of hero coexisted, and therefore it is no wonder that Jerry's quest for masculine identity ends not with a hopeful prospect for his future or the healing of his wounds but with his metaphorical death.

Cormier has objected to having his books labeled "realistic" just because they do not end happily:

> But does an unhappy ending alone make a novel realistic? . . . *I am more concerned with reality* than realism in the novels. . . . I wanted to bring to life people like Jerry Renault . . . who appears for only one poignant moment. . . . But first came the emotions and then the characters. Once the characters are created and they become as real to you as the people you stand in line with at the movies that night, you must follow the *inevitability* of their actions. ("Forever Pedaling" 47–79, emphasis added)

Cormier's interest lies in depicting characters' emotions sympathetically rather than in constructing a realistic environment for his characters. In other words, Cormier depicts the confused emotions of men who are thrown into intense transitional crises. Such a crisis is Jerry's rebellion against gender stereotypes, and it cannot be overemphasized that Cormier, in creating Jerry, became a pioneer for nonconformists like him. Cormier, however, has Jerry pay a high price for his rebellion: his psychic wound.

As the story of Percival suggests, Jerry's psychic wound, recalling the wounded king, is a necessary part of his quest. But the ending of *The Chocolate War* offers no sign of Jerry's wound being healed. So it remains for *Beyond the Chocolate War* (1985) to deal with Jerry's healing or rebirth. Read as accounts of a single quest, the two books actually constitute one story. As the sequel's title indicates, the author depicts a new masculinity "beyond" the old one, a masculinity that transcends the chaos of conflicting models.

In the year *Beyond the Chocolate War* was published, there was a backlash against the counterculture and radicalism and, as evidenced by the Reagan presidency, an emergence of a new conservatism. In the 1980s, according to Rabinowitz and Cochran, "masculinity that defined the male psyche as a simplistic, achievement-oriented black box" returned (xvi). Some youths who found no appropriate masculine model came to identify with a narrow and rigid masculinity in order to protect themselves from possible confusion. It is not surprising, then, that a "mythopoetic perspective" segment of the men's movement became active during this period. Its activities were primarily based on Carl Jung's theory that men's psychological wounds could be healed by probing the archetypes buried in their unconscious and regaining their psychospiritual health. One politicized and feminist contribution to the debate, John Rowan's *The Horned God* (1987), offers insight into Jerry's trajectory of psychological healing. Rowan acknowledges that many men have repressed or excluded their feminine elements from themselves. The rejection of the feminine, he maintains, worsens the wounds men receive when the phoniness of their masculinity is exposed. Rowan believes that men can heal their wounds by reconnecting with the feminine buried in their unconscious, but first "it is important for men to allow themselves to be wounded. The wound is necessary before any healing can happen" (1). This observation is true of Jerry in *The Chocolate War* and *Beyond the Chocolate War,* and his recognition of himself as a beast is a significant part of the healing process. It is important to note that both Rowan's book and a feminist rereading of Percival's quest accomplish what Foucault's work fails to do in that they point toward a reconciliation with femininity.[6]

Although it is not the purpose of this essay to explore *Beyond the Chocolate War* in detail, I would like briefly to analyze the novel's treatment of wounded masculinity and its eventual healing. The story opens with the sinister sentence "Ray Bannister started to build the guillotine the day Jerry Renault returned to Monument" (3). Ironically, it is obedient Obie who rebels against Archie, now the "unchallenged champion of Trinity High School" (37), and conspires to let Bannister kill him, pretending an accident with his magic guillotine. Even though Archie learns of Obie's treachery and the plot fails, he falls from the seat of power. Archie cynically says, "You blame me for everything, right, Obie? . . . I'm an easy scapegoat" (263–64), thus indicating his recognition that power is not an entity that can be possessed but one that lies in the political relations between individuals. He has been thoroughly exposed to the phoniness of his masculinity—the illusions of his power and dominance. This recognition is as indispensable as Jerry's when he recognizes himself to be a beast.

In the meantime, the wounded Jerry has been sent to his mother's home town in Canada, where he is affectionately taken care of by his uncle and aunt. He finds rest in "the Talking Church," where he can smile for the first time since the incident as "he [listens] to the small whispering, chattering sounds" of the wind (107). Significantly, this wounded youth benefits from stereotypically feminine influences and experiences—nurturance, tenderness, affection, warmth, whispering, and chattering—while reconnecting with his matriarchal heritage. If we consider conventional masculinity to be wounded by its separation from femininity, Jerry's communication with the deep feminine side of his nature seems a significant step in the healing process.

Jerry comes back to Trinity High School half a year later, determined to confront his foe Janza once again. Jerry does not respond with violence this time but rather with nonviolence, "knowing where his strength *was,* where it had to be" (219, emphasis in original). Moreover, he smiles at Janza and explains to Goober, who witnesses the scene, "Just now, Janza was beating me up. But he wasn't winning. I mean, you can get beat up and still not lose. You can look like a loser but don't have to be one." He realizes now that "Janza's the loser, Goober. He'll be a loser all his life. He beat me up but he couldn't beat me." He goes on: "They want you to fight, Goober. And you can really lose only if you fight them. That's what the goons want. And guys like Archie Costello. You have to outlast them, that's all" (223–24). Jerry's recognition is empowering because it both discourages Janza from fighting and makes him feel "drained" and "like he had lost something" (222). Symbolically, Jerry's recognition almost coincides with Archie's "execution" by guillotine. In other words, the birth of the new manhood coincides with the death of conventional manhood.

In the guillotine episode Archie seems to undergo a change parallel to Jerry's. The previously power-hungry Archie is transformed into an unresisting fool who meekly accepts the execution. Noteworthy here is the instrument of Archie's intended death; ironically, the guillotine is the ultimate Enlightenment punishment because it completely severs the head from the heart, or reason from emotion.[7] In this sense, Archie's execution is indicative of the transformation he will undergo, a bitter and isolating one compared to Jerry's. Archie's self-recognition acknowledges that he represents what other males hide inside themselves: "I'm an easy scapegoat. . . . I am Archie Costello. . . . And I'll always be there, Obie. You'll always have me wherever you go and whatever you do. Tomorrow, ten years from now. Know why, Obie. Because I'm you. I'm all the things you hide inside you. That's me—" (264). He embodies the conventional manhood that helps create the "rotten" world made up of victims and victimizers. In contrast to Jerry's transformation, which involved getting in touch with the feminine, Archie's takes place without any feminine influence. His attitude toward the feminine is exemplified in his one-sided relationship to his girlfriend, Jill Morton. Not only does he keep himself distant from her, but he is also alienated from the feminine within himself. Moreover, his relationship with Obie contrasts with Jerry's relationship with Goober. In Jerry's rebirth Goober stands as a witness and pledges his friendship to Jerry, but Archie, in his turn, can only say "Good-bye, Obie" once and for all; he is incapable of intimacy or friendship. Archie's transformation, therefore, is only a shallow one; he is still limited by the confines of conventional masculinity.

It is interesting to place these parallel rebirths of two different masculinities within the cultural context of the 1980s. In the early 1980s there was an active discourse on the new man. Goldberg calls this type of man a "new male" who integrates his feminine aspects (*The New Male* 29–39), but Robert Bly in *Iron John* calls him a "soft male" and urges readers to offset this type of manhood by encountering "the Wild Man" within themselves in isolation from women (1–27). As Archie's case indicates, however, rebirth apart from the feminine may not lead to a balanced and well-rounded masculinity. Rowan's criticism of Bly's "Wild Man" is to the point: "For these men who have never done the feminine bit at all, who are unreconstructed male chauvinists, the [Wild Man] is simply an invitation to be even more aggressive" (111).

If we consider that Jerry's "murder" and rebirth coincide with such discourse on changing conceptions of masculinity, we can see that Cormier offers more than despair or Jerry's "death." If the book is read as a mythological quest story, Jerry's despair is undoubtedly a necessary passage to his rebirth. Therefore, Cormier's achievement in revolutionizing masculinity as a social construct cannot be overestimated. In fact, it seems to have anticipated later adolescent novels that deal with changing masculinity such as Katherine Paterson's

Park's Quest (1988), based on the Percival legend, and Le Guin's *Tehanu* (1990). What the protagonist Park finds at the end of his quest are the fallen idols of both his heroic grandfather and his father: the sobbing colonel confined in a wheelchair and the divorced father who was disloyal to his wife. More noteworthy is that Park's uncle, Frank, a gentle farmer who seems to be an identifiable father figure for him, has been married to the widowed Vietnamese wife of his dead brother and has adopted their daughter Thanh, as though to "[mop] up someone else's mess" (142). Similar reconciliations with the feminine occur in *Tehanu* when Ged, a fallen hero who has believed that "both men and magery are built on one rock: power belongs to men" (664), marries Tenar (a once-exploited child) and adopts Therru (an abused girl). By facing the ugly reality of child abuse, Ged not only acknowledges the dark side of conventional masculinity but also finds nurturance, a stereotypically feminine quality, within himself.

In a sense, the fact that Troyes's story of Percival was left incomplete is symbolic. Just as many scholars since the twelfth century have had to imagine an ending for Percival's quest, so today we have to wonder what the ending will be for male youth's quest in a world of changing masculinities. But the second wave of feminism has brought us to the point where the direction of these changes cannot be backward. Clearly, the health and welfare of masculinity is closely connected with the acceptance of femininity. Cormier's *The Chocolate War,* with its acute and sympathetic sensitivity, stands as witness to the need for this connection.

Notes

1. See, for example, Frappier, *Chrétien de Troyes et le mythe du graal.*
2. See Jung and von Franz, *The Grail Legend;* Johnson, *He: Understanding Masculine Psychology;* Corneau, *Absent Fathers, Lost Sons.*
3. According to Foucault, the idea of panopticism is based on Jeremy Bentham's Panopticon, an architectural design for a wheel-like prison with observant guards at the central watchtower behind one-way glass. Because it permitted ceaseless vigilance, this theoretical structure would have been especially effective for internalizing in the prisoners the principle of discipline and punishment. Foucault maintains that the Panopticon is designed "to induce in the inmate a state of conscious and permanent visibility that assures the automatic functioning of power" (201).
4. *The Catcher in the Rye* was originally published in *Collier's* (1945) and *The New Yorker* (1946). In a strict sense, then, this novel does not belong to the 1950s, though the masculine myth was equally strong in the postwar 1940s.
5. In the Japanese name system the family name comes first, followed by the given name.
6. Foucault maintains in *Discipline and Punish* that "docile bodies" are fabricated

by the dominant power. Thus, in the process of their formation, their own voices are silenced and their existence suppressed or marginalized. Here feminism found commonality with Foucault's theory, but he fails to examine the relation of gender to body. As Sandra Lee Bartky says, "Foucault treats the body throughout as if it were one, as if the bodily experiences of men and women did not differ and as if men and women bore the same relationship to the characteristic institutions of modern life" (65). In other words, Foucault's theory does not specify which elements are excluded from the fabric of conventional masculinity and femininity, respectively. It remained for feminists to clarify the lack of femininity within conventional manhood and women's silenced voices in "true womanhood."

7. I am indebted to Professor Jerome F. Shapiro, one of my colleagues at Hiroshima University, for this idea about the guillotine.

Works Cited

Bartky, Sandra Lee. *Femininity and Domination: Studies in the Phenomenology of Oppression.* New York: Routledge, 1990.

Bly, Robert. *Iron John: A Book About Men.* 1990. Reprint. New York: Vintage, 1992.

Branch, Edgar. "Mark Twain and J. D. Salinger: A Study in Literary Continuity." In *Salinger: A Critical and Personal Portrait,* ed. Henry Anatole Gruwald. New York: Harper and Row, 1962. Pp. 205–17.

Campbell, Patricia J. *Presenting Robert Cormier.* Rev. ed. Boston: Twayne, 1989.

Carroll, Peter N. *It Seemed Like Nothing Happened: America in the 1970s.* New Brunswick: Rutgers University Press, 1982.

Clatterbaugh, Kenneth. *Contemporary Perspectives on Masculinity: Men, Women, and Politics in Modern Society.* Rev. ed. Boulder, Colo.: Westview, 1997.

Cormier, Robert. *Beyond the Chocolate War.* 1985. Reprint. New York: Dell, 1986.

———. *The Chocolate War.* 1974. Reprint. New York: Dell, 1986.

———. "Forever Pedaling on the Road to Realism." In *Celebrating Children's Books,* ed. Betsy Hearne and Marilyn Kaye. New York: Lothrop, 1981. Pp. 44–53.

Corneau, Guy. *Absent Fathers, Lost Sons.* Trans. Larry Shouldice. Boston: Shambhala, 1991.

Doyle, Richard. *The Rape of the Male.* St. Paul, Minn.: Poor Richard's, 1976.

Eliot, T. Stearns. "The Love Song of J. Alfred Prufrock." In *Selected Poems.* 1917. Reprint. London: Faber and Faber, 1954.

Esman, Aaron H. *Adolescence and Culture.* New York: Columbia University Press, 1990.

Farrell, Warren. *The Liberated Man.* New York: Bantam, 1975.

Fasteau, Marc Feigen. *The Male Machine.* New York: McGraw-Hill, 1974.

Foucault, Michel. *Discipline and Punish: The Birth of the Prison.* Trans. Alan Sheridan. 1977. Reprint. London: Penguin, 1991.

Frappier, Jean. *Chrétien de Troyes et le mythe du graal: Etude sur Perceval ou le conte du graal.* Trans. Amazawa Taijiro. *Seihaino Shinwa (The Myth of holy grail).* Tokyo: Chikumashobo, 1990.

Gilligan, Carol. *In a Different Voice: Psychological Theory and Women's Development.* Cambridge: Harvard University Press, 1982.

Goldberg, Herb. *The Hazards of Being Male: Surviving the Myth of Masculinity Privilege.* 1976. Reprint. New York: Signet, 1977.

———. *The New Male.* 1979. Reprint. New York: Signet, 1980.

Griswold, Robert L. *Fatherhood in America: A History.* New York: BasicBooks, 1993.

Hamilton, Virginia. *The Planet of Junior Brown.* 1971. Reprint. New York: Macmillan, 1974.

Holland, Isabelle. *The Man Without a Face.* 1972. Reprint. New York: HarperKeypoint, 1987.
Iskander, Sylvia Patterson. "Readers, Realism, and Robert Cormier." *Children's Literature* 15 (1987):7–18.
Johnson, Robert A. *He: Understanding Masculine Psychology.* Rev. ed. New York: Harper and Row, 1989.
Jung, Emma, and Marie-Louise von Franz. *The Grail Legend.* Trans. Andrea Dykes. Boston: Sigo, 1986.
Kamei, Shunsuke. *American Hero no Keifu* (The Heritage of the American heroes). Tokyo: Kenkyusha, 1993.
Le Guin, Ursula K. *Earthsea Revisioned.* Cambridge, Mass.: CLNE/Green Bay, 1993.
———. *Tehanu.* 1990. Reprinted as *The Earthsea Quartet.* London: Penguin, 1992.
———. *A Wizard of Earthsea.* 1968. Reprinted as *The Earthsea Quartet.* London: Penguin, 1992.
Lewis, R. W. B. *The American Adam: Innocence, Tragedy, and Tradition in the Nineteenth Century.* Chicago: University of Chicago Press, 1955.
Lukens, Rebecca. "From Salinger to Cormier: Disillusionment to Despair in Thirty Years." In *Webs and Wardrobes: Humanist and Religious World Views in Children's Literature,* ed. Joseph O'Beirne Milner. Lanham, Md.: University Presses of America, 1987. Pp. 8–13.
MacLeod, Anne Scott. "Robert Cormier and the Adolescent Novel." *Children's Literature in Education* 11 (1981):74–81.
Nodelman, Perry. "Robert Cormier's *The Chocolate War:* Paranoia Paradox." In *Stories and Society: Children's Literature in Its Social Context,* ed. Dennis Butts. London: Macmillan, 1992. Pp. 22–36.
Paterson, Katherine. *Park's Quest.* New York: Dutton, 1988.
Rabinowitz, Fredric E., and Sam V. Cochran. *Man Alive: A Primer of Men's Issues.* Belmont, Calif.: Brooks/Cole, 1994.
Rotundo, E. Anthony. *American Manhood: Transformations in Masculinity from the Revolution to the Modern Era.* New York: BasicBooks, 1993.
Rowan, John. *The Horned God: Feminism and Men as Wounded and Healing.* New York: Routledge, 1987.
Salinger, J. D. *The Catcher in the Rye.* 1951. Reprint. Boston: Little, Brown, 1991.
Skolnick, Arlene. *Embattled Paradise: The American Family in an Age of Uncertainty.* New York: Basic, 1991.
Troyes, Chrétien de. *Le Roman de Perceval ou le conte du graal.* Trans. Amazawa Taijiro. In *Fransu Chusei Bungakushu* (French verses and romances in Middle Age). Tokyo: Hakusuisha, 1991. 2:141–323.

Still a Slave: Legal and Spiritual Freedom in Julius Lester's "Where the Sun Lives"

Paula T. Connolly

Before the end of the Civil War, more than one hundred book-length slave narratives had been published.[1] Although the popularity of these books was aided by the public's interest in plantation life, religious discussion, and the drama of slaves escaping to the North, the primary concern was, of course, the political one (see Foster, esp. 20–21, 54). Indeed, these firsthand accounts of life in slavery became an extraordinarily effective means of political persuasion. As a reviewer of Henry Bibb's narrative noted in 1849: "This fugitive slave literature is destined to be a powerful lever. We have the most profound conviction of its potency. We see in it the easy and infallible means of abolitionizing the free States. Argument provokes argument. . . . But narratives of slaves go right to the hearts of men" ("Life of Henry Bibb"). These narratives went "right to the hearts of men" because they transformed the slave from the object to the subject of his or her own story. Writers such as Frederick Douglass and Harriet Jacobs could provide authentic testimony, they asserted, because they were not only "eye-witness" to the sufferings endured by slaves but were also what William Andrews terms "I-witness" (xxxii), that is, they were able to recount their feelings as individuals who had themselves suffered and survived slavery. The slave narrative—which often recounted the author's childhood and first realization of slavery, details of slave life, beatings, and slave auctions, and the successful escape of the narrator (see Olney)—also provided insights into the slave community and especially into the rebellions that allowed a means of psychological if not physical freedom.

More than a century later, there are a number of stories for young audiences based on actual slave narratives of the nineteenth century, as well as a range of others that purport to tell not of actual lives but instead of events that "could have happened."[2] Julius Lester's

I am grateful to the University of North Carolina at Charlotte, which provided a grant for my research on Julius Lester.
Children's Literature 26, ed. Elizabeth Lennox Keyser (Yale University Press, © 1998 Hollins College).

books about slavery for young adults include both forms. In *To Be a Slave* (1968) Lester weaves together actual excerpts principally from accounts of ex-slaves, and in two later short story collections—*Long Journey Home* (1972) and *This Strange New Feeling* (1981)—he draws on historical fact, then, as he explains, "add[s] details . . . and character motivation where it was lacking in the original source material." This blending is a means, Lester asserts, of "intensifying the human experiences in the story, and . . . of teaching history" (*LJH* 1).

According to Lester, although "history as we know it" is generally made up of "the stories of the lives and works of so-called great men and women . . . they comprise only one facet of that history." Instead, Lester argues, it is precisely the unknown individual who provides the key to the past: "For me these stories, and hundreds like them, comprise the essence of black history. . . . While Frederick Douglass organized against slavery, he would have been an isolated figure if hundreds of thousands of slaves had not run away. . . . History is made by the many, whose individual deeds are seldom recorded and who are never known outside their own small circles" (*LJH* 1–2). Other than "A Christmas Love Story," which is a retelling of William and Ellen Craft's narrative, these short stories originated in frequently overlooked references from a range of sources, and they tell of people who "are [not] . . . known outside their own small circles." Lester's stories, then, are not only a way of telling a new generation about slavery but also of representing a range of people who faced the threat of silence from both slavery and recorded history.

These short stories, largely geared to an audience of young adults, grapple with significantly complex issues of racial and sexual exploitation, physical and psychological abuse, societal repression, and, most central for the characters he presents, the struggle to achieve and maintain identity against extraordinarily aggressive and repressive forces. No doubt readers today could come to these stories with the same range of motives as did readers of narratives in the nineteenth century, and although there is danger of essentialism in connecting issues of identity for people under slavery to current adolescent readers, by focusing on that key struggle for self-determination, writers such as Lester are able to "teach history" by making it real for readers today.[3]

In *This Strange New Feeling,* Lester presents three stories: the title story, "Where the Sun Lives," and "A Christmas Love Story." Although each of the protagonists of these stories is in love, the book's title refers not to that but to "this strange new feeling of freedom" ("SNF" 39). The first story tells of a young man who escapes from slavery, is recaptured, then escapes again with a young woman who kills their master. The last story tells of the Crafts' journey to the North, as well as their later attempts to elude slavecatchers. The center story, "Where the Sun Lives," is perhaps the most problematic, for although it is counterpointed by two stories in which the protagonists achieve physical emancipation, its protagonist does not.

Lester's source for this story is not a narrative but an entry in Helen Catterall's *Judicial Cases Concerning Slavery:* "William Yates, a free man of colour, died in 1829, having first made his will, by which he gave his whole estate . . . in trust for his wife, Maria, who was his slave, to be paid over to her as soon as she could obtain her freedom, and get permission to remain in the State. All the personal assets were insufficient to pay the . . . debts and Maria was sold."[4] Using this citation as the nucleus of his plot, Lester fashioned the story of William (renamed Forrest) Yates and Maria, creating as well the figures of Maria's friend Sukey and the mistress and master of the plantation.

Although "Where the Sun Lives" should not be conflated with actual slave narratives, this story replicates many of the complexities of the narratives, especially in its examination of power structures, identity, and the personal and social ramifications of slavery. Indeed, whereas slave narratives functioned as a way to break the silence surrounding slavery, silence is also broken in this fiction, for Lester presents a story that could not be told by those early writers—the story of a woman who is within and not escaped from the slavery of the South.

Just as the narratives were meant to humanize the slave so that the issues went "right to the hearts" of their readers, so the role of Maria in this story turns the slave from object to subject; Lester personalizes slavery for his young readers so that the story of Maria and Forrest is interwoven with a significantly complex array of issues. In particular, he uses the story of their lives to examine the ways in which slave, freed black, and slaveholder may experience legal or spiritual enslavement. And in Maria, Lester creates a first-person narrator who makes real the experiences of slaves by serving as both an "eye-" and an "I-" witness to slavery and the people caught within it.

"Where the Sun Lives" begins with the issues of rebellion and retribution as Maria is shown tending to her dying mistress. Unable to sleep because she must answer her mistress's constant complaints,

Maria recalls her life with this woman and recounts as well the many beatings that have left her scarred but undefeated. In this early scene, although Maria must overtly agree with Mistress, she carries on an interior dialogue of criticism. When the mistress promises, "When I get well, I'll give you twenty lashes for staring out that window when you're supposed to be looking after me," Maria mumbles, "Yes'm," but thinks to herself, "That's one beating I won't have to worry about. Everybody know she ain't going to lay that rawhide whip on nobody ever again. She know it, too" (45). Within the limitations of her situation, Maria uses silent language to combat this woman. When Mistress stares at her, Maria affirms, "I stare back, trying to put as much life in my eyes as I can. I want her to see all the life that's in me, all the life that she won't be able to take from me" (46).

In *Black Culture and Black Consciousness* Lawrence Levine discusses the ways in which slaves created a "verbal art" of privately encoded messages that then "created the necessary space between slaves and their owners and were the means of preventing legal slavery from becoming spiritual slavery. In addition to the world of the masters which slaves inhabited and accommodated to, as they had to, they created and maintained a world apart which . . . remained their own domain, free of control of those who ruled the earth" (80). It is clear that Maria, despite being physically enslaved, retains as much spiritual freedom as she can, particularly by psychologically battling Mistress Phillips at every opportunity.

The degeneration and death of slaveholders is also a common theme in slave narratives. In his *Narrative,* for example, Frederick Douglass describes his mistress Sophia Auld as "a woman of the kindest heart and finest feelings" whose "cheerful eye, under the influence of slavery, soon became red with rage; [whose] . . . voice, made all of sweet accord, changed to one of harsh and horrid discord; and [whose] . . . angelic face gave place to that of a demon" (77–78). Lester evokes such images here with the depiction of the insidious but inexorable changes slavery has wrought on the mistress. When Maria had first met her, Mistress Phillips had had "yellow hair [like] . . . buttercups" and had been "one of the prettiest girls in Virginia" (46), but by the time she dies, just five days short of her thirtieth birthday, Mistress Phillips's "pretty buttercup-color hair is gray. . . . Now she looks like an old lady and her face is the color of old sour milk" (48).

Although it is the responsibility of running the plantation that has sickened the mistress, her physical degeneration is accompanied by—or, perhaps more accurately, prompted by—a moral one. This physical illness parallels the slaveholder's spiritual collapse. As with Douglass's Sophia Auld, Mistress Phillips's personality undergoes a striking transformation. Maria recalls that when she was seven, "Mistress treated me like I was her little girl. She played games with me, and at night would tell me stories. After she lost her first baby in the fifth month, she told me that it was all right, that I was her baby" (46). Maria's status as the adopted child of her mistress is, however, ultimately a false one that offers her no real protection.

The young girl's realization of that, as well as the change in Mistress Phillips, echoes other frequent foci in slave narratives: the child's first recognition of the realities of slavery through the betrayal or beatings of a slaveholder and the clarification of ostensible paternalism. Indeed, the conflation of *master* and *mistress* with *parent* was often used in pro-slavery tracts to represent the harmony of plantation life,[5] but that conflation is repeatedly critiqued in slave narratives, as it is in "Where the Sun Lives." In these texts, the terms *parent* and *slaveholder* are ultimately antithetical ones: the biological slave parent is powerless, and the slaveholder does not succor the child. Here, although Mistress Phillips calls Maria her child, she comes to see the girl as a reminder of her inability to bear children, and after her third baby dies, the whippings of Maria begin:

> I turned around [Maria recalls] and she was standing in the doorway, the whip in her hand.
>
> . . . Mistress Phillips say that I hadn't done nothing wrong, just that it was time I learned that I was a slave.
>
> . . . After a while I could tell when she was going to get the whip. It was something about the way she would wake up in the morning, a look in her face like her eyes had died during the night. I don't know which I hated more—the whippings or her taking care of me afterward. (47)

This violence becomes more problematic because it signals the sexual vulnerability of female slaves. These whippings, which begin in Maria's early adolescence, are prompted by the mistress's jealousy of the girl eleven years her junior. As slave narratives—particularly those by women—and Elizabeth Fox-Genovese's study *Within the Plantation Household* reiterate, the sexual jealousies of mistresses against slave women were often an important dynamic in their daily interactions, and such tensions are implicit in this early scene. The mistress who cannot have children beats Maria so severely that Maria will never be able to nurse any babies she may have.

Indeed, the wife's suspicions about her husband are not unfounded. At his wife's wake, when Phillips asks Maria to come to Richmond to cook for him, Maria realizes his intent immediately: "We've known each other for a long time, me and Master, and he ain't like a lot of masters are with the slave women. It ain't because he might not want to be. He just don't know how to do it and make it seem all right." Maria tells him simply, "That ain't a good idea, Master" (60), and for now, he hurriedly agrees and does not pursue the subject.

Ironically, the slaveholder who has legal freedom clearly does not have spiritual freedom. Damned because of her enslavement of others, the mistress dies with "no kin and no friends" (57), the scene paralleling slave narratives that detail the torturous deaths of slaveholders as an emblem of God's vengeance. In this story, Maria learns from Sukey that "you can tell how evil a person was by how long it takes them to die. Mistress must've been the Devil. She was all of three months dying" (55). The death is a painful one; Mistress Phillips thrashes about, curses, and suffers fever, and her breathing "sounded like there was rocks and sand in her chest" (56). The view that the mistress's death is direct punishment for her treatment of slaves is clear in Maria's reflection that "the only whipping there's going to be around here now is the one Death is putting on Mistress" (52).

Mistress's death provides a catharsis for those around her. Maria is finally able to sleep through the night, and at the moment of the death Maria notes, "I listened to the silence and wanted it to last forever. It felt like somebody was touching me all over with hands as soft as dandelion fluff" (56). Although the slaves who pass by the coffin the next day "look serious and sad as they file in . . . to look at Mistress. . . . [Maria] sees the smiles on their faces as they go out" (58).[6] There is even "no sadness" (57) in the master, who eats a hearty breakfast the morning he learns of his wife's death. The ostensible peace and retribution brought by this death are compounded by improved conditions on the plantation. There will be no whipping now, food is much improved, Maria's work is lessened, and Maria even suggests that the slaves run the plantation by themselves. Indeed, it seems at this point that Maria will gain physical—although not yet legal—freedom when she leaves the plantation to live with Forrest Yates, a free black man.

One of the ways Lester is able to expand on slave narratives is in his development of the problematic central character of Forrest. A free black man still living in the midst of slavery, Forrest acts as both Maria's liberator and her enslaver. Maria first sees Forrest when she is tending to her dying mistress; his vitality is contrasted with the mistress's debilitation and his ease with Maria's relentless caretaking. He thus becomes an immediate sign of life and freedom to Maria, and that freedom is developed when he takes her from the plantation. Yet his character is not an unambivalent one. Sukey describes Forrest as a man who "never slaved a day in his life. But he cares more about us slaves than a lot of us do for ourselves. White folks think the world of him too" (54). Here, Sukey unwittingly describes the central conflict of the character. Forrest seems to stand in two worlds—slave and free—but fits fully in neither.

"White folks think the world" of this man, but not merely because of his skill as a blacksmith. Forrest serves as a link between the slave and the slaveholding communities, and most frequently he attempts to reify his identity by aligning himself with white slaveholders. When Maria first meets Forrest, she learns that he is hiding Jim, a slave who has run away to avoid one of Mistress's whippings. Yet this man that Forrest protects is ultimately returning, not escaping. At Mistress Phillips's wake, "Forrest comes in, Jim following. Master sees them and rushes forward to shake Jim's hand and to welcome him back to the plantation" (58). This scene of instant reconciliation is the most ideal presentation of slavery in the story and parallels scenes in proslavery plantation novels that depict repentant slaves voluntarily returning to their masters.[7] In "Where the Sun Lives," it is Forrest who choreographs this reunion scene between master and slave, he who returns the hiding Jim to the plantation. This slave seems to function as an object of trade between the two men, and their commerce in people continues later that day when Master agrees to sell Maria to Forrest. Maria loves Forrest, but this transference of ownership initially highlights symbolic parallels between the two men.

Maria, afraid that slaves may be sold from the plantation, calms herself by believing, "Master wouldn't sell me or Mammy [Sukey] or Jim." Yet she soon discovers that she has already been sold. "He [Phillips] is smiling," she remarks. "I don't understand how he can say something like that and smile" (64). When Maria goes to the back of the house, where she has been told her new owner waits, she sees only Forrest and rushes into his arms. Instead of quelling her fears, he teases the clearly distraught woman, following her to the front of the house as she looks for her new master. The instability of Maria's position is exacerbated by this game played out between Phillips and Forrest. The two men have orchestrated the scene in which Maria is left powerless: they determine whether she is sold and to whom, denying her ownership of her person, and they escalate her anxiety by withholding that information. In that regard, Forrest's teasing seems particularly cruel. His insensitivity is evident when he not only smiles, like Phillips, but even laughs at her discomfort. Indeed Forrest, whom Maria realizes "reminds me of Master" (63), reveals what has happened to her with a statement that serves as a frighteningly ironic presentiment—"You got to call me Master now" (66).

Manumission laws would require that Maria leave the state if she were set free, yet as Forrest learns from Phillips, "there wasn't any law against a free black man owning a slave" (66). Thus, despite Maria's pleas that they move North, Forrest chooses to remain in the South, where he can continue working for wealthy plantation owners. Although, as Eugene Genovese points out, it was not unheard-of for freedmen to own their wives and children in order to remain in the state (398–413), Forrest's choice—to become a slaveholder—is supported by his economic and even psychological ties to the white slaveholding community. When he assures Maria that bought "wives" of freed black men are "slaves on paper and that don't mean nothing" (66), he is echoing the ideology and rhetoric of such slavery advocates as Reverend Nehemiah Adams. Adams, who in 1854 detailed his proslavery stance in *A South-Side View of Slavery,* assured his readers that "after all, the bondage is theoretical" (25).

Forrest's view of slavery—unlike Maria's—is also tinged with sentimentality, and their opinions on the topic are, according to Maria, "the one thing me and Forrest argue about sometime." When "Forrest asked me once if I missed the plantation . . . I asked him if he had lost his mind. It don't make no difference how good a master is, you still a slave." Maria's anxiety is not relieved by Forrest's promises that legal slavery means nothing, and she tells him, "I'd rest easier in my mind if I wasn't a slave on paper" (68).

Forrest believes he can create a place of safety within this world, and the two years that he and Maria are together become a conflicted mixture of companionable union and Maria's uneasiness about her continued legal status as a slave. Each day Forrest and Maria make breakfast and do the morning chores together. Later, the two greet the morning as they "sit on the railing of the corral and watch the sun come up" (68). This idyllic depiction of their home is sometimes interrupted when Maria can "see smoke rising from behind the stand of pine trees that blocks the big house from [her] view, and when [she does, she knows] that Master and his new wife are back from Richmond and Mammy is cooking up breakfast" (68). Although the trees seem to provide some initial visual and spatial protection from the plantation, that screen is easily penetrated.

That penetration by the outside world is accentuated by Forrest's value system, for although he has never been a "slave on paper" (68), Forrest defines himself largely through the eyes of white slaveholders. Especially, he seeks equality and freedom through the conspicuous consumption of unnecessary luxury goods, an obsession that Maria cannot understand. Maria assures him that the horses and wagon they have are good enough for her, and she refuses to buy a new dress in town, knowing that she could have made better ones when she was only eight years old. Yet "new" and "fine" things are precisely what Forrest demands for himself and Maria. He explains to her, "I want us to live as good as white people. That means we got to have the things that white people do. That'll prove that we're just as good as they are. . . . It'll prove that I'm as free as they are" (72).

The perversion of Forrest's definition of freedom is made especially clear when he and Maria go into town so that he can buy a new horse. Left on her own, Maria is drawn to a large crowd for what she hopes will be a puppet show but instead finds is a slave auction. Although the horrors of slave auctions are an important component of the narratives, Lester further develops this scene by focusing on the sexual violation of a young woman who is taunted and stripped before a cheering crowd. Such sexual vulnerability of women is revealed in the early narratives. In her 1861 narrative, for example, Harriet Jacobs argues that although "slavery is terrible for men . . . it is far more terrible for women. Superadded to the burden common to all, *they* have wrongs, and sufferings, and mortifications peculiarly their own" (77). Those sufferings entailed the constant threats of sexual harassment and rape. Women such as Jacobs determined to tell the truths of those sexual violations but found they had to be wary of alienating their audience—in particular, northern white female abolitionists. Despite such concerns, narratives tell of the rapes, beatings, and murders of slave women.

In "Where the Sun Lives," Lester builds on such incidents to depict a graphic scene of this woman's suffering as she stands alone and unprotected before the crowd. She is first taunted by the auctioneer. He orders her to strip, and when she does not move, he tells her, "Just pull [the dress] over your head like you do for all the young bucks" (70). When she tries to move away from the man, he "grabs her by the arm and snatches the top of her dress, pulling on it hard. It rips and falls to the floor. The crowd cheers loudly" (70). As the young woman stands naked, the auctioneer "puts his hands on her full breasts and squeezes [saying] . . . 'Now, who'll make the first bid?' " (70–71). Such graphic details show the myriad physical and psychological assaults involved in viewing a person as an object to be sold, as well as in the sexual exploitation of women trapped in slavery.

The objectification of this unnamed woman by the crowd is countered, for the reader, by Maria. As this woman is viewed through the narrator's eyes, she becomes not object but subject, for Maria both sees this woman ("eye-witness") and is herself, still a legal slave, vulnerable to her plight ("I-witness"). Indeed, Maria hopes her presence as the only other woman in the crowd will mitigate the young woman's isolation. Maria tries to fight these men as she stares at the young woman and thinks, "Maybe if she looks at me, she won't cry. She'll know that we can't ever let them see us cry. If they see us cry, then we won't have anything left that's ours" (71). Unlike Forrest, who believes owning objects will signify freedom, for Maria, it is keeping possession of the inner self that is a way to battle total enslavement.

Although Forrest does not attend the slave auction, he is not disassociated from the scene. At the time of this auction he is buying a "shiny black horse" (71) in an attempt to reify his sense of freedom. The two purchases are linked, for not only are the auctioneer's description of the woman as "a finer bit of flesh" (70) and his handling of her as callous as toward any animal, but Forrest's obsession with conspicuous possessions also implicitly accepts and depends on the slave market. Following this scene, Maria and Forrest have their "worst argument yet" (71), and Forrest accuses her of having a "slave mentality" (72) and not enough sense to stay away from the auction. Maria fears that Forrest may be borrowing too much money to buy things they don't need. She responds: "Maybe having the slave mentality ain't all bad. . . . The slave mentality sees white folk and their fine horses and big houses and pretty china and all like that. But we see that they ain't got no love. And that's all I got to say on it" (73). Maria redefines the term *slave mentality* so that it comes to mean, not being trapped by a limited imagination of oppression, but being freed of the cultural values of those who have oppressed her. For her, it comes to mean the awareness of slavery, the ability to empathize with and be angered by the plight of slaves. It is what Levine would term that "necessary space . . . [that prevented] legal slavery from becoming spiritual slavery" (80).

Forrest, although born legally free, never gains this spiritual freedom, and images from Maria's years with Mistress Phillips resurface in these later passages to demonstrate how Forrest's ideology replicates that of the slaveholders, as well as how legally vulnerable Maria is within that system. Anxious to please Forrest, Maria, seeing the new carriage he has bought, "exclaim[s] and carr[ies] on like it's the prettiest thing [she's] . . . ever seen in [her] . . . life." Maria also reflects, "All I know is that I hope he didn't have to borrow too much money to pay for it. But I don't say any of that" (73). This contrast of external support and internal criticism, albeit not as vitriolic, resembles the two-tiered dialogues she had maintained with Mistress Phillips. Here, although she loves Forrest, Maria is as careful to guard her thoughts from him as she was with her mistress. Ironically, it is exactly at the moment when Maria thinks to herself that she will "make a new dress for when Forrest takes me riding in the [new] carriage [for] that'll help him feel free too" (74) that Master Phillips comes with news of Forrest's death. He tells her that Forrest was killed shoeing a horse when a young white boy "thought it would be funny to watch the horse jump around if he flicked some live coals on it. Forrest was kicked in the head and died instantly" (75).

The horrific implications of Forrest's obsession with things are made clear following his death. When Forrest had assured Maria that she would be set free if he died, he had compared his will to the way his mother had been given her own freedom just before Forrest's birth. Forrest, who had escaped slavery by three months, functions in his own life as the slaveholder. Yet his belief that he has mastered the legal system of slavery is false, for in his quest for freedom he has borrowed large sums of money, and Maria, "according to the law . . . the most valuable piece of property he owned" (78), will be sold off to pay his debts. The man who had once returned the runaway slave Jim to his master has now delivered Maria into the hands of the slave trader.

As Eugene Genovese points out, "the great majority of Negro slaveholders . . . owned relatives or friends as a mere formality. . . . Even when relatives were bought, their fate necessarily remained precarious while they were legally slaves" (406–7).[8] That precariousness was something Forrest had continually denied, and his denial marks both his oppression of Maria and his association with slaveholders. Further, the fact that Forrest's will depends on his trust in Maria's "old master" (68), who knows Forrest's wishes and is expected to carry them out, reveals a benevolent view of slaveholders that was frequently denounced in slave narratives. Harriet Jacobs, for example, who points out that slaves had no economic, legal, or social rights against their owners, asserts that "no promise or writing given to a slave is legally binding" (6). Forrest, however, trusts the system and even functions as a slaveholder in his relationship with his wife, for Maria remembers how he had "explained to [her] about his will and how he was giving [her her] freedom" (77).

Narratives by women such as Harriet Jacobs had pointed out the particular vulnerabilities and sexual exploitation of women in slavery, as well as the struggles of black men to protect women from rape and punishment (also see Genovese, 482–94). Any criticism of black women's oppression by black men was stilled in the face of fighting the common and overriding enemy of white oppression. Indeed, such silence was essential, not only because the keenest threat was from white oppressors but also because slavery advocates touted their system as one that protected slave women's virtue; suggestions of abuse by black men would only have been further exploited in proslavery tracts (see Genovese 482–84; Adams 86–88). Not as concerned with the abuse of black women by white men, slavery advocates decried any suggestion of abuse of those women by black men and defended slavery as a protection for women: "The [slaves] are placed under the control of others, who are interested to restrain their excesses of cruelty or rage. Wives are protected from their husbands, and children from their parents" (quoted in Genovese 483).

Nonetheless, women such as Harriet Jacobs would clarify distinctions based on gender and argue that "slavery is . . . far more terrible for women" (77). Later, early black feminists such as Anna Julia Cooper would point out that "the colored woman . . . occupies . . . a unique position in this country. . . . [H]er status seems one of the least ascertainable and definitive of all the forces which make for our civilization. She is confronted by both a woman question and a race problem, and is as yet an unknown or an unacknowledged factor in both" (134). What these women argued against was any essentialism that did not take into account both race *and* gender as factors of oppression.[9]

Lester, too, focuses on the intersection of race and gender in his depiction of Maria, particularly in her relationships with her "old" masters (Mistress and Master Phillips) and her "new" master (her husband and legal slaveholder, Forrest). Maria's relationship with Forrest is encapsulated with images identifying him with Master Phillips. In both her first meeting with Forrest and her final meeting with Master Phillips, Maria notes similarities between the two men, and in a strange conflation of characters and identities at the close of the story, Maria understands Master Phillips both because of his prior "proposal" to her and because she can interpret his look, since "Forrest looked at me like that when he was angry and ashamed at the same time" (79).

Maria's relationship with Forrest is particularly insidious because of the ways in which she relinquishes resistance against the authority that constrains her. In a world in which oppression is based on the collapse of identity, Maria's hope for rescue from Forrest becomes itself another means of her enslavement. Although Maria rebels against the oppression of her mistress as the story opens, she quickly looks to Forrest as a means of her salvation. The first time she sees him she thinks, "If I didn't know better, I would swear he knew where the sun lives" (45). An image of power and freedom, this "sun" becomes her hope for escape, and Maria continues to believe that Forrest "was brother to the sun" (67). Even after her internal rebellion against Forrest—when she criticizes his growing debt and his notion of freedom as based on material possessions—she stills her criticisms when she looks at him later that day: "If he doesn't know where the sun lives, nothing can convince me that he won't find its address" (73). In this relationship, which is in some ways even more dangerous than that with her more overtly oppressive old masters, Maria silences her criticisms and sublimates both her identity and hope for freedom in Forrest.

Yet, once Forrest is killed, Maria reaffirms her sense of independent identity and confronts her old master. Although the cost of Forrest's spiritual enslavement for his own life and Maria's is dear, Maria, who has psychologically battled Mistress Phillips, survived her beatings, refused Master Phillips's advances, and rejected the cultural and commercial values of her oppressors, is still determined to retain her spiritual freedom and reassert herself. Sukey, present when Phillips explains the will to Maria, begs him to pay off Forrest's debts: "Master, you can't let them sell Maria. She's been like a daughter to you. Like a member of your own family" (78). Maria, however, knows that the conflation of *parent* and *slaveholder* is false in this instance, just as it had been with Mistress Phillips.

She also realizes that she and Phillips are reenacting a prior incident: "If I ask Master, he'll say yes. That's what he's waiting for. He did the asking the other time, but he never asked really. I didn't know that I shamed him when I said no." After Mistress Phillips's death, Maria had quietly refused Phillips, but this time the scene is overtly described as a struggle between Master and Maria for "all the power." Maria pulls Sukey from her knees and tells her, "It's all right, Mammy. It's all right. I don't want no new mistress whipping me because she see something in Master's soul he shamed to have there" (79). As Harriet Jacobs, through her narrative persona in *Incidents in the Life of a Slave Girl,* saw victory in thwarting the advances of her master, Flint, so too does Maria make explicit Phillips's implicit desires and choose the auction block rather than acquiesce to her role as slave. Her direct confrontation of her old master and her use of voice to explode the silence of the sexual exploitation of slave women both damns and saves her.

With this refusal, Maria knows she will be sold. She has already recognized the man who accompanies Phillips as the slave auctioneer. And although Maria, having witnessed the earlier scene, knows what lies in wait for her, she resolves:

> I can see myself standing up on that platform, and when he tears my dress off, I won't cry. I'll stand up straight, and when the white men start cheering and applauding, I'll stare every one of them in the eye and make them stop. Won't many of them want to buy me, and whichever one does will wish he hadn't.
>
> 'Cause I know. I know now where the sun lives. (79–80)

Maria, legally enslaved, refuses to be spiritually enslaved and resolves to continue to battle her oppressors. She defines herself in opposition to slavery and, as a woman of strength, independence, and integrity, she redefines *slave mentality* as a state of knowledge and psychological freedom. She remains ready to fight, and in this story the images of the sun evoke this strength as they evolve from a sign of her mistress's death, to her love of Forrest and belief in his power, to the strength within herself.

Slave narratives broke silence by telling of the lives of slaves. In "Where the Sun Lives," Lester breaks silence by presenting a story that could not be told by the escaped slaves of the nineteenth century, the story of a woman who did not gain physical freedom and who could not come to the North to write of her life. He further problematizes the racial exploitation of slavery by intersecting it with the sexual exploitation Maria faces from the masters who attempt to control her life.

Yet he also fashions a tale that echoes many of the issues and narrative techniques found in slave narratives: the transformation of the slave from object to subject, the recollection of childhood scenes and one's first beating as a realization of one's legal slavery, the clarification of language and resignification of terms, the sexual vulnerability of slave women, the characterization of an originally kind slaveholder transformed by her role in slavery, the depiction of counterlanguages and inner criticism to create spiritual freedom for the slave, and the development of a character determined to survive enslavement with selfhood intact. By using the story of Maria and Forrest as the center point of "Where the Sun Lives," Lester both dramatizes and personalizes these issues to make clear to his young audience that, indeed, the men and women who endured slavery were not merely "a repetition of identical forms" (Kibbey 173). In the case of Maria, Lester has drawn a character who not only retains her identity but defies the terms of slavery to demand it.

Notes

1. Regarding the number of published book-length slave narratives, see Gates, ix–xi. For a bibliography of slave narratives, see Davis and Gates.

2. Retellings based on actual slave narratives include Ossie Davis, *Escape to Freedom;* Florence B. Freedman, *Two Tickets to Freedom;* and Mary E. Lyons, *Letters from a Slave Girl.* In the introductory note to *Runaway to Freedom* Barbara Smucker states that her story about the "escape from Mississippi to Canada by two fictitious characters . . . could have happened" (n.p.).

3. The issues and form of stories about slavery vary in significant ways depending on the age of the intended child audience. Picture books, for example, do not deal with the sexual exploitation that forms a central part of Lester's "Where the Sun Lives." Further, although picture books such as Patricia Polacco's *Pink and Say,* Faith Ringgold's *Aunt Harriet's Underground Railroad in the Sky,* and Jeanette Winter's *Follow the Drinking Gourd* describe issues such as resistance to slavery, the intersection of words and pictures often provides a balance of tensions; that is, if the words describe a scene of danger, the pictures often offer ways to mitigate that danger for the young reader. For a discussion of such techniques, see Connolly.

4. This excerpt from Helen Catterall's *Judicial Cases* (1:210) is reprinted in Lester, *This Strange New Feeling,* 161–62. Lester notes that his story "was suggested" by that entry (161).

5. See Kibbey. Also, Eugene Genovese argues in *Roll, Jordan, Roll* that through the manipulation of language and loyalty, paternalism "disguised, however imperfectly, the appropriation of one man's labor power by another" (6). Further, he notes that

"wherever paternalism exists, it undermines solidarity among the oppressed by linking them as individuals to their oppressors" (5).

6. In *Incidents in the Life of a Slave Girl* (1861), Harriet Jacobs tells of a woman who strikes her dead mistress, saying, "The devil is got you *now!*" That woman's action is seen by one of the mistress's children, and the woman is later sold in punishment (48).

7. See, for example, John Pendleton Kennedy, *Swallow Barn, or A Sojourn in the Old Dominion* (1832). Forrest's role here may be an ironic statement about plantation novels, for the close of "Where the Sun Lives" clearly execrates the notion of such idyllic reunions.

8. Genovese cites Carter Woodson's 1924 study, which "found cases of husbands who bought their wives and deliberately kept them as slaves to ensure their fidelity and good behavior. One Negro shoemaker in Charleston, South Carolina, bought his wife for $700, found her impossible to please, and sold her some months later for $750" (407). Although such cases were not common, they clearly demonstrate the vulnerability of anyone legally defined as a slave, regardless of who his or her slaveholder may have been. White also cites cases that demonstrate the particular vulnerability of female slaves, as well as the lack of legal protection afforded them (152–53, 161–63). Rape by white men was never deemed illegal, and in an 1859 Mississippi case a judge released a black man convicted of raping a female slave under ten years of age, arguing that both common law and the statutes of Mississippi "charge[d] no offense known to either system. . . . There is no act which embraces either the attempted or actual commission of a rape by a slave on a female slave" (Catterall 3:363).

9. Cooper confronted a range of ways in which black women were oppressed, from marriage (68–73) to the political sphere, where, she argued, they "may yet seem almost a nonentity, so far as it concerns the solution of great national or even racial perplexities" (137). In particular, Cooper took to task black men for not offering more support to the efforts of black female reformers (see 75). I am grateful to Dr. Sandra Y. Govan for our discussion of the gender dynamics involved in early black feminist discourse.

Works Cited

Adams, Nehemiah. *A South-Side View of Slavery: Or, Three Months at the South in 1854.* 1854. 3d ed. Reprint. Port Washington, N.Y.: Kennikat, 1969.

Andrews, William L. Introduction to *Six Women's Slave Narratives.* Ed. Henry Louis Gates Jr. The Schomburg Library of Nineteenth-Century Black Women Writers. New York: Oxford University Press, 1988. Pp. xxix–xli.

Catterall, Helen, ed. *Judicial Cases Concerning American Slavery and the Negro: Cases from the Courts of England, Virginia, West Virginia, and Kentucky.* Vol. 1. 1926. Reprint. New York: Octagon, 1968.

———. *Judicial Cases Concerning American Slavery and the Negro.* Vol. 3. 1932. Reprint. New York: Octagon, 1968.

Connolly, Paula T. "Imagining the Escape: Picture-Books and the Flight to Freedom." *Journal of Children's Literature* 22 (Spring 1996): 8–13.

Cooper, Anna Julia. *A Voice from the South by a Black Woman of the South.* 1892. Reprint, with an introduction by Mary Helen Washington. The Schomburg Library of Nineteenth-Century Black Women Writers. New York: Oxford University Press, 1988.

Craft, William, and Ellen Craft. *Running a Thousand Miles for Freedom: Or, The Escape of William and Ellen Craft from Slavery.* 1860. Reprint. Salem, N.H.: Ayer, 1991.

Davis, Charles T., and Henry Louis Gates Jr., eds. "A Selected Bibliography: Black Narratives, 1760–1865." In *The Slave's Narrative.* New York: Oxford University Press, 1985. Pp. 319–27.

Davis, Ossie. *Escape to Freedom: A Play About Young Frederick Douglass.* New York: Penguin, 1979.
Douglass, Frederick. *Narrative of the Life of Frederick Douglass, an American Slave, Written by Himself.* Ed. Houston A. Baker Jr. 1845. Reprint. New York: Penguin, 1982.
Foster, Frances Smith. *Witnessing Slavery: The Development of Ante-bellum Slave Narratives.* Westport, Conn.: Greenwood, 1979.
Fox-Genovese, Elizabeth. *Within the Plantation Household: Black and White Women of the Old South.* Chapel Hill: University of North Carolina Press, 1988.
Freedman, Florence B. *Two Tickets to Freedom: The True Story of Ellen and William Craft, Fugitive Slaves.* New York: Peter Bedrick, 1971.
Gates, Henry Louis, Jr. Introduction to *The Classic Slave Narratives.* New York: Mentor-New American Library, 1987. Pp. ix–xviii.
Genovese, Eugene. *Roll, Jordan, Roll: The World the Slaves Made.* 1972. New York: Vintage-Random House, 1976.
Jacobs, Harriet. *Incidents in the Life of a Slave Girl, Written by Herself.* Ed. L. M. Child. 1861. Reprint, ed. Jean Fagan Yellin. Cambridge: Harvard University Press, 1987.
Kennedy, John Pendleton. *Swallow Barn, or A Sojourn in the Old Dominion.* Ed. Jay B. Hubbel. 1832. Reprint, New York: Harcourt Brace, 1929.
Kibbey, Ann. "Language in Slavery: Frederick Douglass's *Narrative.*" In *Prospectus: The Annual of American Cultural Studies,* ed. Jack Salzaman. Cambridge: Cambridge University Press, 1983. 8:163–82.
Lester, Julius. *Long Journey Home.* New York: Scholastic, 1972.
———. *To Be a Slave.* New York: Scholastic, 1968.
———. "Where the Sun Lives." In *This Strange New Feeling.* New York: Scholastic, 1981. Pp. 41–80.
Levine, Lawrence. *Black Culture and Black Consciousness: Afro-American Folk Thought from Slavery to Freedom.* Oxford: Oxford University Press, 1977.
"Life of Henry Bibb." *The Anti-Slavery Bugle* 5 (3 November 1849). Reprinted in *The Slave's Narrative,* ed. Charles T. Davis and Henry Louis Gates Jr. New York: Oxford University Press, 1985. Pp. 28–29.
Lyons, Mary E. *Letters from a Slave Girl: The Story of Harriet Jacobs.* New York: Scribner's-Macmillan, 1992.
Olney, James. "'I Was Born': Slave Narratives, Their Status as Autobiography and as Literature." In *The Slave's Narrative,* ed. Charles T. Davis and Henry Louis Gates Jr. New York: Oxford University Press, 1985. Pp. 148–79.
Polacco, Patricia. *Pink and Say.* New York: Philomel, 1994.
Ringgold, Faith. *Aunt Harriet's Underground Railroad in the Sky.* New York: Crown, 1992.
Smucker, Barbara. *Runaway to Freedom: A Story of the Underground Railway.* 1977. Reprint, New York: Harper and Row, 1979.
White, Deborah Gray. *Ar'n't I a Woman? Female Slaves in the Plantation South.* New York: Norton, 1985.
Winter, Jeanette. *Follow the Drinking Gourd.* New York: Dragonfly-Knopf, 1988.

"To Sleep, Perchance to Dream": Sleeping Beauties and Wide-Awake Plain Janes in the Stories of Jane Yolen

Tina L. Hanlon

> *The power of the tales is that they are . . . as evocative, as sensual, as many-faceted, as disturbing, as slippery as dreams. They offer a moral, they speak to the human condition, but it is not always the condition or the moral one immediately sees.*
>
> —Yolen, *Touch Magic*

After at least twenty-five years of intense debate, there is still much disagreement about how to interpret gender roles in fairy tales. Folklorists and fairy-tale historians have provided overwhelming evidence that the tales reflect the cultural biases of the societies in which they are retold and that they affect children and adults in complex ways. Marina Warner and Maria Tatar have revealed how easily misogynist tellers of the past exploited "the way in which a few quick strokes can reorient a story" to serve the moralist's purpose (Tatar 101). Throughout this century fairy tales have been neglected, condemned as escapist or satanic or useless, and trivialized through shallow caricatures and modernizations by new breeds of moralists and realists. In the 1970s, critics such as Marcia Lieberman and Madonna Kolbenschlag drew attention to the preponderance of passive and victimized female characters in the best-known fairy tales, warned us about their pervasive effects on the acculturation of women, and advised us to kiss these detrimental influences good-bye. Yet their hold on our psyches is so powerful that allusions to fairy tales permeate popular culture, as well as many studies in the fields of folklore, the arts, and the social sciences. While a storytelling revival has grown in recent decades, psychoanalytical critics such as Bruno Bettelheim and, more recently, Clarissa Pinkola Estés and Rollo May have emphasized the therapeutic value of folk tales and myths, which, like dreams, reflect symbolically our subconscious fears and desires. Thus, although the motif of the sleeping beauty appears to be one of the most blatantly sexist images in fairy-tale traditions—the innocent, passive vic-

Children's Literature 26, ed. Elizabeth Lennox Keyser (Yale University Press, © 1998 Hollins College).

tim waiting for just the right prince to rescue her—a multitude of diverse voices invites us to reconsider the significance of the old tales. Present writers such as Jane Yolen continue to portray images of sleeping beauties in a variety of ways: retelling the classic tales as well as satirizing them and reviving more obscure and unfamiliar old tales, creating new tales that preserve the familiar motifs and magical atmosphere of the old "wonder tales," and writing startling new stories using a variety of experimental techniques to combine fairy-tale motifs with realistic contemporary and historical themes. Yolen's work is remarkable because, since the early 1960s, she has employed all these approaches in many books for children and adults that feature the adventures of strong women without severing their ties to the ancient fairy-tale realm of magic and dreams. She weaves traditional motifs into the fabric of her tales so persistently and intricately that we recognize familiar patterns even as we are startled and delighted by amazing original ones. As she has written, "There is an eclecticism to modern telling. Stories lean on stories, art on art. I can only trace my own sources so far before I realize that, in the end, it is the story that matters, not the parts: the tapestry of the tale and not the individual threads" (*Tales of Wonder* xi–xii). In a number of her stories, interwoven images of shadow and light, sleep and dreams, briars and roses, spinning wheels and golden threads, forests and castle towers, hair and fur, fairies and mortals create so many subtle connections that we never lose sight of the tapestry—although it is wondrously complex—while we trace the individual threads.

Although Yolen's picture book *The Sleeping Beauty* has an unusual history in her career, its appearance in 1986 allows us to compare her retelling of the Grimm Brothers' "Briar Rose" with the sleeping beauties and wide-awake Plain Janes she created before and afterwards in her parodies of classic tales, her more original fairy tales, and her very innovative contemporary stories for older readers, including the novel *Briar Rose.* Typically her stories derive from personal experience and the emotional exploration she describes as "going down into the heart's cavern"; she usually does not write for hire, predict the course a tale will take, or predetermine its primary audience (Roginski 229–30). Before a completed narrative goes to an illustrator, she revises it carefully with skills enhanced by her experience as an oral storyteller, a poet, and an editor. In an unusual set of circumstances, however, Yolen agreed to write the text of *The Sleeping Beauty* after her friend Ruth Sanderson had created the illustrations for the publisher (with Yolen and her husband posing as the cook and the king). Yolen recalls that "it was put together less like a storytelling and more like a jigsaw puzzle" (E-mail, 27 Feb. 1997).

Nevertheless, the result is an enchanting blend of lyrical text and beautiful illustrations inspired by Pre-Raphaelite paintings. Unlike most of Yolen's fairy tales, which combine motifs from a number of sources, this picture book follows the Grimms' version of "Briar Rose" quite closely. It reminds us that "The Sleeping Beauty" is the most romantic and idealistic of tales. As in Yolen's more original stories, however, there are subtle details of language and image that resonate with echoes of many other old and new tales, leading us to reexamine the implications of old motifs. At the heart of critical debate over the sleeping beauty archetype are widely divergent interpretations of the heroine's long sleep. Does it represent passive victimization, sexual exploitation, a healthy process of growing toward individual self-fulfillment, or a natural desire to protect loved ones from danger? Yolen has observed that each individual's perceptions of a tale can change as he or she is influenced by reading and by personal experience. For example, reading "Snow White" as a parent made her understand the impulse to put a teenage daughter in a safe place "until the right person or job or college comes along to wake her up" (Roginski 232). Warner believes that "the idea of awakening, sometimes erotic but not exclusively, goes to the heart of fairy tale's function" (417). Yet she and other feminists remind us that before and after the awakening, Sleeping Beauty and the prince have very different roles and points of view. Women traditionally appear inferior when they are depicted as dreamers while men are the doers. In Yolen's tales dreamers are not weak characters, since both men and women need to recognize that dreams and stories reflect our most profound human fears, desires, and ideals. Without departing from the traditional plot and idyllic atmosphere of the Grimms' tale, Yolen's text and Sanderson's illustrations unite Sleeping Beauty and the prince by putting more of the doer into the princess and some of the dreamer into the prince.

This tale dramatizes the dream that love transcends the limitations of time and death, one of the most seductive of human myths. But no matter how appealing we find the fantasy of pure romantic love and spiritual union, it is difficult to deny that at the heart of this fairy tale lie classic images of female passivity and patriarchal domination. Some critics refer disparagingly to the stereotype of the "comatose" or "catatonic" princess waiting for her prince.[1] Bettelheim argues that the gender of the hero is insignificant and that the enchanted sleep in fairy tales symbolizes universal stages of adolescent development, with periods of introspective withdrawal and dreaming followed by active exploration, confrontation, and loss of innocence (225–26). As feminists have emphasized, however, in the best-known fairy tales beautiful maidens spend more time sleeping and waiting, being sacrificed and rescued, while virile men are exploring, conquering, and protecting the helpless. Although some storytellers observe that the prince in this tale has little to do besides appear at the right time, he still has to choose to enter the briars and risk death.[2] Yolen's prince is brave when he sees corpses in the briars because "the dream was still strong within him," while naive Briar Rose is instantly rendered unconscious by the protective spell of the good fairy when her dangerous adventure begins. As Kolbenschlag observes, "At the universal level of meaning, Sleeping Beauty is most of all a symbol of *passivity,* and by extension a metaphor for the spiritual condition of women—cut off from autonomy and transcendence, from self-actualization and ethical capacity in a male-dominated milieu" (5, emphasis in original).

"Sleeping Beauty" is interesting historically as a dramatic demonstration of the futility of society's efforts to suppress women's internal development and shelter them from knowledge and experience of the external world. In Yolen and Sanderson's book we see just one image of Briar Rose's girlhood before the more animated depictions of her exploration of the tower: she is a languid maiden in white gazing narcissistically into a reflecting pool, while her father supervises the burning of all the spinning wheels. He is "content" after protecting her from external threats, yet her inner needs appear to be neglected. His misguided action is accepted by all as a loving attempt to protect the beloved princess. It not only removes from the kingdom a vital instrument of female productivity, however, but it ultimately makes Briar Rose all the more curious to touch a spindle when she sees one, on the day when she is left alone to explore her world for the first time in her life. Her initiation experience is cut short at the very moment she approaches maturity and interaction with female culture.[3]

Although Briar Rose's active adventure is brief, Yolen and Sanderson put extra emphasis on her curiosity in "exploring all the parts of the castle where she had never been before." She feels "herself drawn toward the dustiest of the chambers, where spiders spun their elusive dreams." She fights off dizziness to climb the winding stairs, resolved "to find where the stairs led." Her determination in looking behind a heavy tapestry and using a rusty key, as well as her eagerness to try spinning, shows that she is ready and willing to begin a more independent life of action and inquiry. Although women are often punished for curiosity in fairy tales—and for their efforts to maintain ties with the past as well as determine their own future—from a modern perspective we can see that these are potentially very productive inclinations. When Yolen adds that "a shaft of light from the window touched the spindle and the thread shone like purest gold," we are reminded of other stories in which golden threads represent desirable and dangerous things. For example, in Yolen's own "Weaver of Tomorrow" a curious girl who stubbornly seeks the truth about the future meets an old woman weaving the golden threads of human life. Learning after years of apprenticeship that the threads all lead to death, Vera realizes that her curiosity has brought her sorrow as well as a beloved mentor and an inescapable destiny as the weaver for the next hundred years. The black loom of life is "like a giant ebony cage with golden bars as thin and fine as threads" (*Tales of Wonder* 116–17).

Briar Rose begins her hundred-year sleep before she learns anything of life or death, yet she is linked with symbols of sexual desire, worldly experience, and death. Yolen and Sanderson connect her in subtle ways with the old, evil fairy and also with the prince and the briars. The old woman she greets as Granny, spinning in the tower, looks like the Thirteenth Fairy, who had emerged from another dark tower to curse the infant Briar Rose.[4] The visual details of candles snuffed out in the presence of the evil fairy, while shafts of sunlight follow Briar Rose and light the key in the door, suggest that exploring the dark, looking beyond the sheltered home, is inextricably linked with danger. The traditional associations of the spindle and thread with female productivity and with life and death, along with the symbolism of the finger prick and blood, also indicate that Briar Rose is confronting her own sexual maturity and mortality.

The name Briar Rose combines the beauty and purity of the rose with the "fierce brambles," which are also symbols of sexual desire and danger. The prince sees "briary fingers" giving way to blossoms and then he finds the sleeping beauty's face "as lovely as a flower." The lovers descend the wide castle stairs very close together, "their fingers laced like briars in a hedge." Yolen tells us that the prince has dreamed of Briar Rose every night for a year. At the end the couple "lived in contentment all the rest of their days, as if—they often said—they had met and married within the longest and most beautiful of dreams." In the final idyllic scene the prince is shown in a languid, dreamy posture as Briar Rose plays music at his side. The Grimms' "Briar Rose" never mentions dreams, whereas versions by Perrault and others suggest only that Sleeping Beauty dreams of and waits for the valiant prince.[5] Yolen's prince and princess are true devoted lovers united by their dreams, destined to be together. Bettelheim emphasizes that "this union is as much one of the minds and souls of two partners as it is one of sexual fulfillment" (232). As Kolbenschlag observes, "In general, the Perrault and Grimm versions portray the 'sleep' as a concentration of powers, a period of quiet preparation for fulfillment and an exclusive relation to an ultimate Other. In these versions, *being* is idealized" (5, emphasis in original). Kolbenschlag uses Sleeping Beauty as a central metaphor in her appeal to contemporary women to progress beyond the cultural memories represented in the fairy tales, to seek new levels of awakening and spiritual maturity. Her book *Kiss Sleeping Beauty Good-Bye* illustrates the value of reexamining the classic fairy tales from a feminist perspective and learning from their powerful, timeless images, rather than trying to ignore them or replace them completely with other kinds of stories.

Whereas critics such as Kolbenschlag, Warner, and Zipes explore the social and historical significance of these traditional fairy-tale images, other feminists have used satire to expose the outdated rituals and cultural biases of old tales. First published in 1925, E. Nesbit's *The Last of the Dragons,* with a rebellious princess who refuses to be victimized, is a forerunner of comical parodies in children's books that have been especially popular since the 1980s. Picture books such as Robert Munsch's *The Paper Bag Princess* and Babette Cole's *Prince Cinders* and *Princess Smartypants* are full of role reversals and male-bashing, with outspoken feminist princesses who rescue their prince or defend themselves from undesirable suitors and monsters. Although some of these clever girls merrily dance or drive off into the sunset alone, the accomplishments and rewards of these independent heroines are severely limited by the portrayal of emasculated opponents and suitors who are so easily duped and so undeserving. In Frances Minters's 1996 picture book *Sleepless Beauty,* a clever girl outwits a witch by setting her clock radio so that a rock star's voice will wake her up before a lengthy enchantment can take effect. Although this resourceful heroine defends herself without assistance, the ending also allows for a modern form of wish fulfillment when the rock star appears in person and goes out with Beauty.

Yolen has written several parodies that poke fun at patriarchal and elitist traditions, but hers preserve more of the utopian spirit of serious tales, with deserving men as well as virtuous heroines who choose their own dreams and develop the potential for fulfilling romantic love. Among her earliest books is *Gwinellen, the Princess Who Could Not Sleep* (1965), a comic reversal of various tales about sleeping beauties and stubborn princesses. Princess Gwinellen disrupts the life of the castle, not by falling under a magic spell that puts maiden and court to sleep, but by staying perpetually awake. Rather than being immobilized when she touches the instruments of female productivity, Gwinellen spends her sleepless nights overindulging in tasks traditionally assigned to females in life and in fairy tales: her sewing is burying the royal army in surplus mittens and scarves, and her spinning of flax into excess gold is inflating consumer prices. She inconveniences her parents by keeping them from getting the amount of sleep customary for monarchs and by remaining single, since "all the available princes married sleeping princesses long ago." After wizards and others fail to put Gwinellen to sleep, a humble, dust-covered traveler who describes himself as "a dreamer, a schemer, a plotter, a planner"—not a tramp but "a poet-traveler and a teller of tales"—discovers that Gwinellen has never heard of dreams. Explaining that "a dream repeats what is in your heart while you sleep," he claims her face has been in his dreams. After they talk in the castle gardens all day and night, Gwinellen interrupts his lecture at dawn by abruptly going to bed.

Since the king has offered his "daughter's hand and/or one-half of [his] kingdom" to any "eligible young man" who would put Gwinellen "into a deep sleep—by fair means or foul," this story appears to be following a conventional structure, with a wayward princess who is reformed by a wiser man and then offered to him in marriage as a reward. This independent, sensible princess continues to violate tradition, however, by going to bed in the morning, when she chooses, now that she has something to dream about. Although the king eagerly anticipates the wedding, on the last page everyone is still waiting for her to wake up, and her future remains open-ended. This gentle parody mocks traditional tales in which the rhythms of a princess's life are dictated by parents, magical beings, and valiant princes. Yet it also conveys a heart-warming theme that runs throughout Yolen's subsequent writing, stressing the wondrous relationship between stories and dreams, between physical and psychic needs, and by showing that a young woman must develop her own dreams in her own time.

Sleeping Ugly, Yolen's 1981 story for beginning readers, parodies different fairy-tale conventions associated with "Sleeping Beauty" and other tales.[6] Like the heroines in some of Yolen's serious stories, Plain Jane is a virtuous girl who lives in the woods with the animals that love her. Miserella, a very beautiful but selfish princess, causes a series of disasters with her temper tantrums and arrogant demands. An angry fairy who decides to get rid of her by putting her to sleep accidentally puts Plain Jane, Miserella, and herself into "one of those famous hundred-year-naps that need a prince and a kiss to end them" (44). Years later Jojo is the only prince passing by who happens to enter the house. "Being the kind of young man who read fairy tales," he knows what to do when he finds a beautiful sleeping princess (49). However, since he is a romantically inexperienced youngest son with no wealth or property, he practices by kissing the fairy's nose and then kissing Plain Jane. Jojo also knows princesses well enough to recognize that Miserella, who appears to be enjoying her bad dreams, is like his three cousins: "Pretty on the outside. Ugly within" (59). Plain Jane, remembering the prince's kiss "as if it were a dream," wisely asks the fairy, who owes her a third wish, for the prince's love (56). He gladly marries the homely but sweet-smelling heroine. When they settle down "happily every after" in Jane's cottage and have three children, the sleeping princess is used as a conversation piece and an occasional coat rack, with a sign around her neck forbidding anyone to kiss her. "Moral: Let sleeping princesses lie or lying princesses sleep, whichever seems wisest" (64).

These satiric tales are fun, using laughter to expose the outdated formulas that have limited women's roles in fairy tales and in life. But Yolen, in *Touch Magic,* and Jon Stott, in a 1990 article on teaching old stories and parodies to children, have expressed concern about children who learn the archetypes primarily through the weakened cartoon and video game imitations and shallow caricatures so prominent in popular culture, without knowing the richer folk traditions that lie behind them. A more productive response to the sexist stereotypes of so many traditional tales involves revising the canon of classic fairy tales, digging deeply into oral and written folk history to resuscitate strong heroines who were not sleeping but were neglected in favor of the submissive and self-sacrificing beauties sharing the literary spotlight for generations. Yolen's 1977 article "America's 'Cinderella'" is a well-known defense of a seemingly passive fairy-tale princess who is more active in older variants than she is in popular watered-down versions by American storytellers such as Walt Disney. Thanks to the extensive research of writers and editors such as Yolen and many others, we now understand that male translators, editors, illustrators, and interpreters through the centuries have given us a biased view of gender roles in the tales that were most often written down.[7] For example, Angela Carter and Alison Lurie have published little-known tales in which sleeping princes are rescued by adventurous women.[8] The Scottish tale of Tomlin or Tam Lin, another story of a captive hero and a powerful heroine, has been reprinted by Lurie and other recent anthologists. New collections like theirs are helping to make tales of strong women more accessible and familiar.

Yolen's reworkings of lesser-known folk tales highlight the triumphs of courageous heroines. She explains that the "Literary" or "Art Fairy Tales" for which she is best known "use the elements of old stories—the cadences, the magical settings or objects—but concern themselves with modern themes" (Chevalier 1077). In *Tam Lin,* published in 1990 with colorful illustrations by Charles Mikolaycak, Yolen retells the ancient Scottish ballad in which brave Jennet McKenzie rescues her lover from the curse that turns him into a hideous monster. The opening description of "a strange, forbidding castle with ruined towers" and the adults' warnings about "prickers and briars, thistles and thorns" bring to mind Sleeping Beauty's castle. People who went there "had bad dreams for many nights after," just as the rumors of evil and death surrounding Briar Rose's castle are emphasized in Yolen's *The Sleeping Beauty.* Yolen has added descriptions of Jennet as a girl who "always had a mind of her own, even as a wee girl. The villagers all said . . . she always spoke what she thought. And *what* she thought was never quite proper for a fine young lady" (emphasis in original). Rather than waiting in a sheltered chamber for a prince to rescue her and her kingdom, Jennet has to fight to reclaim her castle from the outside, because her father's father lost it to the Faeries. When she goes there on the night of her sixteenth birthday, she laughs at others' fears, ignoring the shadows and briars to pluck the one remaining object of beauty—a rose "the color of spilled blood"—as her pledge to restore the land to humankind. Her voice calls a handsome laird's son "back to the world of men." Like

Sleeping Beauty, Tam Lin has been removed from the natural flow of time; he is an idealized, saintly victim forced to live with the Fey, the Ever-Fair, for 160 years without aging. Jennet has to rescue Tam Lin at the right time and place, on All Hallow's Eve by a holy well, where he has ridden with the Fey every seven years. To save him from becoming their human sacrifice this year, Jennet is willing to risk death, like the prince in "The Sleeping Beauty." After Jennet wins a fierce midnight struggle that requires great strength of will and body, Tam Lin emerges from his monstrous transformations naked and reborn. Jennet covers him with her mantle, freeing him and her ancestral lands from the power of the Faery Queen. As Yolen explains in her notes to this tale, "In most of the other old ballads, it is the man who does the rescuing. But in this one, it is Jennet . . . who braves the wrath of the Faery Queen herself to win her own true love."

In *Dove Isabeau* (1989) Yolen has helped revive interest in another strong heroine from ancient British ballads, again skillfully interweaving motifs that evoke more familiar tales while also incorporating some striking feminist revisions. Dove Isabeau appears gentle and submissive at first, although her bad dreams reflect her dissatisfaction with her jealous stepmother-witch. We are reminded of "The Sleeping Beauty" when Dove Isabeau sheds innocent blood by pricking her finger on the door of the witch's tower room and when she is shocked to see that her mother's spinning wheel and other cheerful domestic furnishings have been replaced by instruments of "dark magicks." After Isabeau is immobilized by an evil spell, however, her transformation into a bloodthirsty red dragon differs dramatically from the initiation experiences of fairy-tale heroines such as Briar Rose or Snow White. Now the woman herself as a fierce dragon, not a protective briar hedge, encircles the castle and destroys foolhardy suitors. This story parallels the legend in which Childe Wynde of Northumberland rescues his bewitched sister Margaret by kissing her in her dragon shape.[9] Yolen's use of the lover Kemp Owain in place of the brother, her images of the dragon weeping while it devours young men, and the ironies involved in Isabeau's resulting loss and recapturing of innocence suggest that the dragon transformation represents the destructive as well as the redemptive powers of female sexuality and strength. In both *Dove Isabeau* and *Tam Lin* the women are more powerful than the men they rescue. It is Isabeau's prince, not the beautiful heroine, who experiences a period of paralysis as a stone statue after he kisses the dragon and saves Isabeau, until she rescues him in turn. Whereas Jennet is able to restore and rename her ancestral property with Tam Lin at her side, Dove Isabeau and her wise prince rule their kingdom equally at the end of their tale. Isabeau shocks her wedding guests by wearing a red gown, but her prince has always loved "his glorious dragon queen . . . for her spirit and for the fire that lay beneath the skin."

Yolen has devoted most of her creative efforts to revising old folk materials so dramatically that they almost become new tales, as in *Dove Isabeau,* and to crafting more original stories such as *The Girl in the Golden Bower.* Zipes lists Yolen among the many writers who, "especially since the 1970s," have written "more aggressive, aesthetically more complex and sophisticated" tales that exemplify "the restructuring and reformation by feminists of the fairy tale genre itself" (*Spells of Enchantment* xxvi–xxviii). Her best tales take us into a fantasy world in which old symbols and old gender roles are subtly reworked, without disrupting the utopian atmosphere of magic and wonder found in traditional fairy tales. *The Girl in the Golden Bower,* a 1994 picture book illustrated by Jane Dyer, is another story of a sleeping beauty, but it gives the young girl, Aurea, a more active role in defending herself and stronger ties with a powerful female heritage. Aurea's sorceress stepmother, like Dove Isabeau's, has green eyes and uses materials from nature for evil purposes. Although Aurea is trusting at first like Briar Rose, Snow White, and Dove Isabeau, while she is still a young child she realizes that the sorceress wants her magic comb, and she bravely refuses to give it up. When the sorceress leaves her in the woods among the roses, "casting a spell to deepen [her] natural sleep" and assuming she will starve, the animals keep her warm and build her a nest. They comb her hair until it grows longer; it "twine[s] about her in an intricate bower and cover[s] her over with a golden cloth . . . embroidered with a pattern of thistle and briar." When the sorceress cuts the hair, it wraps around her and binds her tightly, while a beast's roar frightens her.

This appears to be yet another tale in which magical sleep protects the maiden from evil until men rescue her, since the woodland animals and magic beast all turn out to be enchanted men. But Yolen's original plot and Dyer's lush images of golden figures on gold pages build to a climax in which the heroine's luxuriant hair and protective bower function primarily as symbols of strength in the child of nature who can defend herself. Aurea may not be as spunky and independent as the girl in Yolen's *The Emperor and the Kite,* who rescues her father from a tower and then shares his throne, or the adventurous child in *The Girl Who Loved the Wind,* who escapes from her overprotective father's mansion by flying away alone. Aurea is younger and less headstrong than Jennet in *Tam Lin,* yet she achieves a similar triumph when her fortitude in protecting her mother's magic comb restores her grandfather's castle, transforming briars back to roses. Aurea is never sacrificed to a beast that frightens or deceives her, as some fairy-tale Beauties are; rather, she always recognizes her kinship with the animals and nurtures them. Like the "wronged daughter of fairy tale" discussed by Warner, Aurea finds refuge with the animals when she is threatened by crimes she abhors, but she does not have to abase herself by assuming a bestial form—typically "donkey, cat, or bear"—in order to escape (354–55). She has taken an active role in taming the animals, maintaining a positive identification with nature by combing their fur and interweaving strands of her golden hair. Thus she has prepared them for releasing protective magic by combing her hair, and when she awakes she can approach the roaring beast without fear, combing his mane and leading him into her bower. Her beneficial relationship with nature and her mother's family, represented by green and russet accents against the predominant gold of the illustrations, contrasts with the jealous sorcerer's evil uses of nature, emphasized in a night-time scene that is dominated by green shades and shadows.

In her sleep Aurea does not escape the turmoil of adolescence or wait for a predestined lover to arrive; she grows into a beautiful princess who can stand up to the sorceress, but after her hair is cut and the beast arrives, they return to their original forms as a little girl "in a tattered dress" and a grandfather. As in *Dove Isabeau,* maiden and man rescue each other from sorrow and evil enchantment. The grandfather, revealing that he was attracted to the bower by the magic of his wife and daughter, does not recognize Aurea in her tatters, so she figures out how they are related and identifies herself to him. As Yolen has explained in relation to gender roles in her Arthurian tales, she likes a female to be an "action character" and "do some take-charge things"; however, the man needs "a magic *outside* himself. Hers comes from within" ("Interview" 36, emphasis in original). The language associated with "happily ever after" fairy-tale weddings is used at the end, but Aurea can still live out her childhood, while the man who lost his humanity when his daughter was taken has recovered a child more precious than gold (like

Silas Marner, the rural miser in George Eliot's classic novel who re-establishes his relations with humanity after his lost gold seems to be replaced by a golden-haired, disinherited foundling). The idea of the magic sheltering a sleeping child from abuse and neglect, and then restoring her to her family as a child, is more appealing to contemporary readers than the fate of Sleeping Beauty and Snow White, whose fathers disappear or fail to protect them. Snow White starts her adventure at age seven and, like Sleeping Beauty, she is awakened and claimed by a husband she has chosen only in her dreams. Some modern writers try to alleviate our discomfort with predestined or arranged fairy-tale marriages by including prior meetings or extended courtships in their tales. For example, Disney's Snow White and the princess in John Stewig's "sleeping prince" story, *Princess Florecita and the Iron Shoes,* both meet their kind princes before their dangerous adventures begin. In Yolen's more innovative plot, Aurea's transformation reveals her potential as a powerful woman, but her ability to reclaim her interrupted childhood and family heritage is a refreshing change from the traditional fairy-tale solution of marriage to a prince from afar.

Aurea's strong bond with her mother, represented by the images of hair and the inherited magic comb, illustrates the powerful, enduring legacy of mother-daughter relationships, a dominant theme in many of Yolen's stories that is missing in *The Sleeping Beauty.* In one of Yolen's best-known tales, "The Moon Ribbon," a heroine who is not beautiful inherits a magic ribbon interwoven with strands of silver hair from several generations of women—a treasure that she will pass on to her daughter. The ribbon enables Sylvia to escape from her stepmother's house, protect her mother's gifts from the greedy, and learn to choose wisely how to share her heart with others. Jennet in *Tam Lin* refuses gold when the fairy queen tries to bribe her, saying that she has enough gold in her mother's hair and silver in her father's. Dove Isabeau is linked with her mother not through such explicit images of the female body but through the relatively traditional magic of the silky white cat that has healing powers and gives advice, as well as the hideous, unconventional dragon images in her mother's last illness and her own transformation. Her naive and subservient attempts to develop intimacy with the stepmother lead to her violent suffering, but she takes her own revenge on the stepmother with the prince's sword. The punishment of the stepmother in *The Girl in the Golden Bower* is especially intriguing. The green-eyed sorceress turns into a green bird in a cage in the woods surrounded by the images of love and nature that she had misused. The cage is open but the bird is held captive by irrational fear and "strong bars of gold, though there are none to be seen. Except in its heart. Except in its heart." Thus Aurea's golden hair and magic comb become a complex symbol of female strength that works externally and internally.[10] The luxurious hair that symbolizes sexuality and vulnerability in other tales, when woven together with the animals' fur and the golden mane of the beast, has the magical power to form a protective bower with golden gates for the growing girl, tame the rage of the man, and immobilize the sorceress by exposing her to her own fears of natural goodness.

Rollo May believes that Briar Rose never should have been burdened with the passive label Sleeping Beauty, that she should be given more credit for protecting her own "emerging femininity" (symbolized by roses and blood) from envious and untimely aggressors (196). Through her "creative waiting" and her natural defenses, represented by the briars, she avoids a premature sexual awakening that would preclude "an awakening on all other levels of the self" (205–14). Aurea is like a younger sister of the Briar Rose that May describes so idealistically. As critics have sought the reminders of female potential and power hidden behind the sexist stereotypes in old tales, storytellers like Yolen have brought these positive themes to the foreground of their new tales.[11] The wish fulfillment of *The Girl in the Golden Bower* goes beyond a desire for some hero or magical helper to protect a virtuous maiden. Dramatizing the hope that a girl can inherit the ability to defend herself from evil without losing her childhood, Yolen and Dyer have created images that transform the links between golden hair and animal fur, roses and briars into symbols of the heroine's natural innocence and strength.

These modern wonder tales appeal to readers of all ages as they reaffirm our belief in the ideal dreams of fairy tales, while some of Yolen's stories for older readers, including "The Thirteenth Fey" and *Briar Rose,* represent postmodern experiments with the fairy tale form. Like many other contemporary authors, Yolen uses alternative points of view and injects realistic and ironic details that threaten to undercut the magic of the tale and the suspension of disbelief required to enter the fairy tale world. Ursula K. Le Guin and Leon Garfield have surrounded Sleeping Beauty and her castle with frame stories that reveal the mundane realities of life for a medieval peasant lad, in Le Guin's "The Poacher," and a contemporary middle-class bridegroom, in Garfield's *The Wedding Ghost*.[12] In "The Thirteenth Fey" (1985), Yolen keeps the focus on a female protagonist but subverts the medieval patriarchal society of "The Sleeping Beauty" by expressing the bitterness of the thirteenth fairy in her own voice. In "The Sleeping Beauty" the uninvited fairy is old and spiteful, and in *Tam Lin* the Fey are evil creatures who steal castles and men from the heroine's human world; this point of view is reversed in "The Thirteenth Fey." The narrator's fairy family is forced to serve a corrupt, self-indulgent monarchy that has weakened and impoverished them. This focus on the decadent life of the court, and the princess's name, Talia, connect Yolen's tale with seventeenth-century Sleeping Beauty stories by Basile and Perrault. Warner contrasts the "macabre excesses" of their tales with the "Grimms' more romantic and innocuous account" (220–22). In Yolen's tale the sickly youngest fairy dooms the princess by mistake when she unintentionally breaks the thread of life on the old spindle she carries to the christening as a gift. Fifteen years later the spell cast by the fairy's mother puts the princess to sleep until the knot in the thread of life can unravel. In the meantime, the thirteenth fairy has been educating herself in her father's library. Foreseeing that a new religion called Democracy will destroy monarchies as well as magic by elevating the common man and technology, the fairy gloats over the expectation that the young man who comes in the future will realize that the sleeping princess is "only a musty relic of a bygone era whose bedclothes speak of decadence and whose bubbly breath of decay. He will wed the scullery out of compassion, and learn Computer Science. Then the spell of the land will be broken" (44–45).[13]

In this tale Yolen demonstrates how cleverly a skillful writer can make use of the slippery nature of the genre to give a different sociopolitical slant to an old fairy tale. She uses the traditional plot of "The Sleeping Beauty" but stops when the princess's sleep begins and the briars grow magically. She sets a complex trap for the modern reader by making the young fairy the victim of human corruption and the source of an accidental magic curse, as well as an educated voice of logic and prophecy. The conflict between good and evil is not so clear-cut in this postmodern fairy tale. The fairy's experience demonstrates that analyzing the old tales politically and realistically can spoil their timeless, utopian ideals of beauty and goodness. The christening scene also shows that fairy magic must be shared freely, that it is dangerous for the king to demand it for selfish reasons. We sympathize with the fairy's desire for revenge on the unattractive and obsolete types of humans who oppress her, but do we believe her prophecy that Democracy will eradicate magic? The elements of grotesque parody in this tale reflect the same fears Yolen expresses in *Touch Magic*—that the most dreaded evil curse would be for modern skepticism and technology to destroy the idyllic dreams and magic of our belief in fairy tales. If we do not appreciate and nurture the magic around us and within us, if we pursue empty lives of dissipation and self-indulgence like the royal characters or rely on studying a haphazard array of subjects like the young fairy, we may lose sight of the deeper truths that stories represent and thus lose our humanity, just as the fairy's "tatty Cloth of Invisibility" works at the wrong times and leads to the inadvertent sentence of death (34). "The Thirteenth Fey" does not reveal whether the cynical fairy's prophecies come true, except that the story itself, and the other fascinating fairy tales of many kinds being written at the end of this century, assure us that our storytelling traditions are still alive. *The Girl in the Golden Bower,* for example, shows that we can experience the wonder of old fairy tales within an enlightened social context in which childhood innocence and female strength are celebrated. As Zipes has noted, contemporary fairy tales such as "The Thirteenth Fey" transform the traditional "tales into problems without solutions," searching for a balance "between the creative forces of the imagination and the reality principle of the world." He also points out that these open-ended postmodern experiments are still rare, that most American writers in this genre, including Yolen, continue to "retain a strong element of hope, especially [in] the longer fiction" (*Fairy Tale as Myth* 153–59).

Yolen's 1992 novel *Briar Rose* links fairy-tale symbols of evil with the modern atrocities of the Holocaust, but without lapsing into cynicism or despair. It has won awards for fantasy and young adult literature, and it has been burned by censors who disapprove of its controversial content.[14] The novel is a fascinating exploration of the imaginative and emotional power of fairy tales in relation to the frightful realities of modern world history and the complexities of family history. With a more intricate structure than the time-travel plot of *The Devil's Arithmetic,* Yolen's 1988 children's fantasy about the Holocaust, *Briar Rose* tells three interwoven fairy tales in the adventures of the contemporary American heroine Rebecca, her grandmother's frequent retellings of "Briar Rose," and the testimony of a Holocaust survivor.

First, the life of "Becca," a young writer living with her parents in Massachusetts, follows the structure of a folktale quest with some modern revisions. The youngest of three sisters, Becca looks like her grandmother, with the same red hair, which her father calls "the family roses," and she is closer to "Gemma" than the others. Misunderstood by her more worldly sisters, she feels "morally oppressed" in their presence (93). At eight she dressed like a princess on Halloween, carrying a king's scepter even though her sister disapproved. At Smith College her mentor, a lesbian named Merlin Brooks, taught her about writing and fighting oppression, while her reading of Robin McKinley's fairy-tale novel *Beauty* in times of trouble suggests that she is a dreamer and an adventurer like Yolen's other heroines. Becca promises her dying grandmother that she will find the castle that Gemma mysteriously refers to as her only legacy when she insists she *is* the princess Briar Rose. Becca's father, the family member most sensitive to the feelings of his favorite, encourages her independent efforts, unlike many fairy-tale and real-life fathers. Becca ignores others who call her and Gemma obsessive-compulsive about Briar Rose. Her search for clues to Gemma's past makes the novel an exciting mystery story that keeps first-time readers spellbound to the end, while the novel's division into sections labeled "Home," "Castle," and "Home Again" reinforces the archetypal structure of her quest. Becca plans to retell her adventure in a magazine article with the encouragement of her editor, Stan. He gives her wise advice about finding the past because it is "prologue to the present," so she travels to a World War II immigrant camp in Oswego, New York, and then to Poland.

Becca's symbolic burden and family heritage are contained in the heavy wooden box she lugs to her office, later "cradling it in her arms as if it were a newborn" (71). The box of treasures her grandmother had kept secret, with a carved rose and briar on its top, holds clues to family mysteries in "a rat's nest of photos and papers" (29). On the flight to Poland, a woman calls Becca Sleeping Beauty because she has not traveled much. In Poland she is aided in her quest by a priest and by a student translator who becomes a trusted confidant and guide, helping her understand Polish folk life and the effects of the repressed horrors of Poland's past. Magda and Becca travel through beautiful scenery, the forests and villages of Gemma's youth, and find ugly reminders of the Holocaust, including guilt and fear in the hearts of citizens who refuse to speak about the war. After they unearth some of the secrets of Gemma's past, Magda announces that

Becca is Polish and calls her an "American Princess." When Becca returns home, she and Stan joke about being awakened with a kiss and living happily ever after. Having completed a similar quest himself when he searched for his biological mother, Stan has waited for Becca to discover her past and her own identity before they begin their romance as kindred spirits.

The relatively frivolous sprinkling of fairy-tale motifs in the descriptions of Becca's comfortable American life contrasts with the haunting blend of fairy tale and historical fiction in the other parts of the novel. Interspersed throughout Becca's story are flashbacks containing the novel's second layer of narrative—fragments of the "decidedly odd" version of "Briar Rose" Gemma tells her grandchildren obsessively (37). The reader gradually realizes that Gemma has altered the tale to reflect her own experience; she was resuscitated after being gassed in a death camp, Chelmno, a ruined castle surrounded with briars or barbs that was shrouded in a mist from which few woke up. Refusing to explain the barbs to the inquisitive children, Gemma emphasizes that "*no one cared to know about the sleeping folk inside*. . . . So no one told about them and neither will I" (55, emphasis in original). She does not reveal that she experienced the Nazi horrors represented by the bad fairy "in black with big black boots and silver eagles on her hat," who cursed the princess and "all the people who bear [her] name" (22, 37). When other children object to her version of the tale, Gemma insists, "That's how it goes in this house" (34). The prince disappears after the wedding in Gemma's "Briar Rose" because her own husband, a medical student nicknamed Avenger who rescued her from a pit full of bodies outside Chelmno, was killed after they were married in the woods. But Gemma's red-haired princess lives happily ever after with her baby more beautiful than herself. Becca has no idea that the baby represents her own mother until she discovers the truth in Poland.

The flashbacks that reveal this tale in stages demonstrate how children respond to fairy tales at different ages and how powerful the old tale's symbolism becomes when it is fused with the adult's unspeakable memories. The fairy tale is a timeless blend of truth and fiction, linking generations of the family and the world through shared memories, yet its details, emotional effects, and meanings change for individual listeners and tellers in different settings. In the novel's first scene, baby Becca asks for "Seepin Boot." Her grandmother, named Eve here, feeds her bites of apple while her sisters help recite the opening of their special tale: "Once upon a time . . . which is all times and no times but not the very best of times" (9). The novel closes with the continuing family ritual: Gemma's two-year-old great-granddaughter says "Seepin Boot?" while she drifts off to sleep, and Gemma reassures the adult Aunt Becca that, in spite of the unexplained absence of the prince, "happily ever after . . . means exactly what it says" (200). Like the psychiatric patients described by Rollo May in *The Cry for Myth,* Gemma has unconsciously reinterpreted and compulsively retold an ancient narrative that mirrors her own psychic conflicts, trying to find "meaning and significance . . . in a senseless world" (May 15). Unlike May's patients, Gemma has never sought psychoanalysis or discussed her secrets, but she does recognize before her death that Becca has the imagination, love, and courage needed to confront the tale's hidden meanings.

In several flashbacks Becca's sisters pretend they are too old to listen or their bickering interrupts the tale, while Becca insists at age five that she will always want to hear it because it is Gemma's story. The terrors of Gemma's version send Becca's first overnight guest home frightened, an incident Becca understands years later when she thinks about a child at bedtime hearing that most of the characters except the princess remain "under the wicked fairy's sentence of death. Death by sleep" (34). Even Becca's sisters object on Halloween to the familiar but scary section about the prince walking along the path of thorns where "the white birch trees gleamed like the souls of the new dead." When Gemma insists that "it is as true on Halloween as any other time," the children argue about whether the story is ever true (116). Although Gemma never changes her version, even when children misunderstand the language or ask for clarification, she tells the girls another time that their own princess can have hair any color they choose. One year Sylvia is brave enough to ask a question that has "puzzled" the girls: how can the many dead princes have "past and present and future lives"? Gemma answers, "The future is when people talk about the past. So if the prince knows all their past lives and tells all the people who are still to come, then the princes live again and into the future" (96). Becca keeps the peace by going along with her sisters when they admit they don't understand, yet she and Gemma know she always comprehends instinctively. While the sisters outwardly develop the skepticism of the modern adult, Yolen quotes P. L. Travers's assertion that "the shock [our grandmothers' tales] give us when we first hear them is not of surprise but of recognition" (187). In the next flashback after this epigraph, little Becca helps retell the popular "kissing part" of "Briar Rose," dramatizing the climactic moment by sharing an impulsive peanut-butter-flavored kiss with Gemma (190). This storytelling within the novel, like Yolen's other stories, demonstrates her belief that fairy tales are eternal, although our responses to them change because "we are all different readers at different ages" ("With a Lacing of Spindrift"). Because of Becca's intuitive, loving acceptance of the teller's devotion and the tale's magic—its horrors and sadness as well as its joys—she inherits the privilege and the responsibility of reclaiming her family's lost heritage, like generations of daring young folk heroes before her who returned from their adventures to tell their own tale of the past, present, and future.

In the novel's third story, the "prince" whom Becca finds in Poland reveals the specific historical and personal meanings of Gemma's "Briar Rose." Josef Potocki is not Becca's biological grandfather, as she assumes when he recognizes her and begins to weep; he is a homosexual who loved her real grandfather, revived her grandmother with mouth-to-mouth resuscitation, and shared his aristocratic family name with her so that she could escape to America. He says to Becca at the end, "I told you more of the truth than I have ever told anyone. I gave [her] the breath of life and she in turn gave it to you" (193). Although he is willing and able to discuss the past, he distances himself from it and reinforces its parallels with fairy-tale traditions by telling it in the third person. His nightmare tale of Nazi horrors is interlaced with fairy-tale motifs—confusion about his identity as a homosexual son of an aristocratic stepfather and a bestial father, his association with real woodcutters who turned partisan and assumed names such as Rat and Mutter Holle, his storytelling while they hid in the woods, and the apparent return of the dead years later when he meets the young American with the magic ring he gave to her grandmother. His story explains why Gemma had so many different names in her American life and in the documents she left behind. The names Dawna Prinz, Eve/Genevieve Stein, and Gitl Rose Mandlestein link her with Eden, fairy-tale princesses, and rebirth. At her makeshift marriage the rabbi named her Eve, the first Jewish woman married in those woods. But Josef had begun calling her Księżniczka, which is Polish for young princess, when she regained consciousness with roses in her cheeks, remembering nothing but a first-person version of the fairy tale "Sleeping Beauty in the Wood."

Josef acknowledges that, like Oskar Schindler, he was a dishonorable man who found himself transformed into a hero "of the moment" (139, 165). As a character in a realistic novel, he is a combination of vice and virtue, yet he is also akin to generations of folk heroes who appear as outcasts and drifters until they are tested by extraordinary circumstances, confronted by evil forces beyond human comprehension. Like Gemma, he is both an eloquent storyteller and a main character in his tale; "even the awful things he had to say were beautifully said" (191). At the end of his life when Becca meets him, the heroism of this frail old survivor is also different from that of the woman he saved, who fled to America to start a new life with her child. Josef has endured decades of solitude in his old home, "drawn back by the souls of the dead," according to the priest (126). He is outwardly a dignified gentleman, inwardly a victim tormented by vivid memories of the violent deaths of his loved ones and uncertainty about the fate of Księżniczka. On days when his worst memories and physical wounds ache, he has imagined her and her baby among the dead. He tells Becca he is glad that Gemma had buried her memories and did not have the painful dreams he has endured. At each level of story in this novel the characters are scarred permanently by injustice and grief, by the realization that sleeping isn't "so bad" for the sleeper but for "the ones left behind, awake" (37). It is Becca's determination to seek the truth, however, and Josef's willingness to discuss the past that set them apart from others in her family and his community, enabling these heroes to find each other and share their stories before he dies.

Although the survivors of the Holocaust are not protected from suffering as are all the inhabitants of Briar Rose's castle, who sleep along with her in the traditional fairy tale, and Becca cannot magically recall her real grandfather, as Aurea does in the modern children's story, Yolen shows that storytelling traditions provide essential sources of comfort and hope for the living. All kinds of stories, from old fairy tales to *Hamlet* to postmodern novels and testimonies of real Holocaust survivors, explore the alluring parallels between sleep and death; our desire for the restorative powers of sleep and dreams conflicts with our fear of separation and our dread of nightmares that result from encountering evil in the world or within ourselves. While Hamlet backs away from the temptation to escape into "that sleep of death," fears "what dreams may come" in that "undiscovered country," and then loses himself in layers of stories about his own family's fate (3.1.66, 79) Yolen points out that stories are "dangerous" and "awe-ful" mazes ("With a Lacing of Spindrift"). But neglecting to explore those mazes can be more destructive than facing the nightmares lurking in their corners. In Chelmno, those who cannot tell their stories of the past are cut off from the help and divine forgiveness their priest wants them to seek. They are dark, shadowy figures in Yolen's novel, cursed by guilt and cursing openly at strangers who ask about the past. Josef's testimony reveals what they hide—historic atrocities as outrageous as those imagined in *Hamlet* or in Anne Sexton's modern fairy-tale poems. Sexton's "Briar Rose" emphasizes the unspoken psychological horrors she sees beneath the surface of the old tale, including the awakened princess's later fears of sleeping and dreaming of death, as well as grotesque parallels with a victim of incestuous abuse (*Transformations* 107–12). Sexton's graphic description of the hideous thirteenth fairy is quoted in Yolen's novel before Josef's story begins. Rather than dwelling on the nightmares of persecution and suffering, however, Yolen has written a fantasy of escape. Although she in her Author's Note and a Holocaust survivor within the novel point out that there is no record of any women escaping from Chelmno, Yolen has imagined one who rejoined the living by embracing the dreams of love and renewal that in fairy tales always triumph over evil. Whereas Gemma lost most of her past and never told her story directly, her instinctive identification with the fairy-tale princess who was cursed and revived enabled her to pass on her legacy of bitterness and love in a symbolic form that her heirs could absorb as children and reinterpret as adults. The interwoven stories in this novel, as well as Yolen's shorter reworkings of tales about sleepers and dreamers, illustrate the Cree view of storytelling as Kay Stone has interpreted it: "The storyteller goes backward into the past while looking forward to the future which one brings to the old tales" ("Uses and Abuses" 96). In *Briar Rose,* the characters' bad dreams are overshadowed by the knowledge that the dead have a future when people retell the past and by the moving story of a survivor who escaped to save her baby and nurtured two generations of strong women.

Brian Attebery has observed that feminist writers, like Le Guin's peasant hero, who struggles through Sleeping Beauty's acres of briars in "The Poacher," have to "break into" the magic spell with the help of metafiction and other devices. They rearrange the contents and transform the tales, crossing sociocultural boundaries so that formerly marginalized characters and readers can sneak in and share the narrative tradition that once depicted female speech as suspicious and dangerous. These observations could apply as well to Yolen's exploration of the misunderstood fairy's point of view in "The Thirteenth Fey" and especially to her achievement in giving a voice to historically oppressed victims of the Holocaust within the framework of a fairy-tale novel. Her belief that any story is "infinite" helps make these transformations possible ("Meddlefurs" 64). "The Thirteenth Fey" almost breaks the magic spell with its infusion of cynical parody, but our enjoyment of this innovative version of "The Sleeping Beauty" leaves us hoping that the fey will be restored to health and that modernism won't eradicate fairy-tale magic after all. In *Briar Rose* we "break into" the magic spell by examining the storytelling process, the old fairy tale, and the horror story of the Holocaust from several angles, gaining more direct access to the hearts and minds of heroes who struggle against evil and ignorance than we would within a traditional fairy tale, but the novel never breaks the magic spell of our belief in the restorative power of fairy tales.

Many readers today may be inclined to reach for new tales that feature independent and outspoken women while avoiding those that seem too closely aligned with old images of passive princesses depending on valiant princes. Yolen's various interpretations of the sleeping beauty motif, however, and the connections she creates with other tales of wide-awake heroines and plain but strong women through her poetic style and her intricate use of recurring images, make it difficult for us to ignore the inevitable links between old and new storytelling traditions. If we reject our fairy-tale heritage, we will be in danger of becoming like Gwinellen or the characters in "The Thirteenth Fey" and losing our dreams. That would be tragic because, as Yolen writes in her collection *Dream Weaver,* "The stories that touch us—child and adult—most deeply are, like our myths, crafted visions, shaped dreams . . . the larger dreams that belong to all humankind, or as the Dream Weaver says, 'The heart and soul made visible' " (Introduction).

Notes

1. See, e.g., Jones 72.
2. Sanderson's lecture and Travers's book mention this interpretation of the prince as a relatively inactive character, but Travers points out that the Grimms made him

into a hero by showing that he must choose to enter the briars where the corpses of other princes are seen (58–59).

3. The image of the spinning wheels seems especially ironic in light of Jack Zipes's recent critique of misreadings of "Rumpelstiltskin." He discusses the historical rise and decline of women's spinning "as a creative and productive act" associated with female initiation and social life, then appropriated by men during industrialization (*Fairy Tale as Myth* 49–71). Travers's version of "The Sleeping Beauty" is among those in which characters complain about the social and economic consequences of the king's decree that all spinning wheels be destroyed (18–19). Zipes also mentions "The Sleeping Beauty" as an example of the traditional fairy tale that "reflects feudal agrarian conditions"; "the head of the extended family is an authoritarian male, who makes most of the decisions," the women have more passive roles, and the young protagonists "do not reject the institution of the patriarchal family. . . . The 'dream' of the . . . oppressed person is fulfilled not through the creation of a new social order and family relations, but through living up to the expectations of defined roles and gaining recognition both inside and outside the family" (*Art of Subversion* 148–49).

4. In Mercer Mayer's 1984 picture book the Blue Faerie is both the creator of the curse and the spinner in the tower. Trina Schart Hyman, like Ruth Sanderson, depicts the thirteenth fairy and the spinner as physically similar in her illustrations. Travers comments on this implicit connection between the two characters and on the spindle as an erotic symbol (55–62). As Yolen and Ursula K. Le Guin also observe in their nonfiction, the fairy-tale antagonist, whether wicked stepmother or monster, represents the dark forces within us all. For Sleeping Beauty, the evil fairy is both an outsider who intrudes on her christening and a symbol of her inner compulsion in adolescence to face the dangers of adult life.

5. For example, Travers and Mayer describe Sleeping Beauty dreaming of the prince.

6. In "The Brothers Grimm and Sister Jane," Yolen describes *Sleeping Ugly* as "a parody of several fairy tales," including the Grimms' "The Three Little Men in the Woods" (287).

7. For example, Jack Zipes, Marina Warner, Suzanne Barchers, Angela Carter, Rosemary Minard, Ethel Johnston Phelps, and Alison Lurie have commented extensively on this aspect of fairy-tale history.

8. Tales called "The Sleeping Prince" appear in Carter 123–24 and Lurie, *Clever Gretchen* 74–83. John Warren Stewig explored Lurie's Spanish sources to produce his picture-book retelling of the same tale in *Princess Florecita and the Iron Shoes.* Illustrator K. Wendy Popp has painted Princess Florecita as a strong figure against a misty romantic background, bravely traveling alone to rescue the handsome sleeping prince who had demonstrated his kindness in an earlier encounter.

9. Compare also *The Loathsome Dragon,* a 1987 picture book by David Wiesner and Kim Kahng with a plot very similar to that of older tales such as Andrew Lang's "The Laidly Wyrm of Spindlestone Heugh."

10. See *From the Beast to the Blonde* for Marina Warner's extensive discussion of hair as a manifestation of the "language of the self," revealing "the beastly and the human selves present in each individual" (371–72). Her many examples from fairy tales and popular culture show that hair—especially blonde hair—has been used to associate women with both strength and vulnerability, with youth and sexual maturity, with base bestiality as well as natural and worldly treasures. Rapunzel is one popular fairy-tale heroine who tries to attain freedom by utilizing the physical strength of her hair.

11. Jill May's 1995 article on Yolen's writing and revising methods confirms that Yolen has earned her reputation as an American Hans Christian Andersen because she maintains a firm commitment to her modern themes while masterfully restructur-

ing folk material. Warner observes that Yolen and other contemporary writers "who draw on fairytale motifs and characters . . . are conjuring up dream worlds as personally idealistic, as politically and socially contentious, and often as spiritedly wary and iconoclastic, as their apparently more sophisticated precursors" (411–12). For a related discussion of contemporary fairy-tale revisions, see Joe Winston's essay "Revising the Fairy Tale Through Magic."

12. "The Poacher" shows that romance and dreams are far removed from the real world of hunger, deprivation, and hard labor represented by a young peasant who spends two years hacking a passage through the briars. He lives out his life enjoying the comforts of the castle, including the luxury of learning to read fairy tales, and like all ordinary mortals he dies while the enchanted court sleeps on. He has no dreams inside the briar hedge, recognizing that he must not wake Sleeping Beauty and interrupt her dreams. In Garfield's *The Wedding Ghost* (with grotesque and haunting illustrations by Charles Keeping), the modern bridegroom Jack cannot resist kissing the Sleeping Beauty during a dreamlike quest on the eve of his wedding. Trapped by the realization that he will die in the briars if he tries to escape without kissing the princess, Jack is doomed to a life of discontent after kissing her, when the cathedral in his fairy-tale world suddenly collapses and he finds himself in the village church with his fond but unexciting middle-class bride. Garfield uses the figure of Sleeping Beauty and the song "O Mistress Mine" from *Twelfth Night* to show that the persistence of fairy-tale fantasies causes frustration and disillusionment in the context of ordinary domestic life; marrying without the ideal romantic love he has tasted is a kind of death for Jack.

13. A more graphic infusion of realism can be seen in the sketch "Sleeping Beauty" by the German poet Günter Kunert (1972), who exposes the romanticism of the tale as an impossible dream of eternal beauty preserved only in the minds of those who died in the hedge, while the victorious prince finds a hideous, aged, "toothless . . . dirty . . . snoring trollop" (in Zipes, *Spells of Enchantment* 701).

14. In a panel discussion on censorship and fantasy held at Clemson University (12 October 1996) and elsewhere, Yolen has discussed the burning of *Briar Rose* on the steps of the Kansas City Board of Education building, caused primarily by censors' disapproval of the character Josef Potocki, a homosexual Holocaust survivor. She has also explained that, in addition to drawing on her own Jewish heritage, she had to undertake difficult research in order to tell Josef's story (E-mail, 12 December 1995). My undergraduate students, some of whom had no knowledge of the persecution of others besides Jews, have affirmed the importance of this novel in familiarizing them with the fate of Holocaust victims. One student, Bernice Cobbs, wrote in 1996, "I have learned a great deal about history from reading this novel and will carry this knowledge when I speak of the Holocaust to my class."

Works Cited

Attebery, Brian. "Gender, Fantasy, and the Authority of Tradition." *Journal of the Fantastic in the Arts* 7 (1996):51–60.

Barchers, Suzanne I. *Wise Women: Folk and Fairy Tales from Around the World.* Englewood, Colo.: Libraries Unlimited, 1990.

Bettelheim, Bruno. *The Uses of Enchantment: The Meaning and Importance of Fairy Tales.* New York: Vintage, 1975.

Carter, Angela, ed. *Strange Things Sometimes Still Happen: Fairy Tales from Around the World.* Boston: Faber, 1993.

Chevalier, Tracy, ed. *Twentieth-Century Children's Writers.* 3d ed. Chicago: St. James, 1989.

Cole, Babette. *Prince Cinders.* New York: Putnam's, 1987. N. pag.

———. *Princess Smartypants.* New York: Putnam's, 1986. N. pag.
Eliot, George. *Silas Marner.* 1861. Reprint. New York: Signet-Penguin, 1981.
Estés, Clarissa Pinkola. *Women Who Run with the Wolves: Myths and Stories of the Wild Woman Archetype.* New York: Ballantine, 1992.
Garfield, Leon. *The Wedding Ghost.* Illus. Charles Keeping. Oxford: Oxford University Press, 1985.
Grimm, Jacob, and Wilhelm Grimm. *The Complete Fairy Tales of the Brothers Grimm.* Trans. Jack Zipes. New York: Bantam, 1987.
Hyman, Trina Schart. *The Sleeping Beauty.* Boston: Little, Brown, 1977. N. pag.
"An Interview with Jane Yolen." *Mythlore* 13, no. 1 (1986):24–26, 48.
Jones, Steven Swann. *The Fairy Tale: The Magic Mirror of Imagination.* New York: Twayne, 1995.
Kolbenschlag, Madonna. *Kiss Sleeping Beauty Good-Bye: Breaking the Spell of Feminine Myths and Models.* Garden City: Doubleday, 1979.
Le Guin, Ursula K. *The Language of the Night: Essays on Fantasy and Science Fiction.* New York: HarperCollins, 1992.
———. "The Poacher." In *Xanadu,* ed. Jane Yolen. New York: Tom Doherty, 1993. Pp. 11–27.
Lieberman, Marcia. " 'Some Day My Prince Will Come': Female Acculturation Through the Fairy Tale." *College English* 34 (1972):383–95.
Lurie, Alison. *Clever Gretchen and Other Forgotten Folktales.* Illus. Margot Tomes. New York: HarperCollins, 1980.
———. *Don't Tell the Grown-Ups: Why Kids Love the Books They Do.* New York: Avon, 1990.
May, Jill. "Jane Yolen's Literary Folk Tales: Legends, Folktales, and Myths Remade." *Journal of Children's Literature* 21 (1995):74–78.
May, Rollo. *The Cry for Myth.* New York: Delta-Bantam, 1991.
Mayer, Mercer. *The Sleeping Beauty.* New York: Macmillan, 1984. N. pag.
Minard, Rosemary, ed. *Womenfolk and Fairy Tales.* Boston: Houghton, 1975.
Minters, Frances. *Sleepless Beauty.* Illus. G. Brian Karas. New York: Viking, 1996.
Munsch, Robert. *The Paper Bag Princess.* Illus. Michael Martchenko. New York: Annick, 1980.
Nesbit, E. *The Last of the Dragons.* 1925. Reprint. New York: McGraw-Hill, 1980.
Opie, Iona, and Peter Opie. *The Classic Fairy Tales.* New York: Oxford University Press, 1992.
Phelps, Ethel Johnston. *The Maid of the North: Feminist Folk Tales from Around the World.* New York: Holt, 1981.
———, ed. *Tatterhood and Other Tales.* New York: Feminist, 1978.
Roginski, Jim. "Jane Yolen." In *Behind the Covers: Interviews with Authors and Illustrators.* Littleton, Colo.: Libraries Unlimited, 1985. Pp. 224–36.
Sanderson, Ruth. "The Art of the Fairy Tale." Lecture. Hollins College, Roanoke, Va. 21 September 1995.
Sexton, Anne. *Transformations.* Boston: Houghton, 1971.
Shakespeare, William. *Hamlet.* Ed. R. C. Bald. Arlington Heights, Ill.: Crofts-Harlan Davidson, 1946.
Stewig, John Warren. *Princess Florecita and the Iron Shoes: A Spanish Fairy Tale.* Illus. K. Wendy Popp. New York: Apple Soup Books-Knopf, 1995. N. pag.
Stone, Kay F. "Feminist Approaches to the Interpretation of Fairy Tales." In *Fairy Tales and Society: Illusion, Allusion, and Paradigm,* ed. Ruth B. Bottigheimer. University of Pennsylvania Press, 1983. Pp. 229–36.
———. "The Misuses of Enchantment." In *Women's Folklore, Women's Culture,* ed. Rosan Jordan and Susan Kalcik. Philadelphia: University of Pennsylvania Press, 1985. Pp. 125–45.

———. "The Uses and Abuses of Traditional Oral Tales." In *The First Steps: Best of the Early Children's Literature Association Quarterly*, ed. Patricia Dooley. Purdue University: ChLA, 1984. Pp. 95–96.
Stott, Jon. "Will the Real Dragon Stand Up? Convention and Parody in Children's Stories." *Children's Literature in Education* 21 (1990):219–28.
Tatar, Maria. *Off with Their Heads! Fairy Tales and the Culture of Childhood.* Princeton: Princeton University Press, 1992.
Travers, P. L. *About the Sleeping Beauty.* Illus. Charles Keeping. New York: McGraw-Hill, 1975.
Warner, Marina. *From the Beast to the Blonde: On Fairy Tales and Their Tellers.* New York: Farrar, Straus, 1994.
Wiesner, David, and Kim Kahng. *The Loathsome Dragon.* New York: Putnam's, 1987.
Winston, Joe. "Revising the Fairy Tale Through Magic: Antonia Barber's *The Enchanter's Daughter.*" *Children's Literature in Education* 25 (1994):101–11.
Yolen, Jane. "America's 'Cinderella.'" *Children's Literature in Education* 8 (1977):21–29. Reprinted in *Writing and Reading Across the Curriculum.* 4th ed. Ed. Laurence Behrens and Leonard J. Rosen. New York: HarperCollins, 1991. Pp. 355–63.
———. *Briar Rose.* Fairy Tale Series. New York: Tom Doherty, 1992.
———. "The Brothers Grimm and Sister Jane." In *The Reception of Grimms' Fairy Tales: Responses, Reactions, Revisions,* ed. Donald Haase. Detroit: Wayne State University Press, 1993. Pp. 283–89.
———. "Dealing with Dragons." *Horn Book* 60 (1984):380–88.
———. *The Devil's Arithmetic.* New York: Viking Penguin, 1988.
———. *Dove Isabeau.* Illus. Dennis Nolan. New York: Harcourt, 1989. N. pag.
———. *Dream Weaver.* Illus. Michael Hague. New York: Philomel, 1979.
———. E-mail to the author, 12 December 1995.
———. E-mail to the author, 27 February 1997.
———. *The Emperor and the Kite.* Illus. Ed Young. New York: World, 1967. N. pag.
———. *The Girl in the Golden Bower.* Illus. Jane Dyer. Boston: Little, Brown, 1994. N. pag.
———. *The Girl Who Loved the Wind.* Illus. Ed Young. New York: HarperCollins, 1972. N. pag.
———. *Gwinellen, the Princess Who Could Not Sleep.* Illus. Ed Renfro. New York: Macmillan, 1965. N. pag.
———. "Meddlefurs." *Journal of Children's Literature* 20 (1994):62–64.
———. *The Moon Ribbon and Other Tales.* New York: Crowell, 1976.
———. *The Sleeping Beauty.* Illus. Ruth Sanderson. New York: Ariel, 1986. N. pag.
———. *Sleeping Ugly.* Illus. Diane Stanley. New York: Coward-McCann, 1981.
———. *Tales of Wonder.* New York: Schocken, 1983.
———. *Tam Lin.* Illus. Charles Mikolaycak. New York: Harcourt, 1990. N. pag.
———. "The Thirteenth Fey." In *Dragonfield and Other Stories.* New York: Ace, 1985. Pp. 31–45.
———. *Touch Magic: Fantasy, Faerie and Folklore in the Literature of Childhood.* New York: Putnam's, 1981.
———. "With a Lacing of Spindrift: The Alchemy of Change—Idea into Book." Children's Literature Symposium: The Art of the Children's Book. Clemson University. 12 October 1996.
Zipes, Jack. *Fairy Tales and the Art of Subversion: The Classical Genre for Children and the Process of Civilization.* New York: Methuen, 1983.
———. *Fairy Tale as Myth, Myth as Fairy Tale.* Lexington: University Press of Kentucky, 1994.
———, ed. *Don't Bet on the Prince: Contemporary Feminist Fairy Tales in North America and England.* New York: Routledge, 1987.

———, ed. *The Outspoken Princess and the Gentle Knight: A Treasury of Modern Fairy Tales.* New York: Bantam, 1994.
———, ed. *Spells of Enchantment: The Wondrous Fairy Tales of Western Culture.* New York: Viking, 1991.
———, ed. *The Trials and Tribulations of Little Red Riding Hood: Versions of the Tale in Sociocultural Context.* 2d ed. New York: Routledge, 1993.

Varia

Writing Kate Greenaway: Carrier-Bag Autobiography

Anne Lundin

> *The first cultural device was probably a recipient. . . . Many theorizers feel that the earliest cultural inventions must have been a container to hold gathered products and some kind of sling or net carrier.*
>
> —Elizabeth Fisher, *Woman's Creation*

Ursula K. Le Guin, in her provocative essay "The Carrier Bag Theory of Fiction," suggests that fiction writing is much like the prehistoric gathering of wild-oat seeds from the husk and carrying them away in some kind of carrier bag, bearing them home—home being another, larger kind of bag—to be shared and honored by the family. This process resembles the fictional one of gathering words that bear meanings and hold "a particular, powerful relation to one another and to us" (169). Those early gatherers, who collected from the fruit of the earth and then returned it to the community to share and to hold sacred, restore Le Guin's faith in humanity. As she writes, "If to do this is human, if that's what it takes, then I am a human being after all. Fully, freely, gladly, for the first time" (168).

Perhaps "writing a woman's life," in Carolyn Heilbrun's words, is even more like bearing home seeds in a carrier bag. Perhaps scholarship in a special collection library is also similar in its bending, unfolding, and collating process. In so doing, I located an extraordinary holograph manuscript—a fragmented autobiography of Kate Greenaway—in a botanical library at Carnegie-Mellon University in Pittsburgh. The location of the manuscript in a botanical library seems

I wish to express my appreciation to Mary Kay Johnsen, special collections librarian at the Hunt Institute for Botanical Documentation, Carnegie-Mellon University, for her generous assistance with my research.

Children's Literature 26, ed. Elizabeth Lennox Keyser (Yale University Press, © 1998 Hollins College).

somehow fitting to the process of organic growth and gathering. At the same time, a botanical library seems to be a curious site for a picture-book collection. How did a scientific archive come to obtain many of the original works of a Victorian picture-book illustrator? What would this abbreviated autobiography reveal about the relationship between Greenaway's childhood reverie and her art?

Original artworks and related materials of Kate Greenaway were donated to the Hunt Institute for Botanical Documentation by Frances Hooper in the 1970s. Hooper, a bibliophile with a collection of Greenaway materials spanning more than thirty years, initially became interested in the artist through a rare book collector from Chicago named Walter M. Hill. Beginning with an instinctive attraction to a pencil-and-watercolor drawing of a girl in an old-fashioned red pelisse, Hooper was finally able to acquire a sizable collection of Greenaway items owned by Arnold Shircliffe, a Chicago restaurateur known for his eclectic acquisitions. She collected original artworks, first editions, holograph letters, and other manuscript material. Hooper finally donated the collection to the Hunt Institute largely because of her affinity with Rachel McMasters Miller Hunt, herself a woman with extraordinary interests in horticulture, rare books, and graphic arts. Hunt was intrigued not only with botanical works on flowers but also with related works, such as the "Language of Flowers" books, popular in the Victorian era. Although Hooper never met Hunt personally, she grew close to Hunt through participation in groups Hunt founded that were related to fine printing and book collecting.

I learned about the existence of the autobiography in 1990 from working in the de Grummond Children's Literature Research Collection at the University of Southern Mississippi. This collection contains large holdings of original Greenaway materials as well as related source books and catalogs. In a 1980 exhibition catalog published by the Hunt Institute, *Kate Greenaway,* was the following citation: "Autobiographical journal, text in pencil, with sketches. One volume, soft bound, *ca.* 110 pp., 22.5 × 18 cm" (105). I was aware of the existence of a journal through biographical works on Greenaway, although I never imagined that I would have the opportunity to read and study the penciled scribblings myself. Frances Hooper purchased the journal at a London auction held at the direction of Greenaway's grand-nephew and donated the work to the collection in 1971. As a librarian, I was struck by the largesse and wisdom of the donor who sensed in Greenaway's work a quality—her floral motif—that transcended traditional archival patterns of where to give what. As a scholar of Greenaway, I was closer to my quarry than ever before.

Kate Greenaway's autobiography as literary text is virtually unknown. The work belongs to the genre that Richard Coe calls "the Childhood," an adult autobiographical foray into childhood and adolescence. As Coe points out, such discursive work takes as its subject matter the quotidian life, the trivia that essentially define childhood experience in its "minutiae of child-delight or torment" (xii). This writing presents an alternative world written not from the vantage of a historian's accuracy but, instead, of a poet's truth (2). Sidone Smith considers autobiography to be a form of fiction, of "assigning meanings to a series of experiences, after they have taken place, by means of emphasis, juxtaposition, commentary, omission" (45). Such elasticity is not always valued as process or product. Greenaway's first—and still most definitive—biographers, M. H. Spielmann and G. S. Layard, purge the manuscript for the same reasons that postmodern critics privilege women's autobiography. In the words of their 1905 biography of Greenaway: "What she left behind is a long detailed record of undigested recollections and sensations as she recalled them, marked by discursiveness and lacking in literary form" (9). What they do acknowledge is her "unusually retentive memory" —of childhood colors, flowers, clothing, dolls, gardens, and family relations. Like that in other women's autobiographies, the writing celebrates homespun and natural details, a rich quilt of sensual experience and genealogy. In this the autobiography is similar to the ancient act of gathering seeds in a carrier bag to bring home to others.

Considering that Greenaway's health was failing during the process of its writing, the mere existence of the journal, however inchoate, is extraordinary. Greenaway wrote this journal in the last years of her life, when she was stoically suffering from breast cancer before her premature death in 1901 at age fifty-five. The journal begins and ends rather abruptly, without introduction or conclusion. A summary of the contents exists in the Spielmann and Layard biography of 1905, extracts of which reappear in various biographical sketches of Greenaway ever since that publication. Despite this visibility, no one has yet examined the autobiography as *autobiography*, as a unique form of women's writing, by a woman who was distinctly a children's book author and illustrator. Indeed, few have considered her late-in-life notebook an autobiography. Yet she conceived of an audience, as her various markings on the page show. She illustrated the text with numerous sketches, corrected names, inserted words, and included "see also" references for the implied reader.

Writing in her early fifties, beset with health problems, Greenaway began the story of her childhood in a simple penciled notebook. No record exists as to what prompted this self-expression, nor if it was ever read, except by her biographers after her death. Greenaway was clearly interested in the art of autobiography, as evidenced by letters quoted in Spielmann and Layard's biography. Two letters to her friend Violet Dickinson (later intimate with the young Virginia Woolf) in 1897 suggest her interest in the genre:

> What an interesting thing nearly every one's life would be if they could put it down; but it is only the horrid ones who will, like Marie Bashkirtseff or Rousseau—but if nice people could tell all their mind it would be charming. Did you ever read Goethe's *Life*—the autobiography? All the early part is so charming—only there you feel he also was very heartless. And he was, but it is so charmingly told. Sometimes frankness is curious. I once met a young man who told me he was a coward and a liar—and it turned out he was, to my great surprise. It isn't often people know themselves so truthfully, or, if they know, they don't say. (9–10)

And again:

> I am longing to read the Tennyson *Life*—shall send for it next week. I don't know, I'm sure, who is best to write a Life—outsiders don't know what any one is like, and relations often get a wrong idea of you because you are cross at little points in your character that annoy you. I feel an autobiography or diary is best. A person must reveal himself most in that. (10)

And reveal Greenaway does in more than a hundred pages of recollections of her childhood.

Greenaway's personal storytelling begins, cryptically, with a crest on the first page with emblem figures appearing to be ducks (fig. 1). With little ado, the first page of text fixes the geography of Rolleston, the quaint country town in Nottinghamshire where she spent her earliest years and every childhood summer thereafter. This is the heart of the matter: where she spent her formative years. She then turns to family, to the relations who nurtured and housed her dur-

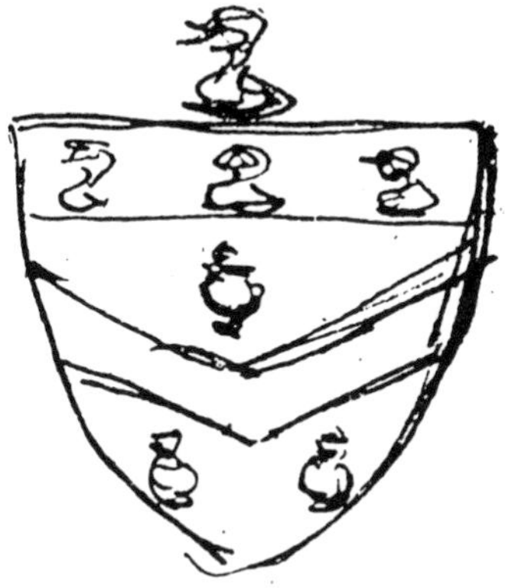

Figure 1. The first page of Greenaway's autobiography begins with these rough resemblances of ducks as a kind of cryptic family crest.

ing her frequent stays. Her most intimate connections there were not with family members, however, but with their servants. When Greenaway was taken seriously ill as a young child, she was sent to her Aunt Wise's house and then to nurse at the home of her aunt's servant Mary Barnsdale, married to Thomas Chapell. Mary soon became "Maman," her husband "Dadad," and Mary's sister Ann "Nanan." Their names appear on the top of the first page of the manuscript, along with the mysterious crest.

Her earliest memories include, curiously, the mention of baskets. She was two years old and being carried by Ann into a hayfield with a basket containing tea, bread, and butter. Greenaway states that for the rest of her life she has recalled the look of the sun, the smell of tea, the perfume of the hay, the feeling of happiness from her perch on Ann's arm. She then recounts picking up tiny stones and pebbles and putting them into a little round purple-and-white basket. Greenaway even remembers what she was wearing—a pink cotton frock and a white sun bonnet. As she writes, "Everything impressed me very strongly early on" (4).

Her next strongest images recollected from childhood are of flowers. There was the snapdragon that opened and shut its mouth as she touched it. There was the pink moss rose that grew by the dairy window. There were the gooseberry bushes, the plum tree, and the laburnum in the garden near the road. There was a purple phlox on one side of the gate and a Michaelmas daisy on the other side.

Flowers—their color, scent, and form—shaped "a real fairy ground" for this young girl (6).

Still in her toddler years, Greenaway reveled in the cornfield and flower bank, which she visited with Ann on free Sundays. She remembers the flowers and the foliage growing along the stream: purple vetch and blackberry bushes. Nearby was a mill with its network of pools and streams, forget-me-nots ablaze on the banks and apple trees overshadowing. In the autumn, fallen apples would float atop the water. Young Greenaway felt these sodden fruits "a Mystery, thinking they might float on and on to the sea to a new land altogether" (7). The only jarring notes in these reveries were sounds of church bells, which seemed "so mournful," or sightings of recalcitrant cows she tried to herd, which caused great terror.

At about this time Greenaway returned to London, where her family struggled with finances and with frequent moves. Although Kate was unaware of the circumstances—her father losing much of his business as an engraver and her mother recouping with her own dressmaking enterprise—she was sensitive to the atmosphere of each location. Greenaway's perspective is always that of a child; she gives no background or explanation of the events that engaged her. She was particularly struck with the house at Islington, where her mother ran a small shop. It was a rambling place with a large garden in the back, then a lane and a field of sheep—in Greenaway's words, "Houses and gardens all rather mixed up with each other" (11).

Part of the mixture involved dolls, a major preoccupation of her childhood. She was enchanted by the Punch and Judy shows in the streets, with the puppets playing out their own dramas. She longed for the dolls that she could not buy. She writes of—and sketches—the dolls that she played with during her childhood, remembering their every garment and imaginative re-creation (fig. 2). Dolls were often brought outdoors, wheeled in carriages, and dressed up in old handmade clothes. She owned a small set of figures of the royal family as well as paper dolls and toy animals.

Another persistent interest involved books and their imaginative worlds. Greenaway recalls how she learned to read by herself at an early age from the old fairy tales in their colored paper covers. The servants passed on scary stories, such as "Pepper and Salt" and "Bluebeard," which created states of terror in the young child. Some of her favorite stories were those by Maria Edgeworth; she mentions, in particular, "Cherry Orchard" (which she was later to paint), "The Purple

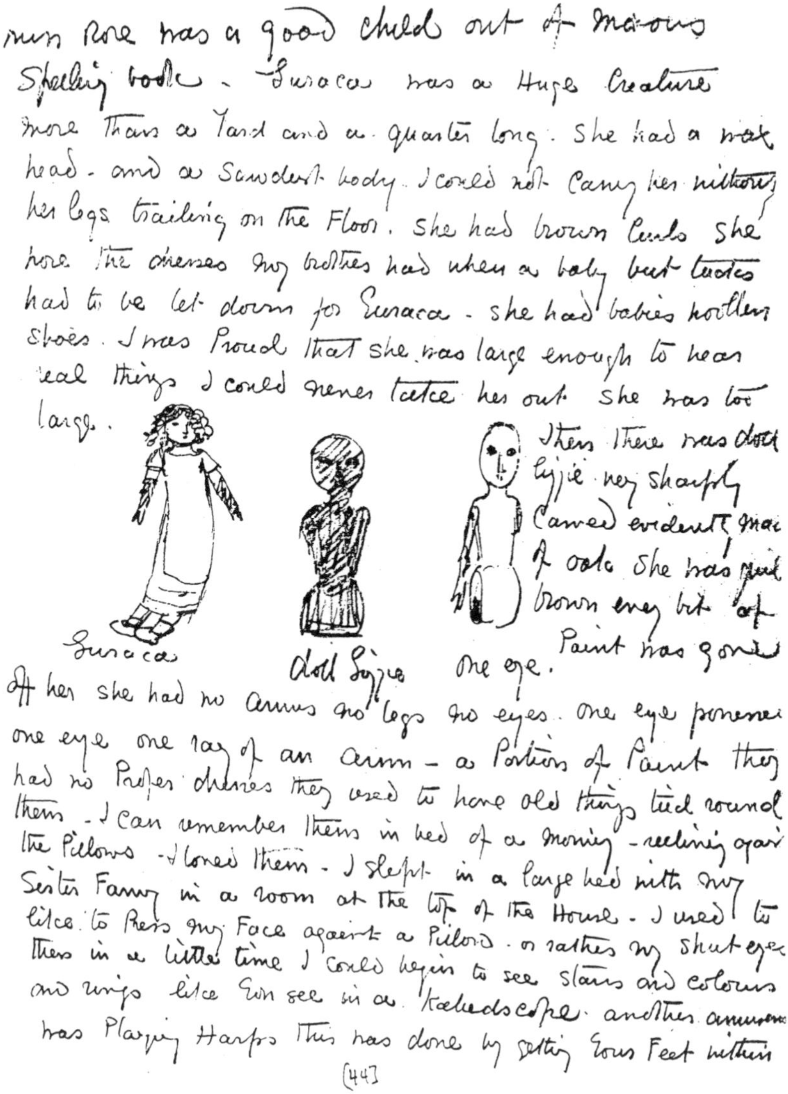

miss Rose was a good child out of Mavors Spelling book - Susaca was a Huge Creature more than a Yard and a quarter long. She had a wax head - and a Sawdust body. I could not Carry her without her legs trailing on the Floor. She had brown Curls She wore the dresses my brother had when a baby but tucks had to be let down for Susaca - she had babies worsted shoes. I was Proud that she was large enough to wear real things I could never take her out she was too large.

Susaca

Doll Lizzie

One eye.

Then there was doll Lizzie very sharply Carved evidently made of oak She was quite brown every bit of Paint has gone off her she had no arms no legs no eyes. One eye possessed one eye one leg of an arm - a Portion of Paint they had no Proper dresses they used to have old things tied round them - I can remember them in bed of a morning - reclining against the Pillows - I loved them - I slept in a large bed with my Sister Fanny in a room at the top of the House - I used to like to Press my Face against a Pillow - or rather my shut eyes then in a little time I could begin to see stars and colours and rings like you see in a Kaleidscope - another amusement was Playing Harps this was done by getting your Feet within

[44]

Figure 2. The figures depicted are Greenaway's remembrance of favorite childhood dolls and their dress.

Jar," and "Frank, Harry and Lucy." She was also enamored of the poetry of Ann and Jane Taylor, which she would later memorialize in her own illustrated volume, *Little Ann and Other Poems* (1882). Greenaway's beloved fairy tale was "Beauty and the Beast," a story of transformation. She responded actively to what she read. She was quite distressed, for instance, by a book of rhymes for which her father engraved the wood blocks. One of the selections was "The Wonderful History of Cocky Locky, Henny Penney, and Goosey Gander," which seemed to her a brutal story. She also pored over the illustrations from *Illustrated London News* that were collected by her father in the course of his business as an engraver. She was horrified at the pictures of fleeing women and children during the Indian Mutiny and would attempt to draw the scenes on her slate, with the innocent victims rescued.

In the midst of depicting a street scene—replete with puppet shows, singers, and vendors selling their wares—she describes one man who marched along proclaiming the end of the world. This intrusion into her blissful world produced "months of gloom." She began to envision the creation of the world, if it were indeed ending. She imagined herself in a dark space with a burning world floating about it and drew circles on the page of the manuscript to illustrate (fig. 3). Such thoughts as to what came before the beginning and into what state the world would evolve created distress. "I can well remember wishing away the despairing thought and seeking forgetfulness of the thought" (42).

Much of the terror aroused by fairy tales, the media, and philosophical questions became woven into her first book, *Under the Window* (1879), in which she combined street cries, nursery rhymes, and some of the fear and trembling of childhood. The pages that include the witch on a broomstick and the hooded man capturing a child show the influence of a fiery imagination, which helps to balance some of the more bucolic pictures and the stasis. Unfortunately, under John Ruskin's tutelage, all images of darkness were expunged from later editions, which conceivably stunted the artist's—as well as the reader's—growth. We will never know how her work might have matured had she been allowed to convey the despair as well as the enchantment she experienced as a child because, from that point on, her work became patterned into a more prettified world.

Greenaway's focus was never far from the family. She describes happy domestic scenes with her mother reading, her father close by,

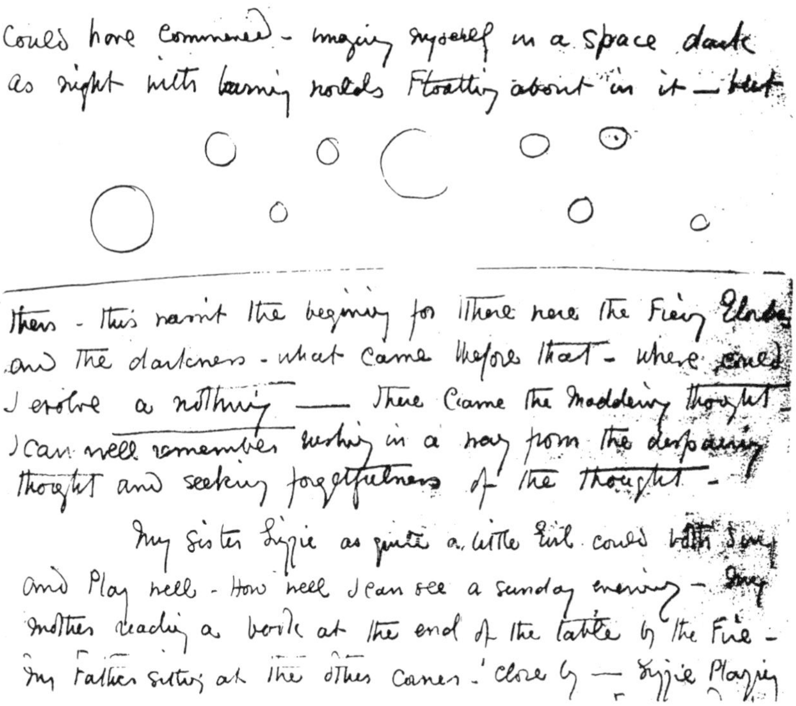

Could have commenced - imaging myself in a space dark
as night with burning worlds floating about in it — but

then - this wasn't the beginning for there were the Fiery Elements
and the darkness - what came before that - where could
I evolve a nothing — There came the maddening thought
I can well remember seeking in a way from the despairing
thought and seeking forgetfulness of the thought -
My sister Lizzie as quite a little Girl could both sing
and play well - How well I can see a Sunday evening - my
mother reading a book at the end of the table by the Fire -
my Father sitting at the other corner close by — Lizzie Playing

Figure 3. Greenaway drew these circles to depict her apocalyptic vision of a world ending and beginning.

her sister Lizzie singing, and her and her sister Fanny sliding off the sofa to the floor or playing with carpet stools as stepping stones across an imaginary stream (fig. 4). She introduces all of her relatives at Rolleston, as well as their personalities and habits and interactions with her. All of her familial characters are described by their clothing, their gardens, or their teatime. Her sense of family extended to the farmers and workers of the town. At one point she writes, "I know every farmer in Rolleston, every la borer, and nearly every cow" (67). She attributes much of her empathy with farmers to the novels of George Eliot, which, she says, taught her much more about their lives than Thomas Hardy's novels did.

As appropriate to a chronicle of childhood, Greenaway recalls her dreams, unself-consciously revealing some of her psyche as well as leaving many gaps. In one recounted dream she is walking in the

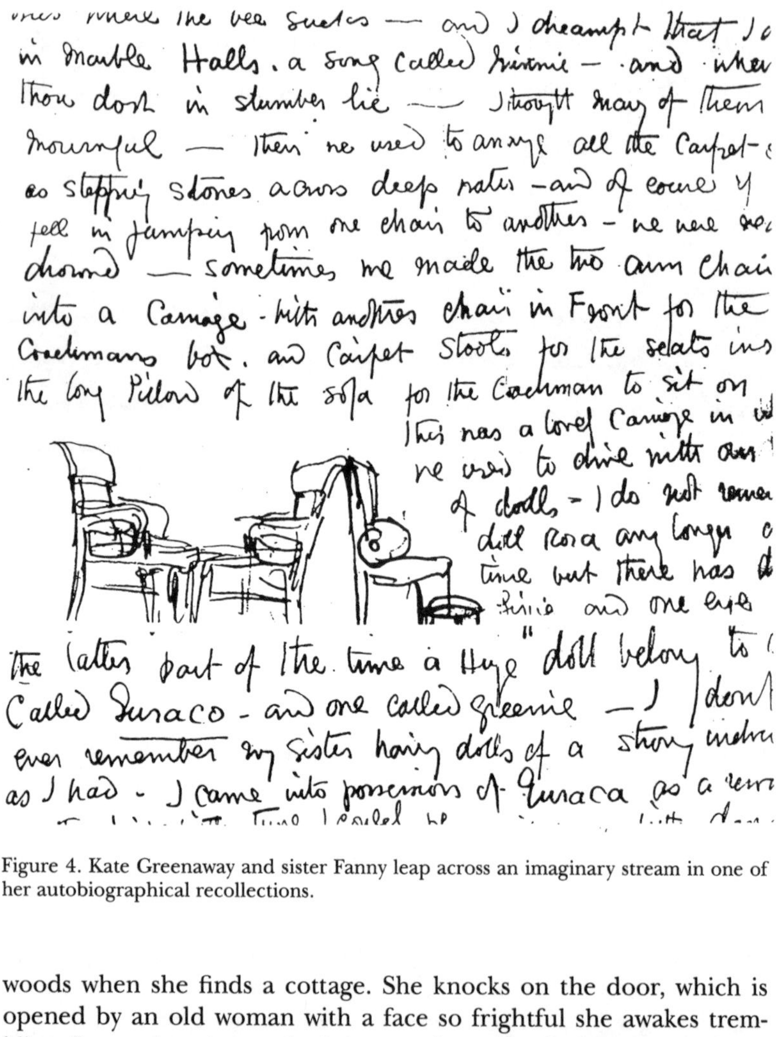
where the bee sucks — and I dreamt that I d
in Marble Halls. a song called Minnie — and when
thou dost in slumber lie — I thought many of them
mournful — then we used to arrange all the Carpet-
as stepping stones across deep water — and of course y
fell in jumping from one chair to another — we were se
drowned — sometimes we made the two arm chair
into a Carriage - with another chair in Front for the
Coachmans box. and Carpet Stools for the seats ins
the long Pillow of the sofa for the Coachman to sit on
This was a lovely Carriage in w
we used to drive with our
of dolls - I do not remem
doll Rosa any longer o
time but there was
Finis and one eye
the latter part of the time a Huge doll belong to
Called Susaco - and one called Greenie — I I don't
ever remember my sister having dolls of a strong indiv
as I had - I came into possession of Susaca as a rew

Figure 4. Kate Greenaway and sister Fanny leap across an imaginary stream in one of her autobiographical recollections.

woods when she finds a cottage. She knocks on the door, which is opened by an old woman with a face so frightful she awakes trembling. In another dream she is in a garden with climbing nasturtiums (a favorite flower). She opens one door after another, only to sense that the door would eventually be opened by the frightful face of the previous dream. In one recurrent dream her father would change faces, and she would desperately try to remove the false one, only to be confronted by another, and yet another. Another repetitive dream was of falling through water, past green weeds, to the very bottom. Or she would dream of flight, of mounting into the air and then floating downward over a steep staircase, out one window and in at another (anticipating some of Maurice Sendak's dreamscapes). Some of these nightmarish and ecstatic dream images resonate in *Under the Window* in the airy feel of the page, in the preponderance of white space, in the water scenes, and in the frightening images that complement the placid expressions (fig. 5).

Her imaginative world was also quite active in the daytime. She would choose circuitous paths through gardens "for my old reason I suppose—the love of the Mysterious, for I could not see the end of it" (49). She would frequent the Rolleston churchyard and occasionally find bones, which created "an awe-struck feeling that they once belonged to people whose descendants belonged now to me. All this gave full scope for my love of the Mysterious and something that was *old" (85; "old" is underlined and starred). She remembers kneeling against the drawing-room window and singing close to the glass. All at once it seemed as if hundreds of voices were singing, until someone came into the room and they vanished. Another day, inspired by the scent of a rose she was carrying, she sensed wonderful scenes, which, when the flower fell, fled too. She writes that when painting flowers and springtime pictures, "I have actually smelt the flowers." Walking into her studio on cold days, she knew she would be in summer as soon as she began to draw. Music was also an elixir. "I have the greatest difficulty to listen to beautiful music, it is so suggestive" (95). Flowers were often enchanted to her. In perhaps the most revealing passage, she writes:

> I have always had a curious feeling whenever I see or smell cowslips or apple blossoms—as if I had known them in some former existence—and I seem always trying to remember something I can't when I smell them. It may be knowing them so young that gives me that feeling. . . . I had a mystical country haunting me—a soul of Eden or Paradise where the air was scented with apple blossom and you walked through cowslips or seemed to live in a sea of buttercups and daisies that were everywhere—a world covered with flowers and blue sky—and divinely fresh air—I never remember primroses there (96).

In her journal, Greenaway captures one posture that seems most emblematic of the unexpressed longings that her picture books express and evoke. She recounts how she loved to climb to the rooftop of her Islington home and look out over the other rooftops and,

Oh, what has the old man come for?
Oh, what has the old man come for?
To run away with Billy, I say,
And that's what the old man has come for.

Ah, what will Billy's mamma say?
Ah, what will Billy's papa say?
What a dreadful fright
They'll be in to-night!—
Oh, what will papa and mamma say?

Figure 5. An illustration from *Under the Window* conveys some of the frightening dreams of young Kate Greenaway as depicted in her dream remembrances and translated into her first picture book.

in the early morning light, imagine a "Hidden dwelling place." She stood high and saw a lovely garden from afar with boxes of nasturtiums. This imprinted image is illustrated in picture and verse in *Under the Window* (fig. 6):

> Which is the way to Somewhere Town?
> Oh, up in the morning early;
> Over the tiles and the chimney-pots,
> That is the way, quite clearly.
>
> And which is the door to Somewhere Town?
> Oh, up in the morning early;
> The round red sun is the door to go through,
> That is the way, quite clearly. (38)

Under the Window reveals much of the self that is expressed in her later autobiography. The gardens, the marketplace, the rooftops all speak of the young Kate who dreamed of waterfalls and flight, who wore a plum-pudding dress of silk with rainbow stripes while herding the cows, who dressed her dolls in the fabric of old bonnet linings, who loved the word *enchanted,* who knew every farmer and nearly every animal in Rolleston, who mentioned more flower names than people in her journal, who sensed the mystery at the core of the world, its very beginnings.

Greenaway's journal is unique as autobiography in its illustrations of these mysteries. Her occasional sketches, which in their fragmentary state seem more spontaneous than designed, signal her full-bodied childhood concerns: toys, architecture, flowers, and, above all, the human form, ennobled by dress. Although most of the illustrations carry little comment, her rough drawings of Rolleston houses include markings as to the function of rooms (fig. 7). The sketches, seemingly more illuminating to the creator than to the audience, suggest that her interests were in her own process of remembrance rather than in communication. There is none of the detail here that characterizes her style of illustration: attention to costume and period, circular relationship of figure to background, her own distinctive sense of perspective. This was her journal—Greenaway writing Greenaway.

Who is the audience, the implied reader? I believe it to be Greenaway herself, with belated overtures toward another reader. Her illustrations, with their occasional corrections or cryptic marks (an X on certain lines), assume a response. My own response is that she intended to complete this inchoate endeavor but sensed the shortness

WHICH is the way to Somewhere Town?
  Oh, up in the morning early;
Over the tiles and the chimney-pots,
  That is the way, quite clearly.

And which is the door to Somewhere Town?
  Oh, up in the morning early;
The round red sun is the door to go through,
  That is the way, quite clearly.

38

Figure 6. An illustration from *Under the Window* reveals the young, dreamy Greenaway looking skyward, outward, toward a "Somewhere Town."

I used to go into the Hayfields with my little Fork and help turn over the Hay. Often I went with Mamam or Ann to take their tea.

The Chappells House was a little House and a kitchen built out at the side -

You went through the kitchen door into the kitchen through another door into a little room with a window looking to the back that answered to a Passage - one door led upstairs another into the dairy - another into the House and from the House a door led into the Parlour also the Front door led into the House upstairs there were ~~three~~ Four Rooms - two large and two small - one large room was the best Room where Visitors slept - Mamam had the other large Room - then there was Anns bedroom and the other smalle room my brother used to sleep in. It is needless to say everything was beautifully clean - our large Four Post bed had Curtains of Red chintz and white in big stripes - we had a white Counterpaine - we had two beautiful old oak chests in the Room. one served as a washstand with a white cloth on it the other as a table - There was a little dressing table with an oval glass and one or two chairs with Rush bottoms

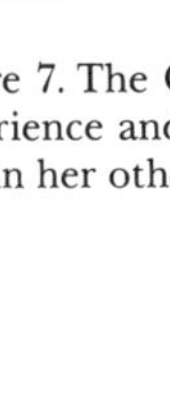

and strips of Carpet laid down. the Floor was a sort of Cement not boards - watch Pockets hung over the Pillows The Kitchen was a true Kitchen. There was a Pump and a Sink in it two ~~a~~ Copper and a large water butt behind the

[70]

Figure 7. The Chappells' house was a significant landscape in Greenaway's Rolleston experience and recollection. The level of architectural detail is unusual compared to that in her other autobiographical illustrations.

of time. Therefore, the creation is intuitive, more a journal of childhood reverie than an autobiography, if those distinctions matter. This language becomes her testament of lasting images, a legacy more personal than that found in her published books. To me, the work exists as a gift. As Lewis Hyde writes in his remarkable book *The Gift: Imagination and the Erotic Life of Property,* "That art that matters to us—which moves the soul, or delights the senses, or offers courage for living, however we choose to describe the experience—that work is received by us as a gift is received" (xii). And so a gift is given to us: a reader, a library, a larger world. For someone as shy as she, who resisted temptations to assume a public persona, this was what could be said, drawn, shared. I as a reader am left with an interior experience of an author and illustrator who has spoken intimately and given much.

Kate Greenaway's autobiography is indeed a frail vessel, a container in which she gathers her seeds, her flowers, her dreamy stuff, however disparate and disjointed. As Carol Shields writes in her novel *The Stone Diaries,* "Biography, even autobiography, is full of systematic error, of holes that connect like a tangle of underground streams" (196). Baskets in all of their brokenness are like that.

Works Cited

Coe, Richard N. *When the Grass Was Taller: Autobiography and the Experience of Childhood.* New Haven: Yale University Press, 1984.

Fisher, Elizabeth. *Woman's Creation: Sexual Evolution and the Shaping of Society.* Garden City: Anchor-Doubleday, 1979.

Greenaway, Kate. *Under the Window.* London: Routledge, 1879.

———. Unpublished holograph journal. The Frances Hooper Collection, Hunt Institute for Botanical Documentation, Carnegie-Mellon University, Pittsburgh, Pennsylvania.

Heilbrun, Carolyn. *Writing a Woman's Life.* New York: Ballantine, 1988.

Hyde, Lewis. *The Gift: Imagination and the Erotic Life of Property.* New York: Vintage, 1979.

Kiger, Robert, ed. *Kate Greenaway.* Pittsburgh: Hunt Institute for Botanical Documentation, Carnegie-Mellon University, 1980.

Le Guin, Ursula K. "The Carrier Bag Theory of Fiction." In *Dancing at the Edge of the World.* New York: Grove, 1989. Pp. 165–70.

Shields, Carol. *The Stone Diaries.* New York: Viking, 1993.

Smith, Sidone. *A Poetics of Women's Autobiography: Marginality and the Fictions of Self-Representation.* Bloomington: Indiana University Press, 1987.

Spielmann, M. H., and G. S. Layard. *Kate Greenaway.* London: Adam and Charles Black, 1905.

Losses and Gains in Translation: Some Remarks on the Translation of Humor in the Books of Aidan Chambers

Emer O'Sullivan
Translated from the German by Anthea Bell

"Every translation entails a loss by comparison with the original" (23), states Wolf Harranth, a well-known translator of books for children and young people. And there is much talk in translation studies of "translation problems" and "malfunctions" in literary translation that no translator can avoid.[1] In Erwin Koppen's opinion such "disturbance factors" (137) include, among other things, "the translation of wordplay and comparable examples of linguistic virtuosity" (138). We need not argue about losses in translation, but gains in translation are seldom mentioned. Can anything of the kind be found in an author such as Aidan Chambers, an expert in wordplay and linguistic virtuoso of the first rank? In this essay I shall argue that generally the translation of Chambers's work into German—when it is carried out by a translator with a high degree of stylistic awareness and creativity—does indeed represent a gain for that literature. On the level of individual texts and passages I would like to concentrate on the production of humor by different means and examine how it fares in translation.

Hal, the protagonist of the novel *Dance on My Grave* (1982), collects epitaphs, most of them funny. The wording on a postman's grave, "Not lost but gone before" (104), is rendered in German as "*Unbekannt verzogen*" (moved to an unknown address [the usual postal marking on mail that cannot be delivered]) (*Tanz* 116). Another epitaph runs:

> He had his beer from year to year
> And then his bier had him (117)

In this couplet the author is playing on the homophony of *beer* (German *Bier*) and *bier* (German *Totenbahre*). The grammatical relation be-

Originally published in the German language within "Hans-Heino Ewers (Editor), Komik in Kinderbuch" © 1992 Juventa Verlag, Weinheim and Munich.
Children's Literature 26, ed. Elizabeth Lennox Keyser (Yale University Press, © 1998 Hollins College).

tween man and [bi:r] changes. The man is the subject in the first line and the object in the second. In the German translation, these two lines become four:

Stets liebte er den Gerstensaft
Bis daß er ihn dahingerafft
Darum bedenke immerdar
Der Weg ist kurz vom Bier zur Bahr (*Tanz* 117)

(He always loved barley juice [= beer, a jocular usage], until it carried him off, so be ever mindful that the way is short from beer to bier.)

This translation conveys the idea behind the joke: an unexpected link between beer and death is established. An element of homophony is also retained in the German text. It comes in the word *Bahr* and refers us to the similarity of sound between *Bahr* as in *Bahre,* a means of carrying the dead, and *Bar,* a place to drink. All the humorous aspects of the source text have thus been successfully shifted to the target text. In addition, something extra has been added. In German, the epitaph adopts the elevated style of didactic verse *Darum bedenke immerdar* only to render it ludicrous with the wordplay of the final line. The moral tone of the warning against death from alcoholism is held up to ridicule with the linking of *Bier* and *Bar.* This additional comic dimension in the German epitaph is a gain in translation, and the appearance of rhymes in the couplets *Saft/gerafft, immerdar/zur Bahr* could also be chalked up as a gain.

We are more inclined to speak of losses than gains in translation; it has something to do with the perspective of comparison. If we read a text first in its original language and then in the language of translation, we risk setting out to hunt for "errors of translation," concentrating on the passages in the translation that represent problems in the form of cultural references, wordplay, and so on. The question about the "failed" passages is then: How far is the individual translator responsible for the failure, and how far is the passage so firmly rooted in its source language and culture that an adequate translation is hardly possible? Using translations of books by Aidan Chambers as examples, I would like to ask to what extent losses in the translation of humor are inevitable and how far gains are feasible. I shall be concentrating on the production of comic effect by use of the graphic dimension of the text, by incongruity between the narrative form and the content, and by wordplay.

Chambers as Author and Critic

The books of Aidan Chambers are particularly suitable for a survey of this kind because of both their textual nature and the theoretical positions adopted by the author. Chambers, formerly a teacher of English and drama and co-founder of a modern Anglican monastery, has been a professional author since 1968. He writes children's plays, short stories, and novels for children and adolescents, is editor or co-editor of various series of books for children and young people, and since 1990 has also been a publisher,[2] concentrating on a field that is rather underdeveloped in the children's literature market of the English-speaking world: translations from other languages. As a critic of literature for children and young people, he received the first annual award for excellence in criticism of the Children's Literature Association for his article "The Reader in the Book."[3] His books have been translated into eight different languages; they are translated into German by Cornelia Holfelder-von der Tann and Karl-Heinz Dürr, among others.[4]

The characteristic feature of his books is his outstanding awareness of linguistic possibilities. To take a small example, there is the name of the protagonist Nik in the book *Now I Know* (1987), translated into German by Karl-Heinz Dürr as *Die unglaubliche Geschichte des Nik Frome* (The Incredible Story of Nik Frome). The letters N - I - K are the initial letters of the words *Now I Know,* making an acronym of a boy's name. Much more important than this formal bit of wordplay in the title, however, is the set of associations shown in figure 1, all of them set off by [nik].

In a book concerned with religious ideas and the explanation of a putative criminal act of crucifixion, the associations of [nik] with prison, arrest, and the devil can be related directly to these themes. The play on words is a play on meaning too. Chambers's books are full of wordplay and employ extremely diverse levels of style and tone. He is constantly making it clear to readers that they are reading a book with a distinctive linguistic structure. On language in the novel he writes, "Whether you . . . want to write in such a way that the reader feels s/he can reach through the book like reaching through a window and touch what is on the other side . . . or whether you are like James Joyce, who clearly wanted his readers to feel the weight and quality of his language on the page, you cannot escape language either as an author or as a reader" (*Booktalk* 18).

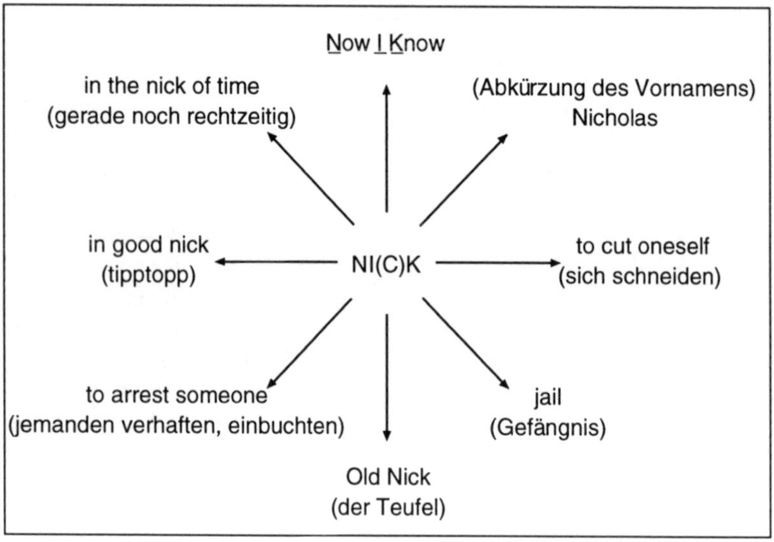

Figure 1. English-language associations of [nik]. From Chambers, *Now I Know.*

Chambers sees himself in the tradition of Joyce. To him, the marks of quality in literary works are a multiplicity of layers, a wealth of subjects, awareness of language, and density (cf. *Booktalk* 19). Language and its part in shaping identity often become the actual subject. The position he takes up leads him to the frequent use of literary references. James Joyce, Kurt Vonnegut, and Flann O'Brien are among the authors he quotes most frequently. He is interested in the various possible ways of telling a story available to an author, and he wishes to make readers of his four novels for young adults[5] aware of this narrative procedure by assembling collages of narrative styles and methods: the books contain texts in the shape of letters, tape recordings, first-person and third-person narratives, newspaper cuttings, cartoons, footnotes, diary entries, graffiti, scenes in dramatic form, internal monologue, film sequences, texts using the slow-motion technique, and so on. In his critical works Chambers has adopted Wolfgang Iser's theories of reception aesthetics. He knows what he is asking of readers, who must not just reconstitute the meaning of his novels but also, for instance, simply get a grasp of the chronology of a story.

All of these qualities in Chambers's prose make life difficult for a translator. But they are an excellent point of departure if you want to discover what happens to humorous passages that are difficult to translate as they move into German.

Humor I: Use of the Graphic Dimension of the Text

The graphic design of the text is very important to Chambers. He has described a book as a "time-space machine: a three-dimensional object that has shape, weight, texture, smell, even taste" (*Booktalk* 10). When humor is produced by the graphic design of the text, translation can range from easy to extremely difficult. A black page[6] such as the one Chambers inserts into *Breaktime,* when Ditto the narrator is knocked unconscious, is of course a black page in the German translation, too. This nonlinguistic element in the text presents no translation problems; the original page is used.

Another page in this book is also taken straight from the English original, but this time there is a loss. Ditto, the protagonist, is at a party political meeting to which an important guest speaker has been invited. Ditto is drunk, and consequently his account of the remarks of the man introducing the speaker runs: "Government people solidarity people people party people policy party left people party-strugglesocialistwelcome" (69). Thereupon the speaker begins to hold forth "with elegant precision." In both the original and the translation, this passage comes at the bottom of a right-hand page. The reader turns the page and sees the illustration shown in figure 2.

The speaker's head and his eloquent remarks are filled in with the letter *Z.* This drawing occupies a whole page, and we are told at the top of the next page that the man then sits down. Instead of giving the content of the speech or describing Ditto's reaction to it, Chambers shows us Ditto's perception of a head droning on and on, letting a torrent of words gush out. This works well enough in the translated version too, but there is a loss, since the letter *Z* is used in English to symbolize snoring, something that will escape the German reader who has not picked up that use of the letter from reading English-language comics.[7]

If a comic effect is made by playing around with features of the grapheme system peculiar to the source language, translation is usually very difficult. At the very beginning of *The Present Takers* (1983) we find a reproduction of notes passed between eleven-year-old Lucy, who like many in the rest of the class is being bullied by Melanie

Figure 2. Graphic reproduction of a speech from the vantage point of the intoxicated protagonist. From Chambers, *Breaktime.*

Prosser, also aged eleven, and her secret admirer Angus, who wants to help her. One of the ways in which Angus's character is depicted is through his creative use of writing. He favors brevity, trying to say a lot as economically as possible. Angus likes using letters or figures where they can replace whole words. This particular kind of wordplay works well in English, because the language often has homonyms for the pronunciation of various letters of the alphabet. For instance, *A* can stand for *hay, B* for *bee, C* for *sea,* and so on. Something similar could be done in German with the German pronunciation of the letters *C* (*Zeh,* toe), *G* (*geh!,* go away!), *T* (*Tee,* tea), and *W* (*Weh,* grief, pain, woe)—even if the possibilities are much more limited in that language.[8] The pronunciation of the English numbers *1, 2, 3,* and *8* means that they too can be used in this way. In the original English, various notes written by Angus to Lucy look like this:

TODAY 1700 RAILWAY CROSSING
GOT PLAN 2 STOP PROSER [*sic*]
xxx Angus (18)

U R THE GREATEST (19)

WANT 2 TALK 2 U
No
Y
Stop sending stupid notes (75)

This is not the first time rendering the pronunciation of the name of the letter *Y*, which in English can serve as a graphic representation of the interrogative *why*, has presented translators with considerable difficulties.[9] In the German translation, these notes become:

HEUTE 17 UHR BAHNÜBERGANG
HABE PLAN UM PROSSER ZU STOPPEN
(Today 5 o'clock railway crossing
got plan to stop Prosser)
xxx Angus (*Melanie Prosser* 22)

DU BIST DIE GRÖSSTE (22)
(You are the greatest)

WILL MIT DIR REDEN
(Want to talk to you)
Nein (no)
YES (yes)
Hör mit den blöden Zetteln auf (92)
(Stop sending stupid notes)

The spelling mistake (Proser) of the original has been corrected here.[10] The figures and single letters have gone, but the three letters *x* for kisses remain, although they mean nothing in German. We can still gather from the translation what Angus and Lucy are saying to each other, but much else is lost. Angus's style shows a high degree of linguistic awareness in his relish for playing with words. At the same time, he can distance himself from the actual meanings in the language system of the expressions he uses. Angus would not have written, in so many words, "You are the greatest": that would have been a serious statement. By playing with words he can still make the statement, but without exposing himself so much. This important aspect of Angus's character, illustrated by his use of language, is lost in translation. It should really be retained in the translated version, either by having at least a few such instances of wordplay in the German, for instance an *8tung* (for *Achtung,* watch out, with a pun on *acht,* eight), or by finding some other linguistic level upon which Angus could be depicted. In general, however, it must be admitted that this is an area where translation is bound to risk losses in the transition between languages, particularly when the linguistic exploitation of graphic form is as intensive as in the following:

> W8 4 U RLY XING 1630 A xxx (*Present Takers* 28)

> WARTE AUF DICH AM BAHNÜBERGANG 16UHR30 Angus xxx (*Melanie Prosser* 160)

This is Angus's last note to Lucy, and in the original, abbreviation has gone so far that at first sight it can present even a native English speaker with problems.

Even in the area of textual design, a difficult one for the translator, gains can be made, however. In the novel *Breaktime* (1978) there is a scene in which Ditto, the protagonist, and Helen are making love out of doors. The narration of the scene is unusual. Three texts interact on the same page: on the left, every alternate line describes what is going on physically from Ditto's point of view. Simultaneously, we get his internal monologue, the voice inside his head, which is set in italics between the lines of the first account. Parallel to these, on the right-hand side of the page, is a text from Benjamin Spock's *A Young Person's Guide to Life and Love.* This text begins by saying that "there is not much point in trying to describe lovemaking," since "it is experienced as a matter of emotion and relationship more than action" (122). Spock, however, then proceeds to quite a detailed description. Three reading processes are involved in the understanding of this passage. The humor lies in the fact that the erotic scene becomes less erotic at each reading, since the reader's attention is diverted from the act itself to the perception of the act and the reading of the description. The gain in translation in the German version here is not linguistic but a matter of printing technology, with a different color—purple!—being used for the text describing the physical course of events (cf. *Fingerspitzengefühle,* 137ff.). This gives greater visual emphasis to the division between the two forms of narrative and perception and focuses attention more strongly on the text as a text, entirely in line with Chambers's intention.

Humor II: Incongruity Between Narrative Form and Content

Where does the humor lie when a literary text takes another text as its model, adopting its stylistic features intertextually, but not aiming for parody, with that genre's disjunction of form and content? In *Breaktime* Ditto masturbates while looking at a photograph of a girl. This scene is written in the stream-of-consciousness style, unpunctuated, just like its model, the final Molly Bloom chapter of James Joyce's *Ulysses.* After this passage the style changes completely, sobering down. Ditto, the fictional author of the whole thing, stands back from himself, writing in a cool, distanced manner, employing the style of an American crime novel by way of contrast to the preceding verbal orgasm. Chambers chooses, from the available repertory of literary styles, one suitable for the time before, during, and directly after orgasm. The humor in the allusion to the Molly Bloom model depends not least on the history of the reception of *Ulysses.* When the book first appeared, this episode, inventing its own narrative technique, was considered shocking and pornographic. *Ulysses* was banned; today it is revered as a great work of literature. When Ditto indirectly quotes Joyce's Molly, he is quoting a now-respectable literary form for the description of sexual acts. But what is Chambers actually describing? A boy masturbating; it is a photograph that sets off his fantasies, but it might just as well have been a picture in a porn magazine. In describing his "dirty" action in a now-accepted narrative form, the boy is trying to give it the gloss of great literature. The discrepancy that makes the passage humorous lies in this play between form and content, quotation and action. A passage such as this masturbation scene does not really present the translator with any serious difficulty. Once the literary reference in the original has been recognized, it should be possible to give a corresponding version in translation.

Another example of incongruity between form and content occurs in *Dance on My Grave.* Here Hal, a boy of sixteen, is standing in front of the bathroom mirror examining his body critically. As the mirror is not large enough to show more than half of him at once, Hal has to perform a rather risky balancing act on the narrow edge of the bathtub in order to inspect his nether regions:

> The problem I have with my knees is that they seem to be too far down my legs. This makes my thighs too long in proportion to the glutei of my nates which have always struck me as nicely shaped, neat and well set under iliac crests that might on some males certainly look too pronounced but on me seem just right. Of course, if your femoral quadriceps are well moulded and smoothly covered, a slight disproportion in their length doesn't matter, at least when viewed frontally. They can even show off your genitalic drapery to good effect. Providing you are flourishing in that feature and not recondite.
>
> I studied myself in that area from as many angles as my precarious platform would allow. On the whole, I decided, my genitalic modelling was passable, though I would have liked a bit more quantity as well as quality. But my rectus and lateralis were okay; the medialis were well developed but they gave too thin an appearance just above the knees, which I suppose exaggerates the boniness of my patellas and further pronounces the length of my thighs. (106)

This raises a smile from the English-speaking reader, not just because of the comic situation of the boy balancing on the bathtub and finally, of course, falling off, but also through the use of medical terminology employing the tone and vocabulary of an anatomy lesson. The boy describes his body with great detachment, as if it were lying on a dissecting table in front of him. The comic incongruity lies in the discrepancy between subject and narrative style. This incongruity is not the only humorous element: readers must also guess what parts of the body are being referred to in the rather abstruse technical terms, which set up an obstacle to understanding at the thrilling moment when Ditto is describing the "most interesting" parts of his body.

This effect is reproduced only partially in the German translation. In the first paragraph, the three anatomical terms are not given their full Latin names (*femoral quadriceps* becomes simply *Quadriceps*). The Latinate adjective *recondite,* unusual in colloquial English speech, is not translated in a way that makes understanding more difficult either, so the translation is not really a functional equivalent. The second paragraph works better; three of the four medical terms are left in their Latin forms:

> Mein Problem mit meinen Knien besteht darin, dass ich finde, sie sitzen zu weit unten. Dadurch wirken meine Oberschenkel zu lang im Verhältnis zu meinen Gesässbacken (buttocks), die ich schon immer als überaus wohlgeformt, proper und im wohlausgewogenen Verhältnis zu meinen für manchen anderen Mann vielleicht zu ausgeprägten, an mir jedoch gerade richtigen Hüften (hips) empfunden habe. Bein einem wohlgestalteten und glatt gepolsterten Quadriceps fällt eine leicht unproportionale Überlänge natürlich nicht so ins Gewicht, zumindest nicht von vorn gesehen. Dann kann sie im Gegenteil sogar die Genitalausstattung besonders gut zur Wirkung bringen, vorausgesetzt natürlich, dies kann sich sehen lassen (providing, of course, it is worth seeing).
>
> Ich musterte diese Region meines Körpers unter so vielen verschiedenen Blickwinkeln, wie mein prekärer Standort nur zuliess. Im grossen und ganzen, befand ich, war mein genitales Erscheinungsbild ganz passabel, obglech ich neben der Qualität ein bisschen mehr Quantität nicht verächtet hätte. Aber alle Muskeln vom Rektus über den Lateralis bis zum Medialis waren gut entwickelt, liessen meine Beine jedoch gerade über dem Knie etwas zu dünn wirken, was wohl die Knochigkeit meiner Kniescheiben (kneecaps) und die Länge meiner Oberschenkel noch deutlicher hervorhob. (*Tanz,* 119 f.)

Humor III: Wordplay

In the opinion of Hans Grassegger, "translation may be considered successful if a passage of wordplay in the source language is rendered in the target language at all, even with another type of wordplay. The invariant in such a version is . . . not the specific form or content, but the *idea of wordplay,* and in rendering it one must often be satisfied with a translation which is only an equivalent" (100, emphasis in original). Translation of wordplay is easiest when a joke in the source text is marked out as a joke and integrated with the text as little as possible. An example of the successful translation of a joke occurs in *Fingerspitzengefühle* (the translation of *Breaktime*). It comes as comic relief in the middle of the description of a break-in. Ditto has been persuaded to join in a burglary. In the description, a joke is inserted, set in italics and visually separated from the rest of the narrative. In the original English it runs, " 'Nobody ever pinches me,' said the burglar's wife to her husband" (89). This would be thought of as a typical music-hall joke in English, involving ambiguity and sexual innuendo. It depends on the two meanings of *pinch,* one literal, the other a colloquial term for "*to steal.*" In Cornelia Holfelder-von der Tann's German translation, the joke runs: " '*An meinem Schätzkämmerchen wird nicht gefummelt,' sagte die Frau des Einbrechers zu ihrem Mann*" ("Nobody fumbles with my little treasury," said the burglar's wife to her husband) (101). The situation is the same, but the joke has not been literally translated. Instead, its function has been recognized—it is an allusion to both the man's profession and his lack of sexual prowess—and rendered with a German equivalent.

Translators do not always find good functional equivalents. At the end of *The Present Takers,* the whole class, aiming to defeat Melanie by means other than her own weapons of violence and blackmail, that is, by means of language, produces a wall newspaper about her misdeeds that contains the following joke:

> Q: What did one bully say to the other bully?
> A: I get a kick out of you. (120)

This joke cannot be translated entirely out of context; it must relate in some way to violence or blackmail. The original depends on the double meaning of the verb *to kick* and the expression "*to get a kick out of something,*" that is, to enjoy it. But since it stands alone, without much in the way of verbal context that must be included, the translator is free to use some other joke on the subject with a double meaning alluding to sadism and, if possible, constructed on the question-and-answer pattern. The German translation of the joke runs:

> *Frage: Was sagt ein Erpresser zum anderen?* (What does one blackmailer say to another?)
> *Antwort: Du machst mir Spass.* (lit., You give me fun)
> (*Melanie Prosser* 149)

Here only the form and context of the joke are reproduced, along with a rendering of only one of the two meanings of *kick* from the original wording. We no longer have a functional German equivalent, however, since there is no real joke any more.[11] In the text itself, this joke has a heading explicitly labeling it as such (and the heading is translated into German too), but the actual joke is lost. This and other examples from *Wer stoppt Melanie Prosser* have to be attributed to the translator's weakness rather than to any insurmountable linguistic obstacle posed by their translation.

As a rule, passages of wordplay are considered nearly impossible to translate because the constituent words, usually homonyms, are just not there in the target language.[12] The degree of translatability depends on various factors, not least on how firmly the references of the wordplay are rooted in the context of the narrative. What can a translator do? A functional equivalent is usually the best that can be provided. Wordplay is not translated literally, but its function is retained with the means at the disposal of the target language. There is a successful example in the German translation of *Breaktime:* Ditto is talking to his friend Morgan. The conversation is notable for its quick repartee, for the associative leaps from subject to subject, and particularly for its playing on words and ideas. The subjects are literature as such and Maureen Pinfold, in whom Morgan is interested. The conversation is a verbal and intellectual game of ping-pong, winning points being acknowledged with a smile or even laughter. Morgan, who thinks literature is "crap . . . A pretence. Ersatz," proposes to draw up charges against it:

> "I'll jot down my Charges Against Literature—I mean fiction—and serve them on you at lunch."
> "A subpoena I'll enjoy discharging," Ditto said. "But why bother? Just tell me."
> "Innocent!" Morgan said. "My Charges will give me just the excuse I need to trap Maureen Pinfold behind her typewriter in the commercial room. While she does me the favour of typing my Charges, I'll prepare the patient for dissection."
> "If this was a story," Ditto said, "you'd call that typecasting."
> Morgan laughed.
> "Thanks for the compliment," said Ditto, and left. (8 f.)

The problem of translation lies in the word *typecasting*. It plays on the fact that Maureen Pinfold can type. The concept of typecasting is from the world of theater and cinema, and to that extent it relates to the subject of fiction, which is under discussion. Furthermore, the word implies a comment on cliché-ridden attitudes toward the opposite sex. The word *typecasting* plays with many possible meanings. A literal translation would render only one of them. What does the German translation do?

> "Ich werde eine Anklageschrift gegen die Literatur genauer gesagt gegen die schöngeistige Literatur verfassen and sie dir zum Mittagessen servieren."
> "Es wird mir ein Vergnügen sein, deiner Vorladung Folge zu leisten," sagte Ditto. "Aber warum dieser Umstand? Erzähl's mir doch lieber."
> "Da zeigt sich mal wieder deine Naivität," sagte Morgan. "Mit der Anklageschrift habe ich genau den richtigen Vorwand, um unsere angehende Sekretärin Maureen Pinfold zu treffen. Sie wird mir den Gefallen tun und meine Anklageschrift tippen, und ich werde die Gelegenheit nutzen, um die Patientin für die Operation vorzubereiten."
> "Schliess lieber vorher eine Haftpflichtversicherung ab," sagte Ditto, "für den Fall, dass dir ein Kunstfehler unterläuft."
> ("Better take out liability insurance first," said Ditto, "in case you commit malpractice.")
> Morgan lachte.
> "Danke für die Blumen," sagte Ditto und ging hinaus.
> (*Fingerspitzengefühle* 8 f.)

Here the translator has recognized that the German semantic field surrounding the verb *tippen* (to type) is not a productive one for this passage of wordplay. She turns instead to the semantic field surrounding the word *Operation,* also present in the original English with the words *patient* and *dissection,* and uses the associations of medicine to get a functionally equivalent allusion referring both to Morgan's designs on Maureen and to literature (*Kunstfehler*). (This German word means literally "*a mistake in art,*" but its usual meaning is "*medical malpractice*").

One of the possible ways for translators to approach passages of wordplay that cannot be directly translated is by metalinguistic methods, including footnotes and other annotations. Such methods are not often used, however, and their legitimacy is disputed in translation theory of the prescriptive type. Another possibility is not to translate at all, that is, simply to omit. This is done if the linguistic or cultural reference of the allusion is so specific that translation would be impossible without lengthy metalinguistic explanation. In *Now I*

Know, Nik spends some time in a modern Anglican monastery. He describes the course of the day—the various church services, activities, and so on—in a letter to his friend Julie. In one passage we read: "The monks included your name in the list of people they prayed for after Compline. (I always thought Compline was that milk powder stuff they give geriatrics who can't eat proper food. Maybe it's spelt differently?)" (141). The allusion is to the brand name of the powdered drink Complan, which is not actually mentioned because the similarity of sound will lead readers to work it out for themselves. The probability of there being a drink for geriatric patients the name of which sounds like the name of the last divine service of the day in another linguistic and cultural area is not very great. Comparison shows that the play on "Compline" is omitted from the translation, but we have to ask how important the loss is. Was any information conveyed at this point in the original that was crucial to the understanding of this passage or the whole book, or does the allusion tell us something about Nik we would not otherwise know? The answer has to be no: the information is incidental and leads nowhere, and there is plenty of other evidence in the book that Nik likes wit and wordplay. The absence of this play on words from the German translation is a loss, but a minor one, and necessary here if the alternative would have been an extensive metalinguistic commentary on the drink Complan, breaking the flow of the translated text with painstaking detail or obscurity.

Since in most cases wordplay in the source language cannot be translated straight into the target language, the translator must try either switching to a form more suitable to the target language or finding some other fitting kind of vocabulary within the same form. This happens, for instance, in the novel *Dance on My Grave,* in which the protagonist Hal has recently moved to the English seaside resort of Southend. At the beginning of the book he writes, "I was still not used to a town whose trade was trippers" (9), that is, people on a day's outing. After seeing all the half-naked bodies on the beach, he modifies this to "I could not get used to a town whose trade was strippers." The specific form of the wordplay is retained in the German translation, where we read first "Noch immer konnte ich mich nicht recht daran gewöhnen, in einer Stadt zu wohnen, die von ihrer anziehender Wirkung auf Touristen lebte" (". . . which lived by its attractive effect on tourists") (*Tanz* 9). In the version emended by Hal, this becomes "Ich konnte mich nicht daran gewöhnen, in einer Stadt zu wohnen, die von ihrer ausziehenden Wirkung auf Touristen lebte" (9f.), ". . . which lived by its undressing effect on tourists"). The German play on words is with *anziehend* (attractive), from the present participle of the verb *anziehen,* which has various meanings but primarily means "to put on" clothes, and *ausziehend,* present participle of the verb *ausziehen,* "to take off" clothes. The translator has not tried playing on the German equivalent of the noun *trippers.* Instead, while retaining the form of the wordplay, she has used an element in the German language that offers good potential for the construction of wordplay: separable verbs. In the original text, the change of meaning is effected by the addition of a letter to the beginning of the noun; in German translation it is done by changing the verbal prefix (using *ausziehen* to replace *anziehen*).

Specific cultural differences in the vocabulary of "bad language" can sometimes cause translation problems. The function of swearing in relieving feelings and shocking hearers is explained by its reference to subjects traditionally taboo in the culture concerned. In the Anglo-Saxon context these are religion and sexual intercourse; in Germany it is the anal area. In general, the translation of bad language is not much of a problem, since the translator does not translate literally but seeks for some functional equivalent in the linguistic and cultural context of the target language. Such words are relevant not for their meaning but merely for the linguistic function of swearing. Translation does become difficult, however, if there are allusions involving actual meaning.

In *Now I Know* a young policeman is talking to an older sergeant. The younger officer has just taken on a case in which someone has allegedly been crucified, although there is no trace of the victim. Part of the dialogue runs as follows:

> "Where is he now?"
> "There you have me."
> "Sorry?"
> "Gone."
> "Gone!"
> "Vamoosed."
> "How come?"
> "You're the one playing detective."
> "This kid was hanging there and we lost him?"
> "Quick on the uptake, I'll grant you that."

"Jeez!"
"Could be him you're after." (11)

The curse is uttered without thinking; taken literally it has a comic effect because it is both unexpected and really means something. The parallels with the Passion of Jesus Christ are no coincidence. The comic effect is possible, however, only because "Jeez!" is an everyday bit of bad language which can be spoken and read without meaning anything at all. In the German translation, "Jeez" is translated by "Jesus."

"Wo ist er jetzt?"
"Weiss nicht."
"Bitte?"
"Verschwunden."
"Verschwunden?"
"Verduftet."
"Wie denn?"
"Ich denke, *du* spielst den Detektiv?"
"Der Junge hat da dran gehangen und ist uns entwischt?"
"Schnellmerker."
"Jesus!"
"Könnt schon sein, dass du hinter dem her bist." (*Nik Frome* 14)

The referential level is retained here, but as "Jesus!" is not a very usual curse in German, the word draws attention to its real meaning from the start, thus detracting a good deal from the comic effect.

This essay cannot enumerate all the possible ways in which Chambers creates humorous effects in his work or comment on their various translations. Using selected areas—the use of the graphic dimension of the text, incongruity between narrative form and content, and wordplay—I have tried to give examples of successful translations and translations that are less successful. Analysis of the translation of humor should not just reckon up the losses and gains made in the translation process; it should also do justice to what may be expected of a good translation—the finding of functional equivalents. The higher the degree of specific cultural and linguistic factors involved in humor, the more difficult it is to translate. In achieving humor, particularly verbal humor, the translator is called upon to reconstruct the stylistic effect of wordplay. But the crucial thing is to retain the play of ideas.

I began with a quotation stating that "every translation entails a loss by comparison with the original." By way of contrast, however, I would like to claim that every successful translation of an innovative author who has a high degree of linguistic and stylistic awareness entails a gain for the literature of the language into which it is translated.

Notes

Author's Note: This essay was originally presented by the author, an Irishwoman, as a conference paper in German and subsequently published in that language as "Transportverluste—Transportgewinne: Anmerkungen zur Übersetzung von Komik im Werk Aidan Chambers'," in *Komik im Kinderbuch: Erscheinungsformen des Komischen in der Kinder- und Jugendliteratur,* ed. Hans-Heino Ewers (Weinheim: Juventa, 1992), 201–21. It was reprinted in the Frankfurt University journal *Forschung Frankfurt* 4 (1993). I sent a copy to Aidan Chambers, knowing that he does not read German but is most interested in aspects of translation. His wife Nancy (editor of the journal *Signal*) then approached the distinguished British translator Anthea Bell and arranged to have the article translated into English as a surprise for Aidan's sixtieth birthday.

What emerged is unusual: questions of translation from English into German are discussed, but because the German "solutions" themselves are rendered back into English, monolingual scholars who otherwise have no knowledge of or access to the kinds of things that happen during the translation process can get an idea of the issues at stake.

Anthea Bell is one of the most acclaimed contempory translators of children's literature into English. In her twenty-five-year career she has translated some two hundred titles for adults and for children, mainly from German and French. Among them are almost all the works of Otfried Preussler, more than a dozen titles by Christine Nöstlinger, and classic texts by the brothers Grimm and E. T. A. Hoffmann, as well as the entire *Asterix the Gaul* comic strip saga (in collaboration with Derek Hockridge).

Translator's Note: Since Dr. O'Sullivan's arguments deal with German renderings, I have given the German passages quoted, with a literal translation of her examples back into English where necessary, and any extra information required to explain her points to readers with no German. In longer passages, I have translated back *only* those words representing a significant departure from the original English. The rest closely follows the original wording. Any additions of mine are in brackets. Quotations from critics who originally wrote in German—Harranth, Koppen, Grassegger, and Levy—have been translated into English for the purpose of this essay.

1. Or so, anyway, say traditional translation studies, which adopt the "prescriptive and production oriented" line, attempting to convey "the rules and principles of good, correct translation" (Frank ix) governed by the question of how one should or must translate. This kind of problem-oriented approach is absent from more recent translation studies of the historical and descriptive variety, where the emphasis is on the product rather than the process. A brief account of the differences between these tendencies may be found in Frank. This essay will touch only briefly on theoretical aspects of translation. There is a more extensive account of the specific nature of translated literature for young people in O'Sullivan 1991/92.

2. The firm of Turton & Chambers is named after him and his Australian partner.

3. The article is reprinted in *Booktalk.*

4. Compare bibliographical details in the notes to this essay.

5. They are *Breaktime, Dance on My Grave, Now I Know,* and *The Tollbridge,* the last published in 1992 and hence not considered in this essay. It was, happily, translated by the most competent and creative of his German translators, Cornelia Holfelder-von der Tann, and published under the title *Die Brücke.*

6. This is a literary reference to Laurence Sterne's *Tristram Shandy.*

7. There is no German letter to indicate snoring.

8. The German language is not rich in homonyms or synonyms.

9. In the Walt Disney animated cartoon of *Alice in Wonderland* the smoke of the caterpillar's hookah keeps changing into pictures or symbols connected with what the creature is saying. When it asks "Why?" the smoke forms the shape of the letter *Y.* The image in the film cannot be changed, so at this point in the dubbed German version of the film the caterpillar says "Ypsilon," the German pronunciation of the name of the letter *Y,* which of course makes no sense at all.

10. Spelling is not Angus's strong point, and in the original he got Melanie's surname wrong. Other spelling mistakes, such as "confidenshal," slightly reminiscent of Richmal Crompton's *William,* are simply corrected in translation and given their proper form in German.

11. Something might have been tried along the lines of "Hier kommt der letzte Schrei" (literally, "Here comes the last scream," but colloquially, "Here's the latest fashion").

12. Because of its wealth of homonyms and synonyms, English offers very good opportunities for wordplay. These are among the "particularly favourable preconditions for certain artistic methods" that languages can often develop "because of their structural characteristics" (Levy 39). The problems of translation are correspondingly great when the target language does not possess these characteristics to the same degree.

Works Cited

Chambers, Aidan. *Booktalk: Occasional Writing on Literature and Children.* London: Bodley Head, 1985.

———. *Breaktime.* London: Bodley Head, 1978.

———. *Fingerspitzengefühle.* Trans. Cornelia Holfelder-von der Tann. Reinbek: Rowohlt, 1981.

———. *Dance on My Grave.* London: Bodley Head, 1982.

———. *Tanz auf meinem Grab.* Trans. Cornelia Holfelder-von der Tann. Würzburg: Arena, 1984.

———. *Now I Know.* London: Bodley Head, 1987.

———. *Die unglaubliche Geschichte des Nik Frome.* Trans. Karl-Heinz Dürr. Ravensburg: Maier, 1990.

———. *The Present Takers.* London: Bodley Head, 1983.

———. *Wer stoppt Melanie Prosser.* Trans. Hans J. Schütz. Würzburg: Arena, 1984 (= Chambers 1984a).

———. *The Tollbridge.* London: Bodley Head, 1992.

———. *Die Brücke.* Trans. Cornelia Holfelder-von der Tann. Ravensburg: Maier, 1994.

Frank, Armin Paul. "Einleitung." In *Die literarische Übersetzung: Stand und Perspektiven ihrer Erforschung,* ed. Harald Kittel. Berlin: Erich Schmidt, 1988. Pp. ix–xiii.

Grassegger, Hans. *Sprachspiel und Übersetzung: Eine Studie anhand der Comic-Serie Asterix.* Tübingen: Stauffenburg, 1985.

Harranth, Wolf. "Das Übersetzen von Kinder- und Jugendliteratur." *JuLit Information* no. 1 (1991):23–27.

Koppen, Erwin. "Die literarische Übersetzung." In *Vergleichende Literaturwissenschaft: Theorie und Praxis,* ed. Manfred Schmeling. Wiesbaden: Athenaion, 1981. Pp. 125–56.
Levy, Jurí. *Die literarische Übersetzung: Theorie einer Kunstgattung.* Frankfurt am Main/ Bonn: Athenäum, 1969.
O'Sullivan, Emer. "Kinderliterarisches Übersetzen." *Fundevogel* no. 93/94 (1991/92): 4–9.

Reviews

Talking About Children's Literature Criticism

Ledia Dittberner
Ian Wojcik-Andrews

Children's Literature and Critical Theory: Reading and Writing for Understanding, by Jill P. May. New York: Oxford University Press, 1995.

The Nimble Reader: Literary Theory and Children's Literature, by Roderick McGillis. London: Twayne, 1996.

Children's Literature Comes of Age: Toward a New Aesthetic, by Maria Nikolajeva. New York: Garland, 1996. Children's Literature and Culture, ed. Jack Zipes.

Teachers, students, and librarians within the worldwide children's literature community cannot fail to have heard about Peter Hunt's *Literature for Children: Contemporary Criticism* (1992), Eric Smoodin's *Disney Discourse: Producing the Magic Kingdom* (1994), or Lois Kuznet's *When Toys Come Alive: Narratives of Animation, Metamorphosis, and Development* (1994), important books that challenge how we interpret the various forms of children's culture. These insightful books, and others like them, are not the only place, of course, where serious discussions about the often contentious relationship between, for example, children's literature and literary criticism occur. In classrooms, in leading journals such as *Children's Literature,* the *Children's Literature Association Quarterly, Children's Literature in Education, The Lion and the Unicorn,* the *Journal of African Children's and Youth Literature,* and at the local, national (MLA), and international (IRSCL) conferences, members of the children's literature community debate the function of children's literature and literary criticism. Jill May, Rod McGillis, and Maria Nikolajeva have been involved in this global discussion, more

Children's Literature 26, ed. Elizabeth Lennox Keyser (Yale University Press, © 1998 Hollins College).

or less, since the beginning; unsurprisingly, their books are well-organized, scholarly, readable, and personable. Using first- and third-person voices, each writer appears to speak directly to an individual reader and to a "community of readers" (May 173). Noting that "critical readers make the best elementary school teachers, parents, citizens, and friends" (ix), May says that the purpose of her *Children's Literature and Critical Theory: Reading and Writing for Understanding* is "to encourage sensitivity to critical theory and to shape real readers into critical readers" (ix). McGillis, in *The Nimble Reader: Literary Theory and Children's Literature,* looks at how different literary theories might be used for reading children's literature texts and for teaching children to become competent, insightful readers. Less directly concerned with the application of literary theory as a pedagogical tool for improving "early literacy" (May viii), Nikolajeva, in *Children's Literature Comes of Age: Toward a New Aesthetic,* examines children's literature from semiotic, intertextual, and metafictional points of view.

May's book addresses issues and questions not easily answered. For example, in Chapter Two, "Literary Criticism and Children's Literature," May argues that both teachers and students should study and know literary criticism in detail. And, "since children cannot become pleasure readers unless they are encouraged to hear the writer out . . . they must have teachers who will show them that a story can have more than one meaning, encourage them to pursue the meaning in the text for themselves, and convince them that it is not always easy to find a personal interpretation for a piece of writing, but is enlightening and invigorating" (16). Teachers knowledgeable about critical theory are thus equipped to show and tell young readers that uncovering the multiplicity of meanings within stories can be both intellectually and emotionally satisfying—an important point children's educators the world over need to hear repeatedly. But what *are* the implications of having teachers and students talk knowledgeably about the way modern critical theory can open up otherwise closed texts for discussion, interpretation, and, from the student's point of view, self-reflection? First, looking at children's literature (and literature in general) from a variety of critical points of view surely democratizes literary studies, revealing that no one single reading or meaning is right and that each student's interpretation of a text (theoretically at least) is as valid as any other, including that of the teacher. Second, children taught to read literary texts critically can also be taught to read political texts critically. The child taught to resist the authority of the literary text can also be taught to resist the authority of the political text. In short, advocating the deconstruction of children's literature through a multiplicity of critical viewpoints has both aesthetic and political implications that surely require discussion not just in classrooms and journals but in bulletin boards around the worldwide web.

May's focus, of course, is education, not politics. Accordingly, her book includes nine chapters on subjects ranging from myth criticism (22) to the racist depiction of Native American history in outdated textbooks and historical fictions by white writers (67) and also a generous helping of student papers that demonstrate how the proper critical tools can empower students to extract levels of meaning that reflect and address the intellectual and emotional issues in their own lives. For example, at the end of Chapter Four, "Rhetorical Style in Children's Literature," May includes Debbie Brunke's "Understanding the Hidden Secrets in Literature." Brunke's student essay concerns Sulamith Ish-Kishor's *A Boy of Old Prague* and Isaac Bashevis Singer's *When Schlemiel Went to Warsaw.* May's ability to show "real readers" how to develop into "critical readers" obviously works. At the end of her essay Brunke writes, "If a child understands that these two Jewish authors have approached their cultural heritage in very different ways, he will see that each author believes that stories hold different things" (quoted in May 86). The struggle toward tolerance and diversity lives on in the hearts and minds of our students—pretty much where it should be.

Declaring himself "fundamentally a formalist" (vii), McGillis nonetheless offers readers with little or no critical background a practical means by which the various critical models that constitute modern literary theory can be used to teach children how to read imaginatively and effectively. What's nice about McGillis's book is that in a clear, persuasive style he makes modern critical theory intelligible for lay readers concerned to prevent what he calls the "debasement of language" (206). Indeed, like May, McGillis argues that interpretation for young readers can be both enlightening and rewarding: Interpretations 'R Us! Thus McGillis hopes that "mothers and fathers, as well as professional academics and researchers, [will] want to know more about the . . . literature children receive either directly or through the mediation of adult readers" (3). If indeed literature has the power to form a reader's social and political values and ideologies it is worthwhile understanding and considering precisely how the literature itself works to shape the reader. McGillis's concern is one of interpretation—and what is more important, the child's interpretation—thus maintaining what Peter Hunt refers to as the "childist" approach. In order to illustrate that interpretations can vary from reader to reader, McGillis offers several readings of the nursery rhyme "Jack Be Nimble." Each interpretation is dependent on what the child reader, or the adult reading to the child, brings to the text. This becomes evident as he investigates the extensions and rewritings of literature by children who change and extend familiar texts in order to "play" with meaning.

McGillis bases his book on the premise that a reader "will employ methods of inquiry that might be 'extrinsic' or 'intrinsic'" (4). He explains that "most extrinsic approaches accept the idea that texts participate in the non-literary as well as the literary world: the text expresses cultural beliefs and emotional content beyond the control of the author" (21). Narrow in focus, the intrinsic approach accepts the idea that "language expresses reality [and] articulates fully and coherently an author's intention" (21). These textual and contextual methods of inquiry become important as we consider questions such as the one posed by McGillis in Chapter Five, "Class Action: Politics and Political Practice." McGillis asks: "How do we make certain that young readers do not unconsciously assimilate the messages encoded in . . . books?" (114). To answer this question, McGillis uses various critical theories—structuralism and postmodernism, for example—to read sections from Lewis Carroll's *Through the Looking-Glass.* In so doing, McGillis demonstrates that even the most apolitical of texts—in particular he looks at "The White Knight"—are often impregnated with subtle political messages, and that bringing to light and discussing with children what Fredric Jameson calls the "political unconscious" helps them to read the text (intrinsic) and also to see the connections between literary text and real world (extrinsic): children *can* become critical readers.

In each subsequent chapter of his book, McGillis focuses on a specific critical approach and integrates portions of children's literary texts in order to illustrate how critical theory can be used to enhance the child's literary experience. Although each chapter points to a particular critical theory, McGillis has added "enough cross-fertilization to indicate that few theoretic approaches are pure" (201). His blurring of critical interpretations reflects the way children extract various meanings from texts in order to make better sense of their world: children's literature, children's criticism, children's meanings.

Like May and McGillis, Nikolajeva is concerned with the relationship between literary criticism and children's literature. Unlike them, however, Nikolajeva eschews pedagogy. Her focus is on semiotics, intertextuality, and metafictionality. Chapter Three, for example, is titled "The History of Children's Literature from a Semiotic Perspective." Drawing on the "Russian semiotic school . . . presented in the works of Yuri Lotman" (61), Nikolajeva says that children's literature "will be viewed as a particular semiosphere" in which the presence "of a double code system consisting of a 'children's code' and an 'adult code'" (61) dynamically converges, diverges, and generally merges into all forces that shape mass culture, including children's culture, at any historical point. This dynamic quality means that although "children's literature can be viewed as a fixed, canonical art form" (61), it also continues to evolve. What Nikolejeva calls a "semiotics of culture" (61) allows us to understand how, for example, "many taboos that existed in children's literature during its early periods are today being withdrawn" (62). She stresses that the "involvement between center and periphery [the intersection of mainstream ideas with marginal ideas and the compromise therein generated] is not a mechanical oscillation back and forth" (64) but instead the result of what Ilya Prigogine call "bifurcation points" (66). After these bifurcation points have been reached, the evolution of children's literature and culture may take an "indefinite number of possible, unpredictable paths" (66). In short, thesis leads to antithesis leads to synthesis. The semiotics of culture is really the dialectics of historical materialism. Finally, Nikolajeva argues that the function of the "semiotically minded historian is to discover these bifurcation points" (67) so that we might know how and why children's literature evolves in the way it does.

Other chapters in Nikolajeva's book examine children's literature from intertextual and metafictional points of view. In the former, she argues that intertextuality is "one of the most prominent features of postmodern literature for adults . . . [and] children's literature" (186). In the latter, she argues that "because it interrogates our own existence, metafiction reflects the chaos and ambivalence of our life and the loss of absolute values and truths. Of all the polyphonic features in children's literature, metafiction is probably the most daring and disturbing, but it also takes the most radical step away from convention and didacticism" (206). Nikolajeva states that children's literature is "evolving towards complexity and sophistication" (207).

No single work of literary criticism can talk about all the issues that inform the study of modern children's literature. True, these books say a great deal. May's "conversation" (172) with the reader about how the ChLA in the 1970s and 1980s disseminated literary theory to the children's literature community is useful, enlightening, and sure to provoke further discussion. Still, teachers and students otherwise interested in May's notion of rhetorical style in children's literature should also read "Conclusion: Political Criticism," the last chapter of Terry Eagleton's *Literary Theory: An Introduction.* Though from different ends of the political spectrum, both May and Eagleton advocate what Eagleton calls "probably the oldest form of literary criticism in the world, known as rhetoric" (205). Those intrigued by Nikolajeva's intelligent yet problematic analysis of postmodernism and metafictionality should also read Geoff Moss's "Metafiction, Illustration, and the Poetics of Children's Literature," a witty, lucid, and thought-provoking essay reprinted in Peter Hunt's *Literature for Children: Contemporary Criticism.* Teachers curious about how class functions ideologically in children's literature should read vol. 17, no. 2 of *The Lion and the Unicorn* alongside McGillis's "Class Action: Political and Critical Practice." In short, educators the world over should read children's literature criticisms in dialogue with one another.

Works Cited

Eagleton, Terry. *Literary Theory: An Introduction.* Minneapolis: University of Minnesota Press, 1983.

Lion and the Unicorn 17, no. 2, ed. Jack Zipes and Louisa Smith. Maryland: Johns Hopkins University Press, 1993.

Moss, Geoff. "Metafiction, Illustration, and the Poetics of Children's Literature." In *Literature for Children: Contemporary Criticism,* ed. Peter Hunt. London: Routledge, 1992. Pp. 44–46.

History or Histories? World Literature for Children— Universal or Particular?

J. D. Stahl

Aspects and Issues in the History of Children's Literature, ed. Maria Nikolajeva. Contributions to the Study of World Literature 60. Westport, Conn.: Greenwood, 1995.

Is it possible to write a universal history of children's literature? Is it desirable to do so? Maria Nikolajeva, the editor of this collection of essays from the Ninth Congress of the International Research Society for Children's Literature, held in Salamanca, Spain, in 1989, regards this volume as a step toward "a comprehensive, universal, and non-biased History of World Children's Literature" (xi), which she sees as "one of the greatest challenges in our scholarship." The ambitious, encyclopedic, Enlightenment goal of a universal history might be regarded as the tantalizing Platonic ideal that lures some scholars of children's literature onward. As the rather vague title of this book suggests, however, this unifying ideal is opposed by the idiosyncratic particularity and diversity of the history of children's literature, which ought more accurately to be called *histories* of children's literatures. Indeed, one section of the volume, titled "Aspects of National Histories," includes a study by Kari Skjønsberg of the role of children's literature in Norway's struggle to become a separate nation from Sweden in the nineteenth century; an account of the evolution of theories of children's literature in the Netherlands from 1880 onward by Anne de Vries; a close feminist psychological reading by Rod McGillis of a nineteenth-century British moralistic tale (a Victorian retelling of "Little Red Riding Hood"); and a biographical study by Dennis Butts of the "almost subversive" undercurrents in the works of Barbara Hofland, the popular and conservative British author for children. These essays all provide valuable insights into their particular subjects, but if anything they tend to confirm the distinctive features of national children's literatures—all European, in this case. Nikolajeva recognizes that "examples from countries other than Western Europe and North America" (xi) are needed before drawing any sweeping conclusions.

Children's Literature 26, ed. Elizabeth Lennox Keyser (Yale University Press, © 1998 Hollins College).

Yet she and others represented in this volume can't always resist the temptation to universalize. Nikolajeva claims, in her introduction, that "children's literature has more or less gone through similar stages in all countries and language areas" (x). Zohar Shavit, in "The Historical Model of the Development of Children's Literature," argues for this Platonist position most rigorously. Her question, "Is it possible to claim a universal structure for the development of children's literature?" (27), is answered with a resounding affirmative: "Since the issue at stake is historical poetics, it is important to stress that the competence to make generalizations about culture, and to describe its dominant structures is at the heart of the matter. It is one of the most important obligations of historical poetics" (27). Thus, Shavit claims that historical poetics cannot exist if we cannot generalize about culture. That may be true, but it does not follow that our generalizations about culture are accurate or that they apply to all cultures. For Shavit, "it is the duty of historiography to explore the structural development of culture," which means organizing the phenomena that can be described structurally, not an "analysis and explanation of all details involved" (27). This emphasis on structural exploration risks excluding the very details that might challenge the resulting generalizations. Whereas Shavit names as fundamental to her claims about the ideological nature of children's literature the Puritans, the Jewish Enlightenment in Germany, and the Egyptian Enlightenment at the turn of the twentieth century, what is silently omitted from her (and Nikolajeva's) more comprehensive accounts is the vast range of cultures and nations ignored in this theoretical narrative. China, India, Japan, and the nations of Latin America do not figure; nor do, closer to the European tradition, Australia, New Zealand, or any of the nations of Africa, new or old. The complicated situation of children's literature in the "literary polysystem" of colonialism and postcolonial nations is not addressed, though this omission does not necessarily invalidate the theoretical model with which Shavit approaches her subject. Ironically, the concept of a literary polysystem would be particularly suitable for exploring the evolution of children's literatures in colonial and postcolonial contexts, but they are not addressed here. These exclusions encourage skepticism about the universality of the claims being made.

More persuasive and intriguing than the Platonic theoretical models with their comprehensive assertions are the Aristotelian thematic and comparative approaches represented in the sections titled "Influence and Interaction" and "Genres, Modes, Styles." Emer O'Sullivan rewardingly examines the complex interrelationships between images of Germany and Germans in British children's books and their dates of publication. Negative, positive, and neutral images of Germans fluctuate, in the children's books studied, in relation to the political and military conflicts between Britain and Germany. The two world wars largely determine the images of Germans in British children's books, generating both stereotypes and efforts to counteract them. Most interesting are the periodic swings in negative and positive portrayals, depending on the ways the political winds are blowing.

Reinbert Tabbert presents a memorable thesis in his analysis of picture books that embody national myths of place for the British, the French, and the Germans: the garden (in *Peter Rabbit*), the city (in *Babar*), and the forest (in *Häschenschule*). He identifies these as first books for each of their creators and argues perceptively for Christian symbolism in Beatrix Potter's illustrations, the ideal of "urbanity" in Jean de Brunhoff's stories, and the threat of the "alien" fox in Fritz Koch-Gotha and Albert Sixtus's story of discipline in a school for little rabbits in the forest. Significantly, he concludes his discussion with a brief examination of the responses of children to whom all three stories were read and shown. Tony Watkins discusses the role of landscape in English fantasy by placing the works of Kenneth Grahame, J. R. R. Tolkien, and Richard Adams in the contexts of nostalgia, heritage, and utopia. Dagmar Grenz seeks to differentiate what she calls "the novel of adolescence specific to young people" in Germany (what has come to be called the young adult novel in the United States and Canada) from novels about adolescence for adult readers and to make critical judgments about their relative literary merit and degree of innovation. She presents a discriminating survey and assessment of contemporary German young adult novels, concluding that "the contemporary novel of adolescence for young people [in Germany] usually achieves only the rank of high-quality light fiction" (180). Maria Lypp provides a historical perspective on the evolution of humor in children's literature by comparing its function in the sixteenth and the nineteenth centuries to the function of humor today. She argues that "contemporary humor often lacks surfaces of friction" because "in liberal education all authority has withered, and there is no binding educational canon that can be parodied" (189), unlike the late Middle Ages and the Reformation, when Grobian, for example, "the archetypal negative hero of children's literature" and a forerunner of Max and Moritz and of Struwwelpeter, represented comic revolt against the teaching of good manners.

These scholars' essays all reinforce the particularity of national children's literature histories, despite important cross-influences and broad parallels among cultures. The volume provides an invaluable international perspective on the complicated histories of children's literature in various Western nations and raises as many questions as it answers. One of the finest essays in the book, Judith Plotz's "Literary Ways of Killing a Child: The 19th Century Practice," appropriately placed first, gives philosophical depth and literary texture to a scrutiny of Victorian images of "embalmed children." Her argument, erudite and wide-ranging, contrasts "the child of the early modern period *and* of the late twentieth century (at least of twentieth-century America)," a "creature of the cultural margins of society," with the nineteenth-century child, "a being of the center (4)." Her assertions are persuasive precisely because they are founded in a close reading of many specific works, some still well-known, many now obscure, and a dense description of the cultural context. As a whole, *Aspects and Issues* casts doubt on the claims of universal historiography while simultaneously providing a wider perspective on national histories of children's literature than is frequently to be found. Unfortunately, the volume is poorly proofread; many errors remain that the editor or the publisher ought to have corrected. Nonetheless, these essays and papers furnish scholars of world literature for children with invaluable stimuli and starting points.

Renewing Our Sources: Children's Literature as Rediscovery

Alida Allison

Rediscoveries in Children's Literature, by Suzanne Rahn. New York and London: Garland, 1995. Children's Literature and Culture 2, ed. Jack Zipes.

As many of us tell our students, one of the primary pleasures of a specialty in children's literature, if occasionally one of its frustrations, is that so much remains to be rediscovered and reassessed. Oddly, as Suzanne Rahn begins her superb book of just such rediscoveries by pointing out, the establishment of children's literature as an academic field has limited, rather than expanded, the number of titles used in college classrooms. Because professors, often new to children's literature themselves, have only a quarter or a semester to present their material, they tend to focus on well-known books that are readily available through publishers mindful of the bottom line. Gary D. Schmidt rues this homogeneity of material in his review (*Children's Literature* 23) of Glenn Sadler's 1992 *Teaching Children's Literature: Issues, Pedagogy, Resources,* in which the syllabi of many contemporary college children's literature courses are collected. And the recycling of the same books is perpetuated: Students who become schoolteachers take the knowledge of authors they obtained in college with them into their classrooms; there they add to these primarily books that have been canonized by having won awards. Books assigned or available to public school students during free reading times thus tend to be of the same kind or, to entice unwilling readers, books with little literary merit such as *Goosebumps* and *The Babysitters' Club.* Time once spent with one's local children's librarian, who would escort young book lovers to treasures such as Eleanor Farjeon's *Martin Pippin in the Apple Orchard* (1922), Edwin Abbott's *Flatland* (5th ed. 1963), or Dodie Smith's *I Capture the Castle* (1948), has been replaced by solitary moments at the impersonal computer to find information on books.

In *Rediscoveries in Children's Literature* Rahn goes a long way toward

Children's Literature 26, ed. Elizabeth Lennox Keyser (Yale University Press, © 1998 Hollins College).

filling in the gaps in scholarship and appreciation that she discusses in her 1981 *Children's Literature: An Annotated Bibliography of the History and Criticism.* She also fulfills, in this second volume of Garland's new Children's Literature and Culture series, the aim of its general editor, Jack Zipes, to encourage "original research in children's literature and culture," especially research dealing with how the "representation and socialization of children" is affected by changes in children's culture (ix). The nine authors she discusses range from Frank Stockton, the contemporary of Mark Twain and author of the ubiquitous "The Lady or the Tiger," to Diana Wynne Jones, whose *The Crown of Dalemark* was published in 1995. Rahn also resurrects the Victorian Toy Theater in a lovingly crafted chapter that builds on earlier research on this form in her *Bibliography* (106–7). In addition, Rahn presents chapters on the works of Selma Lagerlof, Dorothy Canfield, Florence Crannell Means, Maud Hart Lovelace, Beverly Cleary, Ursula Moray Williams, and Raymond Briggs. For each Rahn provides a biographical, cultural, and literary context, as well as comprehensive discussions of representative works. The facts she provides are always of interest: Lagerlof's experiencing writer's block after accepting the Swedish National Teachers Association's request that she write a children's book, the integral relationship between Canfield's writing and her commitment to Montessori's philosophy, or the increasing pessimism and protest that finally led Briggs to use the comic-strip format picture book as a vehicle for adult literature, anticipating authors such as Art Spiegelman. The kinds of stories that are interpreted range from Stockton's fairy tales to Means's groundbreaking ethnic novels to Canfield's interactive *Made-to-Order Stories,* in which her children helped with the plots.

One of the best features of Rahn's superlative book, in addition to the clarity of her prose and the model of research-as-rediscovery she provides, is that it is immediately useful. For example, her chapter on Florence Crannell Means, who wrote in the 1930s and 1940s and whose heroines then were "black, Latino, Hopi, Navajo, and Japanese-American" (19), led one of my graduate students to Means's *The Moved-Outers* (1945) for her research paper.

Let us admit, as Rahn does, that some of the books she critiques are less likely than others to become new favorites among current readers. An example would be Lagerlof's multivolume Nils stories, which—though praised by Konrad Lorenz for their realistic depictions of animals and notable for the breadth with which they accomplished Lagerlof's assignment to write about Sweden's provinces, people, and wildlife—are too long and loosely narrated for current taste. Similarly, Lovelace's Betsy-Tacy stories, very popular in their day, despite their representation of teen-age concerns and joys that are basically timeless, are nonetheless little read nowadays. This is our loss, as Rahn makes clear, one she helps rectify by providing information on yet another resource, a newly formed and growing Betsy-Tacy Society, initiated by a loyal readership in the actual locale of the stories, Deep Valley, Minnesota (102–3). Rahn and others delight in these books' ability to transport modern readers to another period in history. Further, beneath the often "fluffy" surface of these books is a vivid portrayal of adolescent enthusiasm for travel, the diversity of cultures, and, importantly, the kind of lifelong friendship between girls that belies the divisiveness that fairy tales typically reinforce. Betsy and Tacy are friends who take the time to deal thoughtfully, rather than reactively, with the world they and others inhabit.

Rahn's excellent opening chapter on Frank Stockton highlights an author who has received a good deal of recent attention. Jack Zipes and Jane Yolen have edited books of Stockton stories within the past few years, and in the mid-sixties, Maurice Sendak illustrated reissues of *The Griffin and the Minor Canon* and *The Bee-Man of Orn.* Occasionally "sardonic" (19), to use Rahn's word of praise for these stories, which are philosophically challenging, Stockton's rediscovered works are thematically similar to those of another challengingly philosophical and playful current author (though not a subscriber to the fairy-tale form), Russell Hoban, in that they raise metaphysical questions. In his desire to discover his "real" self, Stockton's Bee-Man gets his wish to begin life again as a baby; years later he is found by the sorcerer who granted his wish—and the Bee-Man has again become a Bee-Man, this time pleased to be one.

That many of Stockton's other fairy tales do not end happily—the protagonists' quests may fail or end ambiguously—gives his work an even more modern sensibility. Yet in her chapter on Stockton, as throughout her book, Rahn places her author usefully in literary history by comparing his work to his contemporaries' and sucessors'. In Stockton's case, there were very few contemporary American writers of children's fantasy. Among his notable followers was L. Frank Baum. In a fine section, Rahn discusses Baum, Stockton, and Lewis Carroll. Although Baum was more original in creating imaginary worlds, he did not, Rahn notes, write as well as Stockton did. And works by both of these authors are representative of the clearly identifiable pre–World War I American ingenuity, can-do spirit, and emphasis on cooperation, in contrast to the constant "bickering over status and power" one finds in Carroll (5–6). Classroom teachers are well served by Rahn's reminder that there are alternatives to repetitively revisiting Oz.

In the library copy of *The Bee-Man of Orn* that I checked out, among the words underlined by some assiduous if unprincipled vocabulary student were "resounding," "arbors," "domain," and "abodes." One wonders what this reader would make of the hilarious, often polysyllabic vocabulary Briggs invents in *Fungus the Bogeyman* (1977; American edition 1979): portmanteaux such as "drear," an affectionate term combining "dreary" and "dear," or "milkmuckake," a Bogey delicacy. Briggs's delightful imagination is not limited to neologisms; in this book he invents an entire subterranean society for his Bogeys (slimy citizens of a subterranean world), including the profession of Cow Patty Gatherer, or Pattyman. Bogeys are gatherers of garbage, workers of waste who inhabit the netherworld infrastructures of cities; they come up to our world at night to spook us and—from our point of view—to cause general mayhem. They are, however, loving family members who lead lives that—from their point of view—are as ordinary as ours. Briggs's book satirizes our everyday, unconsidered existences. If Briggs's joking subject matter—the gook, muck, and mud that make up the Bogeys' otherwise recognizably domestic environment—was calculated to "repel adult readers," as Rahn writes (130), those readers nowadays, in these post-*Beavis and Butthead* days, must be fastidious indeed.

In the almost twenty years since Briggs's book first came out, children's culture has accepted as commonplace intricate, detailed, digressive pictorial formats such as Briggs's: the delight is in the details. We have only to look at the copy and layout of many current children's magazines—for example, *Disney Adventures* or *Nickelodeon*—or to think of the success of the Waldo books to realize that Briggs was a pioneer in providing complicated text and pictures for children. But Briggs's books are superior to these 1990s magazines and to the Waldo books, for the literary quality of *Fungus,* and its fundamental message of tolerance for those unlike ourselves, places it among the best of children's books. It, like Briggs's better-known *The Snowman,* expands its readers' perspective.

Rahn's analysis of the development of Briggs's career is insightful.

It is clear that she fully appreciates the contribution Briggs has made to elevating the standards of children's literature through his address to readers who can and will spend the time to savor—if the word will do in describing how Bogeys live—the intricate, intelligent, and inverted world between the covers of his book.

Rahn notes that Florence Crannell Means's multiethnic works of the 1930s and 1940s predate attitudes we usually associate with later decades—ethnicity, diversity, multiculturalism. Means, for example, writes about Moslem African-American families, about Jewish families struggling through the Depression, about Mexican families, about pioneer girls fending off dust storms and grasshoppers. Despite her admiration for Means's subject matter and courage, Rahn's discussion of Means's work is balanced and fair. While pointing out flaws such as avoiding confrontational incidents between black and white characters in stories such as *Shuttered Windows* (1938), Rahn also informs us that Means herself lived to participate in the 1963 civil rights marches. In fact, one of the best features of each of Rahn's chapters is that she carefully presents the entirety of an author's career, providing readers with many books from which to select.

In her chapter on Means, as throughout *Rediscoveries in Children's Literature,* Rahn selects and presents her material so that her analysis of the author's contribution to children's literature is a model not only of research in our field but of good writing. *Rediscoveries in Children's Literature* is a major contribution to children's literature, providing not only food for thought but sustenance for curriculum revision and further research. There is, as this book exemplifies, a great richness to celebrate in children's books. The richness of Rahn's books and many articles (some of the chapters in *Rediscoveries in Children's Literature* were originally published in *The Lion and the Unicorn*) is also cause for celebration. This book is certain to be considered for awards and is one that I hope will be discovered and rediscovered frequently by specialists, students, and literature lovers generally.

Works Cited

Abbott, Edwin. *Flatland.* New York: Barnes and Noble, 1963.

Briggs, Raymond. *Fungus the Bogeyman.* New York: Random House, 1979.

———. *The Snowman.* New York: Random House, 1978.

Canfield, Dorothy. "Jimmy's Made-to-Order Stories." *St. Nicolas* 52, no. 2 (December 1924).

Farjeon, Eleanor. *Martin Pippin in the Apple Orchard.* New York: Frederick A. Stokes, 1922.

Jones, Diane Wynne. *The Crown of Dalemark.* New York: Greenwillow, 1995.
Means, Florence Crannell. *The Moved-Outers.* Boston: Houghton Mifflin, 1945.
———. *Shuttered Windows.* Boston: Houghton Mifflin, 1938.
Rahn, Suzanne. *Children's Literature: An Annotated Bibliography of the History and Criticism.* New York: Garland, 1981.
Sadler, Glenn, ed. *Teaching Children's Literature: Issues, Resources, Pedagogy.* Options in Teaching 11. New York: MLA, 1992.
Schmidt, Gary D. "Children's Literature and Considered Bravado." *Children's Literature* 23 (1995): 243–47.
Smith, Dodie. *I Capture the Castle.* Boston: Little, Brown, 1948.
Stockton, Frank. *The Bee-Man of Orn.* Illus. Maurice Sendak. New York: Holt, Rinehart and Winston, 1964.
———. *Fairy Tales of Frank Stockton.* Ed. Jack Zipes. New York: Penguin, 1990.
———. *The Griffin and the Minor Canon.* Illus. Maurice Sendak. New York: Holt, Rinehart and Winston, 1963.
———. *The Lady or the Tiger?* Ed. Jane Yolen. New York: Tor, 1992.

Carroll and Cohen: On a First-Name Basis with Charles Lutwidge Dodgson

Jan Susina

Lewis Carroll: A Biography, by Morton Cohen. New York: Knopf, 1995.

In what undoubtedly will become the standard biography of Lewis Carroll, Morton Cohen has produced a thoughtful, fascinating, highly readable account of a man best known for writing the most popular children's books of the nineteenth century—*Alice's Adventures in Wonderland* (1865) and its sequel *Alice Through the Looking-Glass* (1872). The world's premier Carroll scholar, Cohen has over the past thirty years produced the standard two-volume collection of Carroll's letters (1978) as well as six other volumes on Carroll. As this massive biography suggests, to limit Carroll's role to that of children's author is vastly to underestimate and oversimplify his wide-ranging interests and accomplishments. Carroll's list of publications includes more than three hundred items. To this list one must add his nine-volume diary and voluminous correspondence. Carroll kept a letter register for the last thirty-five years of his life; the final tally was 98,721 letters sent and received. Cohen estimates that Carroll wrote at least 100,000 letters. What makes Cohen's biography superior to previous Carroll biographies—and there have been a number of excellent ones, including Derek Hudson's *Lewis Carroll* (1954) and Anne Clark's *Lewis Carroll: A Biography* (1979)—is his immersion in every aspect of Carroll's life and work; having attempted to read everything of Carroll's now available to scholars, Cohen has this vast body of information at his fingertips. Ten years in the making, *Lewis Carroll* is the crowning scholarly achievement of Cohen's impressive academic career. Anyone who seriously wishes to understand Carroll's complex and contradictory life must read Cohen's *Lewis Carroll.*

This is not an insignificant assertion, given recent trends in critical approaches to Carroll. Although my students generally have a depressingly limited familiarity with Carroll's books, and that mostly based on a Disney film, they *are* familiar with two "facts" of Carroll's

Children's Literature 26, ed. Elizabeth Lennox Keyser (Yale University Press, © 1998 Hollins College).

life: that he took drugs and that he was too much interested in little girls.[1] I find a similar increase in scholarly speculation that focuses primarily on Carroll's life rather than on his literary texts. For instance, Jacqueline Rose in *The Case of Peter Pan, Or the Impossibility of Children's Fiction* (1984) off-handedly refers to *Wonderland* as the "author's fantasied seduction of a little girl" (3), and James Kincaid in *Child-Loving: The Erotic Child and Victorian Culture* (1992) frames Carroll as a pedophile. Now would certainly seem the time for a careful and detailed examination of the facts of Carroll's life. Since Carroll was an "indefatigable record keeper" (290), a systematic investigation of his records should reduce the need for such critical speculation.

As a biographer who has taken the time to sift through the copious primary material, Cohen takes a fairly dim view of the Carroll scholarship that seems so astonishingly, if not willfully, dismissive of it. Cohen rejects most Carroll criticism as "eccentric readings" that "may amuse" but "do not really bring us any closer to understanding Carroll or his work" (xxii). Indeed if there is a serious flaw in this biography, it is Cohen's refusal to engage in a discussion with scholars whom he views as misguided. But while Cohen chooses to dismiss, for the most part, those critical voices, he is carefully attuned to the multiple voices Carroll assumes in his children's texts, adult texts, diaries, and letters and to the voices of Victorians who knew Lewis Carroll, the writer of children's books, or Charles Lutwidge Dodgson, the more formal lecturer of mathematics at Christ Church, Oxford. Cohen's previous *Lewis Carroll: Interviews and Recollections* (1989), which gathered together all the existing memoirs of individuals who knew Carroll, functions as a companion volume to this biography and provides a useful source for its citations.

What Cohen attempts to create in this biography is an assembled portrait of the entire man, a portrait that makes "fresh connections" and reveals "the real man behind the mask" (198). Cohen presents Carroll as a "formidable figure, a prototype of his time and class, a sharp portrait of an age graven into a single human being" (198). It is astonishing, then, that Cohen chooses to address his subject in the first person—astonishing especially because, as Cohen acknowledges, Carroll was obsessed by rules, rituals, and social conventions; he himself never addressed an equal, a colleague, an associate, or even a friend by a given name. Only children and members of Carroll's immediate family were addressed less formally. Cohen's familiarity is astonishing too when one realizes that even Alice Liddell, the child who inspired Carroll to write *Wonderland,* refers to Carroll as Mr. Dodgson in her famous "Alice's Recollections of Carrollian Days." Cohen is the only person I can imagine who has earned the right to be on a first-name basis with Lewis Carroll. Without a doubt, Carroll would have been horrified by such an invasion of his privacy.

So what does Cohen's intimate portrait of Carroll reveal? It offers surprisingly little new material for those who have read Cohen's previous scholarship on Carroll. Much of the biography is a gathering together and recycling of Cohen's previous Carroll research, and this combination of new and old materials results in a curiously constructed biography, one that is organized thematically rather than chronologically.[2] Nevertheless, Cohen provides some surprises and perhaps one carefully coded bombshell. Although Cohen tends to resist critical analysis, he does present an original reading of *Wonderland:* he argues that Alice Liddell supplied the physical model for Alice wandering through Wonderland but that the spiritual and psychological Alice is Carroll himself. Although *Wonderland* represents the child's plight in Victorian upper-class society, and by extension the universal essence of childhood, the *Alice* books, Cohen suggests, should be read as a metaphor and a record of Carroll's own childhood. The chief taskmaster in Carroll's life, besides his own severe conscience, was his stern father. Carroll is the dutiful son who attempted to practice filial devotion and simultaneously filial rebellion, the latter with limited success, against his clergyman father. Cohen shows that the "grumbling-father theme" is a constant feature in Carroll's work; *Wonderland*'s many tyrants and menacing authority figures provide a revealing gloss on Carroll (334). Carroll's great guilt, which Cohen charts throughout the diary, is the result of not having lived the life that "Papa hoped he would" (341). This disappointing life included Carroll's rejection of Archdeacon Charles Dodgson's High Church belief for a more open Broad Church stance (which allowed Carroll to attend the theater), but more significantly it included Carroll's failure to marry and to follow his father into the church.

Carroll's failure to marry leads Cohen to Carroll's relationship with Alice Liddell and the much-discussed pages for 27, 28, and 29 June 1863, which are missing from Carroll's diary. Whereas many scholars have suggested that Stuart Dodgson Collingwood, Carroll's nephew and first biographer, destroyed these pages, Cohen asserts that it was Carroll's niece, Menella Dodgson, whose sensibilities were so offended that she razored them out. (Despite the vast amount of material that Carroll left behind, scholars are fascinated by what is missing. Cohen prefers to base his judgments on facts, but in this situation he too is forced to speculate, using extant material to fill in the gaps.) Clearly, some sort of rupture between Carroll and the Liddell family occurred during the three-day period. Carroll was exiled from the children, and the Liddells are unmentioned in Carroll's diary for the next five months. Cohen argues that Carroll perhaps introduced the prospect of marriage between himself and his "ideal child friend" Alice to her parents (101). Carroll was then thirty-one years old and Alice only eleven. Cohen, noting that the twenty-year age difference between husband and wife was not uncommon in an era when men were expected to establish themselves financially and professionally prior to marriage,[3] speculates that Carroll might have suggested an extended engagement. Cohen links Carroll's possible proposal to that of his brother, Wilfred, who at age twenty-seven fell in love with Alice Jane Donkin, aged fourteen, another episode that has been suppressed in Carroll's diary. The Liddells themselves offer an example of age discrepancy almost as extreme as that which Carroll may have proposed: at thirty-four, Dean Henry George Liddell had married the nineteen-year-old Lorina Reeve. Her concern for the social and financial advancement of her daughters has been firmly established, as has her dismissal of Carroll, to whom she seems to have attached little importance; when she commissioned H. L. Thompson to write a biography of her late husband, she stipulated that neither Carroll nor the *Alice* books be mentioned. Nor did Mrs. Liddell value the letters that Carroll must have written to Alice and her sisters, although she did cherish a short letter she received from William Thackeray that she mentions in her will.

Although Cohen presents Carroll's intense relationship with Alice Liddell within the context of a marriage proposal, he does not shy away from the troubling issue of Carroll's obsession with young girls, which Carroll preferred to consider as his overwhelming fascination with "child nature" (105). Cohen suggests that Carroll adapted William Blake's ideals of childhood innocence to Victorian sensibilities and argues that William Rossetti's description of Blake as "gentle and affectionate, loving to be with little children, and to talk about them" (107) can be applied to Carroll, but he does not leave it at that. In "The Fire Within," the central chapter of the biography, Cohen makes a somewhat guarded shift from his previous position, articulated in "Lewis Carroll and Victorian Morality" (1984). Cohen still maintains that Carroll envisioned his life as essentially a battleground between good and evil but now acknowledges how perilously close to disaster this struggle brought Carroll, who "successfully transformed a life that might have easily teetered on the brink and fallen into the abyss" (533). Carefully correlating Carroll's "soul-searching, soul-searing" (205) diary entries, Cohen shows that these are directly linked to Carroll's intense emotional involvement with the Liddell children. Cohen argues that the coincidence of increasing self-recrimination and increasing intimacy with the Liddell children cannot be overlooked, nor can the guilt-ridden diary entries simply be attributed to Carroll's sense of his professional shortcomings or perceived indolence.

Whereas critics have long sought a clue in the missing pages of Carroll's diary, Cohen finds one in the adult poem "Stolen Waters." Composed and published in *College Rhymes* in 1862, when Carroll was most involved with the Liddell family, "Stolen Waters" is a young knight's first-person account of having been seduced and deserted by a young maiden and of his regret for his lost virtue. In short, according to Cohen, Carroll's poem reveals that "the man is in trouble" (225). Cohen contrasts the overt references to sex, seduction, and guilty conscience in "Stolen Waters" with the "suppressed sexuality" of the imagery in *Wonderland* (225). Although Cohen resists the temptation to draw absolute parallels between "Stolen Waters" and Carroll's life, he concludes that the poem provides a glimpse into Carroll's "inner fears" and his romantic longing for Alice Liddell (223). This is a compelling reading, but Cohen seems to overlook the distinction between the erotic maiden, who like the knight is an adult, and the voice of the "angel-child," who summons the knight from his fallen state and directs him to a more spiritual, albeit asexual, one. Once rejected by the Liddells, Carroll seemingly reproduces this doomed relationship throughout the remainder of his life, turning to other girls for both aesthetic and emotional satisfaction. Cohen insists that Carroll never allowed himself to cross into the forbidden territory entered by his knight in "Stolen Waters." Thus Carroll's sexual desires and his guilt concerning them were a matter "not so much of deeds as thought" (221), supplying Cohen with his metaphor of "a fire raging beneath the surface" (221). Nevertheless, Cohen insists that it is "mean-spirited" to attribute the composition of the *Alice* books entirely to Carroll's suppression of his sexual desires, although he acknowledges that it may have been one source of Carroll's creative accomplishments (280).

It is indeed unfortunate, if not disingenuous, that Cohen reverts to indirect language when dealing with such important issues as Carroll's attraction to children. The same sort of metaphorical language reappears when Cohen maintains that Carroll's "emotional targets clearly differed from most men's, [and that] the difference affected, even shaped his behavior" (190), and when he suggests that Carroll "recognized earlier than one might suppose that his inner springs differed from most men's, that his heart beat to a different drum, that in order to be true to himself he would be compelled to lead a life that was not only outside the norm but would come under particular scrutiny and raise questions" (190). At least when discussing Carroll's photographs of nude children, Cohen is willing to call naive at best Carroll's claim that his appreciation of nudes was entirely aesthetic. That Carroll felt the need to have another adult present when he photographed nude children points to his recognition, if only on an unconscious level, of that activity's erotic implications.

Cohen concludes his study by suggesting that Carroll's failure to correct his speech impediment was the "overarching symbol of his life" (533). According to Cohen, Carroll's stammer resulted in "a life hampered by inescapable limitations, blotted by imperfections and lacking emotional fulfillment" (533). But though Carroll stuttered, so did most of his brothers and sisters. Some critics have suggested that Carroll's self-portrait as the Dodo in *Wonderland* is the result of the difficulty he would sometimes experience in pronouncing his last name, so that "Dodgson" would come out "Dod-Dod-Dod-Dodgson." While undergoing therapy with James Hunt, the speech correctionist, Carroll first met George MacDonald, whose family's appreciative reading of *Alice's Adventures Underground* persuaded Carroll to revise and publish *Wonderland.* Even Cohen notes that Carroll, though always at ease with his child friends, did not, as some critics have suggested, invariably lose his stammer in their presence, for many children reported examples of his speech impediment as charming. Whereas Cohen attempts to see Carroll's stammer as a symbol of his failures, I see it differently. One could just as easily argue that Carroll's stammer brought him into contact with MacDonald, which eventually led to his greatest triumph, the publication of *Wonderland.* I have always appreciated the headmaster's perceptive report from

Richmond Grammar School informing Carroll's parents that their young son possessed "a very uncommon share of genius" (15).

Cohen's interpretation of Carroll's stammer, like his other attempts to render Carroll's life into metaphor, is one of the rare occasions when this biography falters. Moreover, there is no need for such a rendering, since Cohen's biography makes it clear that Carroll used the material of his own life to create *Wonderland* and *Looking-Glass.* Despite his occasional missteps in *Lewis Carroll: A Biography,* Cohen has written an important critical text that, along with Roger Lancelyn Green's *The Diaries of Lewis Carroll* (1954) and Cohen's own *The Letters of Lewis Carroll,* will become an indispensable volume in Carroll scholarship.

Notes

1. Few scholars of children's literature would debate the importance of *Wonderland* or Lewis Carroll's place in the historical development of children's literature. Cohen maintains that, along with the Bible and Shakespeare's plays, the *Alice* books remain the most quoted in the Western world. I only wish it were so. Each semester I find fewer students who have read *Wonderland,* much less are able to quote from it. Many of the comic allusions that made it such a liberating text for Victorian child readers send contemporary college students to the glosses of Martin Gardner's *Annotated Alice* (1960) and *More Annotated Alice* (1990). Despite the gradual decrease in familiarity with Carroll's texts, there seems to have been an inverse growth in my students' and others' interest in Carroll's life.

2. I find Jean Gattégno's *Lewis Carroll: Fragments of a Looking-Glass* (1976)—which is not strictly speaking a biography of Carroll, in that it abandons any attempt to present its subject chronologically but rather discusses Carroll through a series of thirty-seven short but illuminating interlocking essays arranged alphabetically—one of the most informed sources of biographical Carroll criticism.

3. Consider, for example, the age disparity between Mr. Knightly and Emma in Jane Austen's *Emma.*

Works Cited

Carroll, Lewis. *The Annotated Alice: Alice's Adventures in Wonderland and Through the Looking-Glass.* Ed. Martin Gardner. New York: Clarkson N. Potter, 1960.

———. *More Annotated Alice.* Notes by Martin Gardner. New York: Random House, 1990.

Clark, Anne. *Lewis Carroll: A Biography.* New York: Schocken, 1979.

Cohen, Morton N. *Lewis Carroll: A Biography.* New York: Knopf, 1995.

———. *Lewis Carroll: Interviews and Recollections.* Iowa City: University of Iowa Press, 1989.

———. "Lewis Carroll and Victorian Morality." In *Sexuality and Victorian Literature,* ed. Don Richard Cox. Tennessee Studies in Literature 27. Knoxville: University of Tennessee Press, 1984. Pp. 3–19.

Cohen, Morton N., ed., with Roger Lancelyn Green. *The Letters of Lewis Carroll.* 2 vols. New York: Oxford University Press, 1979.
Gattégno, Jean. *Lewis Carroll: Fragments of a Looking-Glass.* Trans. Rosemary Sheed. New York: Crowell, 1976.
Green, Roger Lancelyn, ed. *The Diaries of Lewis Carroll.* 2 vols. New York: Oxford University Press, 1954.
Hudson, Derek. *Lewis Carroll.* London: Constable, 1954.
Kincaid, James R. *Child-Loving: The Erotic Child and Victorian Culture.* New York: Routledge, 1992.
Rose, Jacqueline. *The Case of Peter Pan, Or the Impossibility of Children's Fiction.* London: Macmillan, 1984.

Nurture Versus Colonization: Two Views of Frances Hodgson Burnett

Elizabeth Lennox Keyser

The Secret Garden: Nature's Magic, by Phyllis Bixler. Twayne Masterwork Studies, no. 161. New York: Twayne, 1996.

A Little Princess: Gender and Empire, by Roderick McGillis. Twayne Masterwork Studies, no. 159. New York: Twayne, 1996.

Phyllis Bixler, in her Twayne Masterwork study, concludes her summary of the ongoing critical debate over Frances Hodgson Burnett's *The Secret Garden* as follows: "It would be inaccurate to consider the appreciative and the more critical scholars . . . as belonging to two armed camps. Few if any of the first group would deny that *The Secret Garden* reflects attitudes about gender and class we would like to believe we have put behind us; . . . On the other hand, critics who set themselves the task of unearthing the various ideologies in Burnett's text discover it to be amazingly fertile in their hands. . . . Finally, it is likely that all the critics whose work I have described would name *The Secret Garden* as . . . certainly among the most important children's books written during the late nineteenth and early twentieth centuries" (20). Bixler's characterization of Burnett's critics as falling into two categories—the appreciative and the more critical—and her collapsing of these two categories into a common recognition of Burnett's achievement aptly distinguish and connect these two new books. Bixler does not hesitate to place herself among the more appreciative of Burnett's critics and in *Nature's Magic* continues to "acknowledge . . . dated attitudes" while emphasizing the "strengths that help explain the book's continuing appeal" (20). Roderick McGillis in his study of *A Little Princess* undertakes "the task of unearthing the various ideologies" in that text and finds it, like *The Secret Garden,* "to be amazingly fertile." He concludes his study, however, on an unequivocal note of appreciation. Quoting the former owner of his paperback edition, he proclaims, "This is an excellent book!" (104).

Twayne's Masterwork Studies series, which now includes more than

Children's Literature 26, ed. Elizabeth Lennox Keyser (Yale University Press, © 1998 Hollins College).

160 titles, is designed for college and university students. Each volume contains a chronology of the author's life and a section on the literary and historical context, including a discussion of the work's reception and criticism. But the centerpiece of each volume is a fresh reading of the work, one that supposedly eschews both theoretical jargon and a narrow polemical approach. The volumes on children's or young adult literature (about a dozen have been published and more are projected) are especially designed for teachers or prospective teachers, and thus they feature an additional final section on approaches to teaching the text under consideration. Ideally, according to its editors, volumes in the Masterwork series should engage their readers and provide them with more than the study guide they may have bargained for. Although it is tempting for the cynical to view these volumes as little more than glorified *Cliff's Notes* (and a few volumes in the series might confirm that suspicion), Bixler's and McGillis's contributions more than meet their editors' expectations, and in fact they transcend the limitations of their genre. As one long familiar with both Burnett novels (*The Secret Garden* from childhood), as one who has taught them repeatedly and even contributed to the debate outlined by Bixler, I found both studies provocative, even inspiring, in their different ways. To me, they are not merely good introductions to the novels—and to literary criticism—for those who may be wary of the critical enterprise; they are also good introductions for experienced critics who may be coming afresh to these works (as, according to his own account, McGillis did to *The Little Princess* in 1993 [37]) or to the field of children's literature. The range of reference in both volumes to classics and lesser-known works for children provides a kind of anatomy (for this reason *Nature's Magic* will be assigned reading in my next introductory graduate course). Even, perhaps especially, for those familiar with the two Burnett novels and their criticism, these volumes offer many pleasures, as I hope the following discussion will show.

Following the Twayne format for its masterwork series, Bixler and McGillis both place the novels in their literary and historical contexts, identify their importance, and discuss their reception and recent criticism. Bixler situates *The Secret Garden* at the end of the golden age of children's literature and suggests that the book is a kind of culmination. McGillis in turn connects *A Little Princess* with other late Victorian and early Edwardian fiction for children but places literary history in the service of his theory about the book: that *A Little Prin-*

cess "is a reworking of the Crusoe story in terms of female experience" (8). Bixler's opening chapters lead the reader to expect a recapitulation of the themes that she and others have identified over years of engagement with the text. Those familiar with Bixler's previous book and several articles on Burnett are prepared to reenter the same garden but also to discover a still richer profusion of growth. McGillis's introductory chapters indicate that he will focus on a single, unexplored aspect of the novel; his reading will offer the adventure of accompanying a critic as he attempts to break new ground.

In their chapters dealing with criticism of the novels, McGillis remarks on the failure of critics to examine *A Little Princess* "in the context of the fiction of Empire" (33), Bixler on the way critics *have* placed *The Secret Garden* in that context. In his chapter on the importance of the work, McGillis suggests that an awareness of the imperial or colonial theme will help us appreciate the value of multiculturalism. After quoting a passage from the novel in which Ram Dass pays homage to Sara, he writes, "The book has it both ways: Ram Dass and the other Indian servants are correct in their subservience to Sara, and Sara in her turn is correct in her resistance to the tyranny of Miss Minchin and her minions" (20–21). One might argue here for a qualitative difference between Miss Minchin's personal vendetta against Sara and Sara's passive acceptance of the homage that she has done nothing personally to exact. One might also argue with McGillis's assertion that "this passage has no irony" (20), for the passage seems to imply that it is a matter of luck and timing rather than merit whether one is insulted or salaamed. Still, McGillis's point—that works such as *A Little Princess* should be studied not only for their aesthetic value and power to move us (to provide, in the words of McGillis's paraphrase of Tolkien, "recovery, escape, and consolation" [25]) but also for their ideological blindness—is well taken.

Bixler, however, responds to critics such as McGillis in the penultimate chapter of her book, the last of her "reading" of the text. While acknowledging that such interpretations can be supported, Bixler reveals more subtlety in Burnett's portrayal of the Sowerby family and manor servants than critics of her ideology have allowed. Not only does Burnett present unsparingly, if unobtrusively, the deprivations and hardships of poverty, she allows her working-class characters to comment on and even offer critiques of their superiors. Bixler concludes this section by remarking mildly that adult readers, in their efforts to excavate a complicated text, are as likely to be selective as child readers. Bixler's own reading of *The Secret Garden* is as generous and inclusive as seems humanly possible, and her penultimate chapter seems as much a matter of giving the critics with whom she disagrees their due as a matter of getting the last word. McGillis's reading, on the other hand, is determinedly selective, and that is *its* particular strength. Had he adhered to that approach even more consistently (had he been less constrained by the Twayne format?), his reading of the imperial theme might have been still more coherent and convincing.

Bixler and McGillis present the readings of their respective texts quite differently. Bixler follows what she identifies as the structure of the novel. According to Bixler, Burnett "uses eight chapters (1–8) to establish Mary's character and get her inside the secret garden and another eight (13–20) to introduce Colin and bring him to the garden. Moreover, each group of eight chapters is followed by a similarly parallel group of four (9–12 and 21–24) depicting Mary's and Colin's transformations within the garden. The book's final three chapters (25–27) can be seen as a coda that recapitulates this theme through an abbreviated depiction of Mr. Craven's transformation and at the same time pulls together various earlier patterns of imagery, especially those related to parental nurturance" (62). The first chapter of Bixler's reading, like the first chapters of Burnett's novel, focuses on Mary, especially her psychology and the way in which the manor servants function as therapists; her second chapter focuses on the garden, Mary's growing friendship with Dickon, and the latent sexual content of these chapters; her third focuses on Colin and the parallels between his experience and Mary's; her fourth and perhaps strongest chapter, on the theme of nurturance and the triangle formed by Mary, Dickon, and Colin. The passage I quoted above, like the chapter it introduces (on Burnett's chapters 21–27), performs the same pulling-together service that Bixler attributes to the conclusion of *The Secret Garden.*

The advantages of this organizational strategy are obvious: whether a college professor preparing to teach *The Secret Garden* for the first time, a college student seeking a better understanding of the book, or a middle-school teacher about to present it to her class, the reader is able to concentrate on a group of chapters, then build on what she has learned as she goes on to the next. As the reader proceeds with Bixler, a plaintive melodic line becomes embellished with rich chords of meaning. These chords are provided by Bixler and the critics on whom she draws, critics such as Gillian Adams, Barbara Almond, Jerry Griswold, and Judith Plotz. Counterpoint, and an occasional dissonance, is provided by reference to "more critical scholars," such as Lissa Paul and Jerry Phillips. The end result is no less a beautifully orchestrated performance of *The Secret Garden* than the 1991 stage and 1993 film adaptations, on which Bixler also draws.

In contrast, each chapter of McGillis's reading of *A Little Princess* makes a separate foray into the territory of the text and in some instances skirts that territory. Most of the first chapter consists of an impromptu essay McGillis wrote in response to an assignment he gave his children's literature class. In this essay McGillis tries to account for the book's appeal to young readers and is disturbed to suspect that Sara's "imperial attitude" (40) gratifies their desire for dominance. As though to counter his repugnance at the possibility, he offers another: that the source of Sara's—and the reader's vicarious—empowerment is her storytelling. Reevaluating what he wrote several years ago, McGillis now finds the second alternative less than satisfactory. Sara's imaginative activity is powerless to effect change, and thus she is a passive rather than an active heroine. Finally, McGillis entertains a third possibility—that Sara's strength is her ability to nurture and create a female community that crosses class lines. The connection between this capacity of Sara's and her—and her creator's—imperial attitude is not yet clear, but the reader anticipates illumination through textual analysis.

The next three chapters, however, offer something of a diversion. The first of these places *A Little Princess* in the context of nineteenth-century thinking about childhood innocence. McGillis's point, that Sara both embodies that innocence and suggests that it can survive childhood, is provocative, but the chapter does not advance the imperial theme. The next returns to that theme as it manifests itself in covers and illustrations of various editions of *Sara Crewe* and *A Little Princess.* The third is actually titled "The Importance of Empire," but the subtitle indicates that the discussion will concentrate on stage versions and film adaptations. This latter chapter contains an odd apology: "I seem to have shifted my attention from the primacy of the visual to the importance of Empire for an understanding of Burnett's story. Actually, the two are difficult to disentangle" (59). The shift instead seems to be from the importance of Empire within the text to its visual representations outside it.

Still, these three chapters have much to offer. The second one concludes by deploring the way modern illustrators have "muted the imperial theme" in the interests of political correctness. Its unabashed presence in the early covers and illustrations accurately reflects "the casualness with which Burnett uses the Empire, her complete lack of awareness that she appropriates another culture and people for her own purposes." McGillis reiterates a point made earlier: "Readers today deserve to know this, not to be protected from this knowledge" (56). The next chapter takes the 1995 film adaptation of *A Little Princess* to task not for its efforts to be "sensitive to racial matters" (61) but for the way it "perpetuates an imperial attitude to" India as well as "Burnett's unconscious championing of a white middle class" (62). I am left pondering the difference between book covers and film adaptations—why one should reflect Burnett's assumptions and not the other. This is the strength of McGillis's study: it makes me ponder.

The next five chapters, in which McGillis's focus returns to the text, constitute the heart of his study. In each the theme of Empire appears to have been dropped only to reappear at the ends of three of them, each time with an interesting twist. In the first of these chapters McGillis picks up on the word *savage,* used by the narrator to describe Sara's attack on her doll: "The message here is that good English girls can, through deprivation, neglect, unkindness, and poverty, sink to the level of a 'savage'" (67). But McGillis seems both to approve and disapprove of this message. On one hand, he praises it as an expression of the novel's realism: "Unlike so many Victorian stories that show adversity and illness as necessary moral agents of renovation, *A Little Princess* shows how one good, if spoiled, little girl might be in danger of reduction to the state of savagery" (67). On the other hand, McGillis, by placing the word *savage* in quotation marks, seems to be blaming the message—or perhaps only its medium—for equating Sara's violent behavior with what its author believes to be the norm for non-European cultures. In other words the message is at once an expression of Burnett's refusal to romanticize, and thus essentialize, her child heroine, and her willingness to demonize, and thus essentialize, cultures other than her own. Or to put it still another way, she acknowledges that Sara partakes of the same nature as "the savage," yet her very use of that word communicates her sense of an ineradicable difference between them.

Two chapters later, having traced Sara's psychological growth, McGillis concludes that it has led her to adopt a mission: "I use the word *mission* precisely because it conjures up an image of Empire—

the mission to the colonies, missionaries and their activities among the 'natives.' Sara's mission is to repatriate the activities of Empire, and in doing this she implicitly offers a criticism of imperial activity abroad" (75). Here McGillis attempts, or sees Burnett as attempting, to reconcile Sara's "imperial attitude" with her propensity to nurture. Sara's imperial attitude, which, however appealing to the child reader, was repugnant to McGillis, has been chastened by both confinement and exposure into a more acceptable domestic imperialism. Thus McGillis begins to deliver on the tacit commitment made to his readers in the first chapter of the reading section: to provide a link between Sara's—and Burnett's—imperialism and their creation of an egalitarian female community. And in doing so he begins to entertain the possibility that Burnett was more self-conscious and critical in her treatment of Empire than he has yet allowed.

The third of these chapters, however, forecloses on that possibility once again. In what is perhaps his most fascinating chapter, the one on Sara's relationship to nature as represented by the rat Melchisedec and Ram Dass's monkey, McGillis seems about to conclude on an approbatory note: "Burnett's position here, as elsewhere in the novel, appears to embrace a liberal humanist ethic that sees everyone as partaking of an essential humanity that transcends class, cultural, and racial differences" (81). But he then goes on: "As we might expect, however, Burnett is not consistent. Ram Dass, like the monkey, is not similar to Sara. Far from it. . . . Class and race separate the little girl and the Indian man" (81). He concludes that Burnett "cannot overcome her sense of his difference; she cannot present him other than stereotypically" (81). The final chapter of McGillis's reading section, on Burnett's narrative voice, clearly identifies that voice with imperial power and privilege: "To maintain an Empire, a ruling state must manage two things: to establish a right to authority and to perpetrate an overriding ideology or pattern of thinking that those within the influence of Empire accept as natural. We can see both these aspects of Empire in Burnett's handling of the narrative of *A Little Princess*" (93). Thus after having tantalized his reader with the suggestion that Burnett might be offering a protofeminist revisionary critique of imperialism, McGillis ends by withdrawing the suggestion, or rather by seeming to forget that the suggestion had been made.

In an early chapter, we recall, McGillis claims that "the book has it both ways" (20). McGillis in his reading of the book also seems to want to have it both ways. At the end of the informal response paper with which he begins his reading, McGillis confesses that the book's appeal to its readers' desire for dominance is "unpalatable" to him, and he seeks "solace in another kind of empowerment to be found in these pages" (40). The image that epitomizes that kind of empowerment is "Sara visiting Anne in the bakeshop to offer charity to the downtrodden" (40). Not only does McGillis's response paper end with this image; no fewer than six of his thirteen chapters (chapters 1, 2, 4, 9, 10, and 11) do as well. Perhaps McGillis keeps returning to this image because it corresponds to his desire to read the text as subversive of imperialism, a desire that he has not been able otherwise to gratify. Perhaps he also wants to leave in his readers' mind a positive impression of a book about which he continues to feel ambivalent. But perhaps the image also recurs because of its ambiguity: is Sara colonizing Anne, and through her other "savage" little children, or is she nurturing her? As recent discussion of children as though they were colonial subjects would indicate, the line between nurture and colonization tends to blur; they seem to constitute a continuum rather than represent moral opposites.

As critics, Bixler and McGillis can be viewed as occupying points on this continuum: Bixler appears to tend the garden of the text, helping its beauties appear to best advantage; McGillis, at least in the present instance, takes us on a journey into the unfamiliar territory of the text, enabling us to identify, understand, and occasionally condemn the way its values differ from our own. It is worth noting that Bixler, although she has written repeatedly about *The Secret Garden,* seldom alludes to her previous work, and then unobtrusively. She seems to have no sense of proprietorship, even though she was the first to explore many of its themes. Seldom does she use the first person singular in *Nature's Magic;* instead, she prefers the first person plural or such constructions as "Burnett calls attention to," "careful reading shows," "as has been noted," "if one remembers . . . her description here reminds one." She writes as though she is collaborating both with other readers and with the author. McGillis, on the other hand, calls attention to himself as an interrogator, interpreter, and sometimes a renovator of the text. He, too, frequently uses the first person plural but as though addressing members of a conducted tour. I am tempted to compare McGillis to the imperious narrator of *A Little Princess,* as he reads it. Yet it occurs to me that, in foregrounding his interpretive efforts, he is almost the antithesis of that narrator. Rather than presenting himself as omniscient, with authority to speak for all, McGillis admits his fallibility and reminds the reader that he speaks only for himself. In fact, Bixler's self-effacement, her quiet but authoritative tone, does more to persuade the reader that hers is the final word and that the mysterious essence of *The Secret Garden* can be no more exquisitely refined. To put it briefly, Bixler's reading is a distillation, McGillis's a drama. The one, for all its inclusiveness, creates a sense of closure; the other, by foreclosing on some of its rich possibilities, reopens the critical debate.

Dissertations of Note

Compiled by Rachel Fordyce

Barron, Frances Marlene. "Doing Books in the Social Context of Montessori Early Childhood Classrooms: Children 'Reading' Without Teachers." Ph.D. diss. New York University, 1995. 261 pp. DAI 56:4332A.

This ethnographic study, involving children aged 2.9 through 5, tries to determine how children respond to books in individual as well as group settings. Not surprisingly her outcome suggests that children's interaction with books is most successful and frequent when teachers create an environment where books are valued and where the classroom is "flooded" with books.

Blyn, Roslyn. "The Folkgames of Celtic-Speaking Children: A History and Classification System." Ph.D. diss. University of Pennsylvania, 1995. 350 pp. DAI 56:1924A.

Blyn suggests that "children's play activities in the Celtic-speaking areas has been over-represented in print due to the desire to present an image that distinguishes the Celts from other ethnic groups." She includes a classification system that combines native Celtic terms with a folk taxonomy.

Bronzel, Patrisha Joy. "An Analysis of Selected Gifted Early Adolescent Protagonists in Children's and Young Adult Literature." Ed.D. diss. Columbia University Teachers College, 1995. 282 pp. DAI 56:4301A.

Bronzel analyzes five gifted protagonists, aged ten through fifteen, in realistic late-twentieth-century fiction. She finds, in a study that surveys many more works than are focused on in the dissertation, that there is a male gender bias in books about gifted children, that the books tend to be limited "in scope of plot and characterization," but that they do reflect the "chaotic reality that is experienced by the gifted early adolescent."

Burmeister, LaVern. "Response to Literature: The Influence of Primary Caregivers' Belief Systems on Eighth Graders' Response to Short Stories." Ph.D. diss. University of California, Riverside, 1995. 154 pp. DAI 56:3034A.

The dissertation indicates that children's value systems are clearly influenced by their parents' beliefs, although students may not be fully aware of the influence or the extent of it. Burmeister also finds that students "appear to respond to literature based on the roles they perceive for themselves within the family."

Carico, Kathleen Marie. "Responses of Four Adolescent Females to Adolescent Fiction with Strong Female Characters." Ph.D. diss. Virginia Polytechnic Institute and State University, 1994. 266 pp. DAI 55:3119A.

Carico's research, based on Mildred Taylor's *Roll of Thunder, Hear My Cry* and Katherine Paterson's *Lyddie,* is informed by Louise Rosenblatt's perception of literature "as human experience and a medium for exploration," as well as the work of Richard Beach. She is concerned with "the enhancement of women's confidence by a validation of their experiences . . . through demonstrations of social constructions of meaning."

Castañeda, Maria Anita. "A Look at Hispanic Children's Reading Choices and Interests: A Descriptive Study." Ph.D. diss. Texas Woman's University, 1995. 141 pp. DAI 56:3448A.

In a semester-long study of five 8- and 9-year-old students Castañeda discovered that the genres they most preferred were realistic fiction, fantasy, and folktales, as well as information and concept books, and that a teacher's influence

Children's Literature 26, ed. Elizabeth Lennox Keyser (Yale University Press, © 1998 Hollins College).

on what students read is much more pervasive than a parent's. She also finds that preferences of both sexes are similar although boys had a stronger preference for legends than girls, and girls liked rhymed text better than boys did.

Cleary, Beth M. " 'Making the Gods' Voices Yell': Performing Theories of the Bread and Puppet Theatre." Ph.D. diss. University of California, Berkeley, 1994. 226 pp. DAI 56:1584A.

Cleary's dissertation is an in-depth analysis of the thirty-year history of the Bread and Puppet Theatre and its founder, Peter Schumann, based on the four years she worked with the theatre. She demonstrates how Schumann draws on sophisticated cultural critics, such as Hannah Arendt, Ernst Bloch, and Herbert Marcuse. He "yolks his papier-mache mass spectacle aesthetics to their sophisticated mass culture ideas [and] asserts the necessity and urgency of [a] critical relationship between the individual and mass culture."

Collins, Pansy Hillin. "Children Responding to Crisis Literature: Fifth Graders and *Bridge to Terabithia.*" Ph.D. diss. University of Missouri—Columbia, 1993. 217 pp. DAI 55:1186A.

Collins designed a study for fifth-graders that tested their ability to experience grief, to sympathize or empathize with characters who deal with grief, and to allow students more deeply to understand what grief means. Post-surveys indicate that most students sympathized with and understood the main character of *Bridge to Terabithia* and that their "level of anxiety or fear toward loss decreased after reading the novel. . . ."

Cook, Nicholas J. "A Survey of Children Audience Members in English Theatre from the Anglo-Saxon to Victorian Eras." Ph.D. diss. The Claremont Graduate School, 1996. 121 pp. DAI 56:4783A.

Cook demonstrates that children were attending theatrical performances as early as the tenth century, that plays were written specifically for them as early as the Tudor period (two centuries before Edgeworth's *Old Poz*), and that most plays were didactic. Types of entertainments he discusses are "tropes, mystery plays, Robin Hood Plays, masques, commedia dell'arte, morality plays, interludes, booth plays, pantomime, comedy plays, opera, *le theatre d'education,* Gilbert and Sullivan, and penny gaffs." He uses "theatre histories, children's literature histories, artwork diaries and playscripts to document specific instances of children attending drama."

Cooper, Connie Sue Eigenmann. "Telling Grimm Tales: Vestiges of German Folklore and Russian Formalism." Ph.D. diss. University of Oklahoma, 1995. 290 pp. DAI 56:4513A.

This dissertation in folklore verifies "a communal construction of the Grimm brothers' fairytales, as opposed to a single author" and is based on "oral narrative traditions reinstituted from literate sources," in this case Jack Zipes's translations and United States oral versions collected and translated in 1994 and 1995. Her study "records a variety of German cultural styles in storytelling, communicative arts of emotional release, and oral narrative. . . ."

Cross, Jennifer Lynn. "Picturebooks and Christopher Columbus: A Cultural Analysis." Ph.D. diss. Ohio State University, 1995. 223 pp. DAI 56:4640A.

Cross shows how the artwork in picture books transmits cultural information. She found that Christopher Columbus was consistently treated as a hero cum dreamer, that books about him were not at all critical, and that they robbed children "of the opportunity to investigate and explore problems of cultural intolerance and exploitation."

Dadson, Fredericka Alice. "A Critical History of the Development of Children's Literature in Ghana." Ph.D. diss. University of Wisconsin—Milwaukee, 1995. 257 pp. DAI 56:4769A.

Dadson discusses the emergence of "Ghanaian" children's literature in the early 1900s. A Western influence is clear and pervasive. The first part of the dissertation is a history of children's literature in Britain and the United States; the remainder demonstrates "the social, cultural, and political factors that influenced the adaptation" of Western literature. In effect, native literature for children is not discussed.

Dashiell, Patricia Michele. "The Literature Potential of Modern High Fantasy: A Case Study of the Exploration of Self Among Adolescent Girls in a Home-Based Literature Discussion Group." Ph.D. diss. Ohio State University, 1995. 257 pp. DAI 56:3486A.

Using a literary discussion group Dashiell studies the reaction of adolescent girls to "high fantasy with strong female protagonists" to determine whether their responses indicate a serious engagement with the characters, on a personal level, and if it is valid for students to use characters as role models to develop a better understanding of themselves. Based on discussions and personal journals she finds that "there is a liberating potential when adolescent girls identify with strong female protagonists faced with oppressive or challenging obstacles."

DeBerry, Paul Clifton, Jr. "The Effects of the Literary Elements of Plot, Characterization, Setting, and Theme in Children's Literature on Interest Levels of Kindergarten Through Sixth-Grade Students." Ed.D. diss. University of Alabama, 1995. 181 pp. DAI 56:3862A.

DeBerry is interested in how children of different ages perceive literary elements as well as the relationship between the reader's interest and the teacher's awareness of it. Generally speaking, the older the child, the less likely teachers were to predict the child's literary interest. Moreover, most studies of a child's literary preferences suggest that characterization is the most recognized and interesting literary element among young children. DeBerry's study did not confirm that, and he indicates that plot is the dominant interest instead.

Dorsa, Deanna. "The Importance of Ritual to Children." Ph.D. diss. California Institute of Integral Studies, 1994. 295 pp. DAI 55:3875A.

This dissertation, in religion, examines the importance of ritual to the entire life cycle but focuses on its impact on childhood and on rites of passage or transition, particularly birth, initiation, marriage, and death. Many literary, dramatic, and storytelling aspects of ritual are analyzed, and "special attention is given to food as an element of ritual—because of its symbolic importance in childhood. . . ."

Everson, Susan Elaine. "A Soldier's War, A Child's Peace: The Dialogue of Adult and Children's War Fiction Since 1941." Ph.D. diss. University of Chicago, 1995. 463 pp. DAI 56:3124A.

Everson focuses on literature published during and after World War II, particularly award-winning books such as *Johnny Tremain* and *The Silver Sword,* for "portrayals of morality, family, self-sufficiency, and the search for meaning in war." She questions "how our cultural attitudes toward the child have determined the construction of young readers with respect to America's history of war." She argues that "the traditional segregation of adult and children's literatures obscures their origin in the same social formation, and, at least in terms of war novels, conceals as well the fact that each literature is a large part of a reaction to the other."

Francis, Christine Doyle, "Transatlantic Translations: Louisa May Alcott and Charlotte Brontë." Ph.D. diss. University of Connecticut, 1995. 287 pp. DAI 56:2680A.

Francis argues that throughout her life Alcott was influenced by Charlotte Brontë, although in different ways as Alcott matured. She finds "intriguing parallels and differences" between the two women and their writing. Alcott's earliest works, as well as the sensational novels and *Little Women* and *Jo's Boys,* most clearly show specific references to Brontë; the early work imitates or adapts; the later resists or "openly" parodies. But "both writers demonstrate great interest in issues of spirituality, interpersonal relationships, and opportunities for self-fulfillment." Clearly Alcott is a "hybrid" writer, "responding as an American . . . but never denying the powerful transatlantic influence."

Frese, Johanna Christine. "Children's Perceptions on the Acquisition of Chapter Book Literacy." Ph.D. diss. Florida State University, 1994. 188 pp. DAI 55:3795A.

Frese is concerned with how fourth-grade children develop literacy while reading picture storybooks, illustrated books, and chapter books and, more important, how literacy emerges after the children develop. She analyzes factors affecting the acquisition and the characteristics of chapter book literacy and notes that there is a "tension" at this age between the desire to read illustrated books and the desire to take on longer, more complex works. Identification with chapter book characters helps to develop literacy.

Gaarden, Bonnie Lou. "The Goddess of George MacDonald." Ph.D. diss. State University of New York at Buffalo, 1995. 157 pp. DAI 56:3973A.

"This dissertation examines the goddess-figures in the fantasies of George MacDonald as indicating the traditionally feminine character of his ultimate values: emotion, intuition, instinct, nurture, interdependence, family orientation, cyclic models of development, and a vision of humanity as a part of nature." *At the Back of the North Wind* is interpreted as "the constant interaction of the motherly and fatherly, dark and light aspects of God in human life." She also discusses "The Lost Princess," "The Gray Wolf," "The Light Princess," and "The Day Boy and the Night Girl," the latter being an example of "pure evil."

Green, Amy Susan. "Savage Childhood: The Scientific Construction of Girlhood and Boyhood in the Progressive Era." Ph.D. diss. Yale University, 1995. 292 pp. DAI 56:2742A.

Green's dissertation in American studies examines two professional movements during the Progressive era: child study and nature study. "These two movements promulgated ideas of childhood that accommodated both the ideological forces of progress and nostalgia so characteristic of the Progressive Era." The latter encompasses the former in that "Child Study experts not only viewed the child as an object of nature subject to the same investigation as [plants and animals], but they maintained that the child, in its progression from infancy to adolescence, recapitulated each stage of human evolution, beginning with the savage and climaxing with the civilized." It would be interesting to trace the effect of these movements on children's literature of the period.

Greever, Ellen A. "Fractured Fairy Tales: Parody in Literary Fairy Tales for Children." Ph.D. diss. University of North Carolina at Chapel Hill, 1995. 164 pp. DAI 56:3863A.

Greever explores traditional fairy-tale parody in literary tales for children by analyzing fifty-seven texts based on nine well-known tales written from approximately 1970 through 1991. She identifies trends and finds that most texts "were both humorous and parodic, with the humor most often appearing in incident and style aspects and the parody most often appearing in plot aspects." Readers needed a fairly high level of sophistication to catch the allusions to popular culture and the satire of contemporary social issues; consequently the audience was usually elementary school level or older.

Hall, Mary Allen. "Images of African-American Males in Realistic Fiction Picture Books, 1971–1990." Ed.D. diss. University of Florida, 1994. 189 pp. DAI 56:4263A.

Hall compares realistic picture books published from 1971 through 1980 and 1981 through 1990 to determine how many of them portrayed African-American males; demographic details and behavioral patterns of characters; the sex and race of authors and illustrators; and the major themes in the books. A total of sixty-six books were identified, and Hall finds some changes in approach to character from the earlier works to the later. Characters in later books are "less active, more emotional and nurturing," and the theme of family relationships predominates. The books, for the most part, are set in homes, and "city and rural settings decreased." The majority of characters in both time periods were children aged four to twelve; "teenagers were not portrayed in 1981–1990 and were included only as minor characters in 1971–1980."

Hoogland, Joan Cornelia. "Poetics, Politics and Pedagogy of Grimms' Fairy Tales." Ph.D. diss. Simon Fraser University, 1993. 259 pp. DAI 56:4302A.

Hoogland analyzes the Grimm tales in the context of language arts classes to determine whether "the tales provide students with insightful metaphors which facilitate better understanding of the human predicament." Not incidentally, she acknowledges the fact that literature is often "used" for its educational value rather than its aesthetic value. She stresses that "curricula . . . need to be balanced with the need for standards . . . , the need for observing literary continuity through mythic themes and images, and the need for understanding literature as a distinct mode of discourse which engages our imaginations and emotions, and by which we are motivated and guided in our response."

Hotta, Ann Miyoko. "Children, Books, and Children's *Bunkō:* A Study of an Art World in the Japanese Context." Ph.D. diss. University of California at Berkeley, 1995. 293 pp. DAI 56:3357A.

Small neighborhood libraries in Japan run by volunteering mothers are called *bunkō.* Hotta examined the influence of *bunkō* on "children's lives, the children's book industry, the neighborhood and the lives of the women themselves, and local government policy." She found that the libraries and the mothers who run them have had considerable social influence: there has been successful lobbying for "new or expanded public library services" and, in small communities, the libraries have been a focal point for information about books and reading (as distinct from the pressure of school reading) and for mothers who want to learn more about parenting.

Huang, Shao-Fang Lucia. "A Study of Fairy-Tale Motifs in Selected Young Adult Novels." Ph.D. diss. University of Tennessee, 1994. 167 pp. DAI 56:1276A.

"Using content analysis, this study examined fairy-tale motifs in selected young adult novels" published in the 1980s. The works studied are *Jacob Have I Loved; Notes from Another Life; Dogsong; Izzy; Willy-Nilly; The Goats, Permanent Connections; Fade;* and *Eve.* The four motifs she examines are "The Helpers; The Unpromising Hero and Heroine; Abandoned Children; Magic." She demonstrates that these are strong motifs in young adult literature, and particularly noteworthy in the books she surveys.

Hundley, Clarence Carroll, Jr. "Fairy Tale Elements in Short Fiction of Nathaniel Hawthorne." Ph.D. diss. University of North Carolina at Greensboro, 1994. 237 pp. DAI 56:553A.

Chapters Three and Four are of particular interest. In them Hundley analyzes fairy-tale elements in *A Wonder-Book, Tanglewood Tales,* "The Snow-Image: A Childish Miracle," "Young Goodman Brown," "Rappaccini's Daughter," and "The Birth-Mark," among others, to determine how familiar Hawthorne was with fairy-tale writers and to what extent his writing is a consequence of his knowledge of the genre.

Jefferson, Maudine. "The Effects of a Literature-Based Subject Matter Unit on African-American Students' Knowledge and Attitudes About African-American Folklore." Ph.D. diss. University of Georgia, 1995. 391 pp. DAI 56:3903A.

Jefferson worked with twenty-one eighth-graders to determine "if a literature-based subject matter unit on African-American folklore would encourage African-American students to increase their knowledge and change their attitudes about the contributions of African-American folklore to their cultural heritage." Results show that students' awareness and knowledge were both increased and that their perceptions were changed or modified.

Jenkins, Christine Alice. "The Strength of the Inconspicuous: Youth Services Librarians, the American Library Association, and Intellectual Freedom for the Young, 1939–1955." Ph.D. diss. University of Wisconsin at Madison, 1995. 734 pp. DAI 57:12–13A.

Jenkins examines a predominantly white, middle-class female group whose activities coincide with the beginning of World War II and end with the Cold War. She shows how they used "the rhetoric and strategies of female-intensive child welfare professions" to counter book censorship and "McCarthy era pressure groups." The most significant issues of the time were "the place of realism in children's literature," the authority of librarians to select Newbery Medal winners, and "the value of books advocating interracial relations and international understanding."

Johnson, Linda June. "Children's Preferences for Text and How These Preferences Contribute to Classroom Literacy Events." Ed.D. diss. University of Nevada at Las Vegas, 1995. 256 pp. DAI 56:2555A.

"In an exploratory study, [Johnson] examined young children's text preferences in the classroom and how those preferences contributed to three literacy events: read-alouds, independent reading, and writing." Findings indicate, among other things, that teachers' "strategic decisions" and choices can both promote and limit "children's use of their preferences in [a] literacy event" and that children were most interested in fiction, primarily fairy tales, fantasy, and books about animals.

Krickeberg, Sandra Kay. "A National Teacher Survey on Young Adult Literature." Ed.D. diss. Northern Illinois University, 1995. 197 pp. DAI 56:3895A.

The purpose of this dissertation was to determine how knowledgeable teachers are about young adult literature, what their attitudes toward it are, and why they do or do not include it in their curriculum. Generally speaking Krickeberg found that four aspects of the literature, "sexual terms, sexual situations, homosexuality, and the occult or supernatural," were repugnant to teachers, or considered too controversial, and that they were ill-informed about young adult literature even though one-third had taken a course in the subject.

Lappas, Catherine. "Rewriting Fairy Tales: Transformation as Feminist Practice in the Nineteenth and Twentieth Centuries." Ph.D. diss. Saint Louis University, 1995. 169 pp. DAI 56:3594A.

While applying feminist criticism, Lappas examines stereotypes and sexism embedded in fairy tales as well as the likelihood that some nineteenth- and twentieth-century writers "appropriate the fairy tale to reflect the experiences and desires of women's invention, rather than those of patriarchal invention." She also demonstrates how some contemporary writers "rewrite" the old tales in order to reestablish "a tradition of female storytelling." She focuses on Charlotte Brontë's *Jane Eyre,* Angela Carter's *The Bloody Chamber,* and Margaret Atwood's *Bluebeard's Egg.*

Lin, Huey-Jen. "A Study of the Responses of Three American and Three Chinese Children to Picturebooks of Chinese Folktales." Ph.D. diss. Ohio State University, 1995. 212 pp. DAI 56:3486A.

Using a home setting to observe children's discussions of picture books, Lin found that there were more similarities within the two cultural groups than dissimilarities. She concludes that "teachers should provide various modes for literature discussion," particularly small groups that allow children to respond personally in a nonintimidating setting.

McIver, Barbara Basore. "Good Girls, Bad Girls, and Heroines: Models from Myth." Ph.D. diss. University of Arkansas, 1994. 106 pp. DAI 55:2379A.

McIver traces the breakdown of the ancient myths about the "Great Goddess" who originally embodied the "dualities of chastity and promiscuity, birth and death, creation and destruction, love and war." She notes that "these are precisely the myths which have most deeply influenced our culture and our assumptions." Unfortunately these myths are contemporarily portrayed as "an impoverishing split of good and bad girls." And "because these [latter] tales have a direct and powerful impact on our vision of our world and our place in it, they limit options for women as well as men."

McKinney, Caroline Smith. "Transforming the Borrowed Words: The Quality of Strength in Female Protagonists in Young Adult Literature, 1967–1993." Ph.D. diss. University of Colorado at Boulder, 1995. 300 pp. DAI 57:89A.

McKinney combines recent research about the way women develop a voice and self-knowledge "with an analysis of the shifting roles for female characters in novels for adolescents" to determine four things: what has been traditionally identified as "strong" in young adult fictional characters, who identifies this quality, how the quality relates to finding identity and becoming independent, and "how female characters develop their self concepts about strength." She examines thirty young adult novels and finds, preeminently, that female characters "demonstrate strength by seeming to maintain connections with others while finding a personal identity."

Moore, John Noell. "Tracing the Weave: Reading and Interpreting Young Adult Fiction." Ph.D. diss. Virginia Polytechnic Institute and State University, 1995. 488 pp. DAI 56:1232A.

"This dissertation demonstrates how the study of young adult fiction can be illuminated by a working knowledge of contemporary literary theories, viewing these theories as strategies, approaches to interpretation." Moore deals with eight literary theories and applies each to a close reading of one text: formalism (Virginia Hamilton's *M. C. Higgins the Great*), archetypal theory (Gary Paulsen's *Dogsong*), structuralism-semiotics (Bruce Brooks's *The Moves Make the Man*), poststructuralism-deconstruction (Lois Lowry's *The Giver*), reader-response theories (Walter Dean Myers's *Fallen Angels*), feminism (Budge Wilson's short story collection *The Leaving*), black aesthetics (Ernest Gaines's *A Lesson Before Dying*), cultural studies (M. E. Kerr's *Night Kites*), and the application of several different theories to Katherine Paterson's *Jacob Have I Loved.*

Morris-Knower, James Pringle. "No Place Like Home: Discourses of Adolescence and the Politics of Space in Contemporary American Coming-of-Age Narratives." Ph.D. diss. University of Michigan, 1996. 265 pp. DAI 57:1194A.

This dissertation, in American studies, is less concerned with adolescents and their sense of place than how adolescence and space are represented in regard to each other "in contemporary coming of age narratives, with specific reference to the ways gender, class and race/ethnicity shape the symbolic landscapes of these political struggles for identity." Morris-Knower also questions traditional American studies "notions of myth, symbol and image, [and] holistic national identity" and supplants them with an argument for "contested American cultures and race/class/gender."

Murphy, James G. " 'I Am Not Like Other Historians': Historical Revision in Nathaniel Hawthorne's Literature for Children." Ph.D. diss. Fordham University, 1995. 205 pp. DAI 56:1780A.

In Jacksonian America children's literature and history for children were "essentially propaganda, presenting a false view of America and her history for social and political ends." Murphy deals primarily with *The Whole History of Grandfather's Chair* and *Stories from History and Biography* to illustrate how Hawthorne "subverts commemorative history" and dramatically revises history as it was normally offered to children. Both works demonstrate that Hawthorne's "consistent response to the culture that produced the nationalistic histories was to illustrate the falsity of their vision of America and her past" while attacking the vaulting rhetoric of contemporary literature for children.

Overstreet, Deborah Anne Wilson. "Winning Hearts and Minds: The Vietnam Experience in Adolescent Fiction." Ed.D. diss. University of Georgia, 1994. 293 pp. DAI 55:2751–52A.

Overstreet examined twenty-five adolescent novels about the Vietnam War published between 1966 and 1993. "The overarching theoretical framework of this study is a combination of critical Marxist educational and critical cultural and literacy theory" drawing on the work of major theorists. She found that the novels were apolitical and ahistorical in that they "did not include significant historical information, nor did they conform to an identifiable historiography." The antiwar movement was rarely mentioned, most books were quite conservative, Vietnamese people and soldiers were stereotyped, and "American soldiers were consistently represented as victims of both the war and the American public."

Palacio, Maria Mata. "Emergence of an Hispanic Oasis in Children's Literature in the United States." Ed.D. diss. University of San Francisco, 1993. 150 pp. DAI 56:3858A.

Palacio points out that, according to the 1990 census, one in eleven Americans in the United States is Hispanic or Latino but that "Hispanic/Latino American writers of children's literature are pathetically under represented in the publishing world in the states." To address this clear need she analyzes the situation, makes recommendations, and includes an annotated bibliography of trade books written by Latino or Hispanic authors.

Patrón, Rose Lee. "Promoting Family Interaction and Literacy Through Children's Literature in Spanish with Spanish-Speaking Parents: A Participatory Study." Ed.D. diss. University of San Francisco, 1988. 174 pp. DAI 57:985A.

The two-fold purpose of Patrón's dissertation was to review, read, and use quality Spanish children's literature in an intervention program that involved parents and parent-child interaction in the home and to use the Johnson and Johnson cooperative learning model "to create a positive interdependence among the parents, to develop interpersonal skills, and to create shared leadership and responsibility roles." She found that using "heritage" language literature enhanced literacy in both Spanish and English and laid a "foundation for cultural and family pride."

Randall, Donald B. "Imperial Boyhood: Representations of Empire and Adolescence in Rudyard Kipling's Fiction." Ph.D. diss. University of Alberta, 1995. 265 pp. DAI 57:1151–52A.

Randall gives an extended analysis of *The Jungle Book, Stalky & Company,* and *Kim,* asserting that the concept of "empire boy" was, for Kipling, "the organizing figure" that he employed "to articulate his envisioning of the British imperial project" and that it "serves yet disrupts [and] asserts yet subverts imperial authority and ideology." Mowgli is "the organizing figure in an allegorization of empire"; Stalky is "an imperial hero who bears an unsettling resemblance to the colonial subjects he dominates"; and Kim is "the hybridized boy . . . , the ambivalent agent and the intractable object of imperial power-knowledge."

Robinson, Elizabeth Kathleen. "George MacDonald's Fantasy: Visions of a Christian Mystic." Ph.D. diss. Texas A&M University, 1995. 274 pp. DAI 56:3597A.

Robinson categorizes the stages of MacDonald's mysticism and its influence on "his theology and philosophy of art." She concentrates on *Phantasies, Lilith,* and *The Princes and Curdie* and believes that MacDonald "portrays Jesus Christ as the redemptive figure who guides Christian mystics to union with God" and that the Great-great-grandmother Irene, in the latter work, symbolizes him. "He also presents to his child readers a vision of the false self similar to that presented in [the adult work] *Phantasies*, and to this he adds a vision of a corrupt society."

Scott, Margaret Gethers. "The Portrayal of Literacy in Children's Picture Storybooks About African Americans: A Content Analysis." Ph.D. diss. Florida State University, 1995. 214 pp. DAI 56:1167A.

The dual purpose of this dissertation was to identify books that portray reading and writing "while featuring African American characters in home, neighborhood, and other non-school community settings and to determine if differences existed in such portrayals by African American and non-African American authors and illustrators." Understandably, most portrayals were by African American authors and illustrators—illustrators portraying African American characters about three times more frequently than authors. When literacy events were portrayed, reading events far outnumbered writing events, and negative portrayals were "minimal."

Sonheim, Amy Loretta. "Picture Miladies: The Illustrating of George MacDonald's Fairy-Tale Women by Arthur Hughes." Ph.D. diss. University of Missouri at Columbia, 1994. 258 pp. DAI 57:487A.

Sonheim demonstrates an unholy alliance between George MacDonald and his illustrator, Arthur Hughes. She demonstrates how Hughes's "pictures provide an iconographic interpretation of MacDonald's fairy-tale women [but] without exception, Hughes differs in his pictorial details from MacDonald's descriptions in the stories" and creates "a new synthesis of meaning." For instance, when MacDonald created a character "modelled after the intellectual, independent New Woman, Hughes inculcates . . . the portrait with his own chivalrous rhetoric. . . ." Together they create "a holy-sexy-independent fairy-tale heroine," a product of MacDonald's associations with suffragettes and Hughes's relationship to the Pre-Raphaelites.

Swartz, Mark E. "Before the Rainbow: L. Frank Baum's *The Wonderful Wizard of Oz* on Stage and Screen to 1939." Ph.D. diss. New York University, 1996. 536 pp. DAI 57:931A.

Swartz traces the performance history of *The Wizard of Oz* from its publication in 1900, through the many plays and silent films that the book generated, as well as the latter's influence on the 1939 MGM musical and its lasting influence on our "cultural bloodstream." He suggests that the film has probably been seen by more people than any other (more than a billion viewings). He is particularly interested in the many live-action early adaptations of *The Wonderful Wizard of Oz* and the way they "laid the iconographic ground for the depiction of Dorothy and her world."

Ueno-Herr, Michiko. "Masters, Disciples, and the Art of *Bunraku* Puppeteer's Performance." Ph.D. diss. University of Hawaii, 1995. 374 pp. DAI 57:35A.

More than 45 percent of the dissertation is a description of the art, history, performance, and craft of *bunraku* puppetry, one of the major theatrical traditions in Japan. It is "story telling accompanied by the *shamisen* (a musical instrument with three strings, played with a plectrum) and enacted by puppets. The three elements—narration, *shamisen* accompanied, and puppets—together constitute *bunraku* in its purest form."

Weaver, Mary Bronwyn. "Empowering the Children: Theatre for Young Audiences in Anglophone Canada." Ph.D. diss. University of Toronto, 1992. 317 pp. DAI 55:3688A.

Weaver describes the influence of Brian Way, the British Theatre-in-Education movement, and the Grips Theatre of Berlin on Theatre for Young Audiences (TYA) of Toronto while she analyzes a performance of John Lazarus's *Night Light* and discusses "commitment shortcuts," a term she uses to describe how children commit to theatre "through emotional identification." The concept includes "accessible iconography, playing on emotional associations of place and time, enactment sequences, victimization of child characters, presenting more than one perspective, ineffectual or absent adults, self-reliant child characters, and open ended hopeful resolutions." She found that commitment shortcuts were an effective, albeit "modest," way to pull an audience into the action and emotion of a play.

Yeoman, Elizabeth. "Tales Told in Schools: Children, Stories and Issues of Justice and Equity." Ph.D. diss. University of Toronto, 1994. 228 pp. DAI 56:2634A.

Yeoman's dissertation is about "disruptive" literature—literature that "challenges the world as it is and suggest[s] a better world that *might* be . . . , particularly concerning issues of race, gender, peace and the environment." She acknowledges that the common wisdom of school boards and others is to have children read "non-violent, non-racist and non-sexist" materials in the hope that these will "contribute to the building of a more peaceful and egalitarian society," but she stresses that choosing these types of materials is no guarantee of "long-lasting social change."

Zincani, John. "Pinocchio Revisited: Tales of a Stringless Puppet." Ph.D. diss. New York University, 1994. 234 pp. DAI 55:2858A.

Zincani's thesis is that "to a critical reader, *Pinocchio* loses its relevance as a favorite children's story providing frivolously harmless entertainment for the child seeking an amusing tale, and becomes a significant document written during the birth of a new nation." He believes that the novel proposes a method of education based on personal experience because Collodi describes "an anarchical world where governmental and parental authorities [do not] protect the individual from himself" and where "a sentient and conscious human [is] able to formulate his own mature ideas without the need for a formal educational indoctrination." Needless to say, Collodi's ideas were rejected. Zincani compares *Pinocchio* with De Amici's *Cuore,* a more conventional work that is contemporary with *Pinocchio.*

Also of Note

Adams, Ellen Louise. "A Descriptive Study of Second Graders' Conversations about Books." Ph.D. diss. State University of New York at Albany, 1995. 194 pp. DAI 56:3894A.

Unlike the typical teacher-centered approach of most dissertations this one analyzes peer-group discussions of books.

Argent, Joseph Edward. "'No More Existence Than the Inhabitants of Utopia': Utopian Satire in *Gulliver's Travels.*" Ph.D. diss. University of North Carolina at Greensboro, 1995. 262 pp. DAI 56:2244A.

Aud, Susan Veronica. "Looking for the Implied Reader in the Picture Storybook: An Analogue to Reader-Response Theory." Ph.D. diss. Southern Illinois University at Carbondale, 1994. 274 pp. DAI 56:2590A.

Aud describes "a developmental progression in young children's narrative thinking through reading picture storybooks."

Brooks-Hodridge, Deborah Ann. "Effects of Interactive Story Reading on Concepts About Print and Journal Writing in First-Grade Children." Ed.D. diss. Texas Woman's University, 1995. 108 pp. DAI 56:3443A.

Byerly, Steven Lee. "Dramatization Within the Secondary Language Arts Curriculum: An Intervention for Generating Analytical/Evaluative Thought Relevant to Story Theme and Characterization." Ph.D. diss. University of California at Riverside, 1995. 149 pp. DAI 56:2981A.

Cirulli Scoboria, Rosemarie. "A Comparative Study of Achievement Gains: Literature

Based vs. Basal Approach to Junior High Reading." Ed.D. diss. Temple University, 1995. 82 pp. DAI 56:3527–28A.

Comey, James Hugh. "Three Moons Till Tomorrow: An Examination of the Interactions, Transactions, and the Construction and Co-construction of Meaning by Elementary School Students, Teachers, and Theatre Professionals with an Original Children's Musical Play." Ed.D. diss. University of Pennsylvania, 1995. 295 pp. DAI 56:3074.

"The intersection of elementary children, teachers, professional children's theatre, literary theory, and teacher research" demonstrates that with teachers in the audience children are equals.

Coxwell, Margaret Jacobson. "Teachers' Reflections on the Importance of Creative Dramatics in Their Elementary Classrooms." Ed.D. diss. Montana State University, 1995. 178 pp. DAI 56:2996A.

Teachers' use of creative dramatics is more dependent on teaching experience and a desire "to seek inventive pedagogical strategies" than on training.

De la Cruz, Rey E. "The Effects of Creative Drama on the Social and Oral Language Skills of Children with Learning Disabilities." Ed.D. diss. Illinois State University, 1995. 173 pp. DAI 56:3913A.

"Interviews demonstrated that the experimental group enjoyed the experience of learning through creative drama lessons."

Demers, Dominique. "Représentation et mythification de l'enfance dans la littérature jeunesse." Ph.D. diss. Université de Sherbrooke, 1993. 506 pp. DAI 55:2416A.

Demers deals with Cynthia Voight's *Solitary Blue* and Raymond Plante's *Le dernier des raisins.*

Ellis, John Robert. "From Ozzie and Harriet to Beavis and Butt-Head: Mass Media's Contribution to the Loss of Self and the Dilemma of Public Education in a Postmodern World." Ed.D. diss. Oklahoma State University, 1994. 168 pp. DAI 55:3341A.

Ellis examines how mass media, "especially television, impacts the development of the American elementary and secondary student's self perception." The implications for literacy, self-esteem, and public education are very negative.

Favor, Lesli J. "Interactions Between Texts, Illustrations, and Readers: The Empiricist, Imperialist Narratives and Polemics of Sir Arthur Conan Doyle." Ph.D. diss. University of North Texas, 1995. 130 pp. DAI 56:4784A.

Ferris, James S. "The Influence of Near-Death and Non-Near-Death Experience Literature on Three Suicidal Female Adolescents in Interactive Bibliotherapy." Ed.D. diss. University of San Francisco, 1995. 215 pp. DAI 56:4323A.

Ferris suggests that interactive bibliotherapy "may significantly reduce suicidal behavior in the seriously suicidal adolescents."

Flynn, Rosalind Mary. "Developing and Using Curriculum-Based Creative Drama in Fifth-Grade Reading/Language Arts Instruction: A Drama Specialist and a Classroom Teacher Collaborate." Ph.D. diss. University of Maryland at College Park, 1995. 290 pp. DAI 57:996A.

Flynn "found creative drama to be a viable instructional tool in reading/language arts instruction."

Gerbracht, Gloria Jean. "The Effect of Storytelling on the Narrative Writing of Third-Grade Students." D.Ed. diss. Indiana University of Pennsylvania, 1994. 194 pp. DAI 55:3741A.

Gerbracht concludes that storytelling [stories told to children] is enjoyable and educational and "has a substantial impact on the development of oral and written language skills."

Gillespie, Catherine Wilson. "A Bedtime Storybook Reading Intervention with Deaf Children." Ph.D. diss. University of Tennessee, 1995. 109 pp. DAI 57:582A.

Gillespie indicates that the children were "highly engaged."

Gruccio, Margaret. "The Integration of Literature into the Secondary Science Classroom." Ph.D. diss. University of Akron, 1995. 140 pp. DAI 56:3072A-73.

Gruccio provides a curriculum guide for earth science teachers and demonstrates ways to integrate literature into the curriculum.

Harlan, Richard Frederick. "The Models for Reading and Writing for Primary-Aged Children Presented in Selected Basal Textbooks Compared to Popular Trade Books." Ed.D. diss. East Texas State University, 1995. 229 pp. DAI 56:3519A.

Compared with earlier, similar studies, the only change in basal texts Harlan found was that there are more examples of literate female characters in recent books.

Jenkins, David Omar. "The Moral Adventure of Childhood: A Critical Study of the Works of Robert Coles." Ph.D. diss. Duke University, 1994. 242 pp. DAI 55:1004A.

Jenkins questions Cole's ability to portray children's moral characters: dissertation is a "theological critique of psychiatry and the philosophical traditions and cultures in which it currently flourishes."

Johnson, Nancy Ogles. "Four Second-Grade Children's Responses to Literature." Ed.D. diss. Rutgers The State University of New Jersey—New Brunswick, 1995. 121 pp. DAI 56:3519–20A.

Johnson examines the ways emerging readers respond to literature by restating the story, working to understand it, extending and expressing feelings, and making connections or value judgments about it.

Johnston, Callum Barnett. "Interactive Storybook Software and Kindergarten Children: The Effect on Verbal Ability and Emergent Storybook Reading Behaviors." Ph.D. diss. Florida State University, 1995. 129 pp. DAI 56:4270A.

Johnston reasons that since adults' reading to children improves children's verbal abilities and reading skills, then interactive software that reads stories might do the same. Results are positive if the software is used for about forty-five minutes a week for seven weeks.

Kandell, Stuart Leslie. "Grandparents Tales: Stories Our Children Need to Hear." Ph.D. diss. Union Institute, 1996. 194 pp. DAI 57:28A.

Krol-Sinclair, Barbara D. "Immigrant Parents with Limited Formal Education as Classroom Storybook Readers." Ed.D. diss. Boston University, 1996. 304 pp. DAI 57:984–85A.

Krol-Sinclair found the experience beneficial for parents and children, with no negative effects.

Landau, Daniel. "Effects of Fairy Tales on Creativity." Ph.D. diss. Wright Institute, 1994. 105 pp. DAI 55:3566B.

"Results indicate that fairy tales can be very valuable in enhancing creativity as measured by the [Holtzman Inkblot Technique] in individuals who are in a relaxed state of mind and who are susceptible to hypnotic induction."

Lindstedt, Delores Elise. "Recount Narratives of Navajo and Mainstream Culture Children." Ph.D. diss. University of Denver, 1994. 146 pp. DAI 55:5310B.

Lo, Deborah Eville. "Social Construction of Meaning in Storybook Reading with Young Children." Ph.D. diss. University of Chicago, 1995. 249 pp. DAI 56:3060A.

Lo concludes that story recall is greatest in the most socially supportive atmospheres.

Manke, Beth Anne. "The Nature and Nurture of Adolescent Humor: Links Between Childhood Family Environment and Adolescent Humor." Ph.D. diss. Pennsylvania State University, 1995. 125 pp. DAI 56:3478B.

Manke, who worked with adoptive and nonadoptive children, concludes that humor is not genetic, that it is more influenced by peers than by adults or reading.

Matsukawa, Yuko. "The Cartography of Expatriation: Mapping the American Girl

Abroad in Fiction, 1874–1915." Ph.D. diss. Brown University, 1995. 165 pp. DAI 56:3127A.

Chapter 4 deals with Burnett's *A Fair Barbarian, A Little Princess,* and *The Shuttle* "within the context of popular romance fiction and [the] dissemination of imperialist ideology."

Matthew, Kathryn I. "A Comparison of the Influence of CD-ROM Interactive Storybooks and Traditional Print Storybooks on Reading Comprehension and Attitude." Ed.D. diss. University of Houston, 1995. 132 pp. DAI 56:2997A.

Matthew indicates no difference in comprehension when students read stories in books and on CD-ROMs.

Olson, John Dennis. "Overcoming Obstacles: Research Use in the Congressional Hearings on the Children's Television Act of 1990." Ph.D. diss. University of Washington, 1995. 122 pp. DAI 56:2468A.

Orton, Peter Z. "Effects of Perceived Choice and Narrative Elements on Interest in and Liking of Story." Ph.D. diss. Stanford University, 1995. 95 pp. DAI 56:3784A.

Orton tests "how manipulation of an index of story strength affects audience interest in and liking of pictorial (film/videotaped) stories."

Philipp, Eva Exter. "Using Fairy Tale Themes in Consciousness Raising Groups for Adult Women." Ed.D. diss. Columbia University Teachers College, 1995. 350 pp. DAI 56:4249A.

Polster, Arnim Henry. "Childhood, Autonomy and Social Order: The Pedagogy of Karl Philipp Moritz." Ph.D. diss. University of California at Berkeley, 1994. 258 pp. DAI 55:2849–50A.

Rabin, Beth Elyse. "Children's Understanding of Emotional Display Rules on Family Television Series." Ph.D. diss. UCLA, 1994. 201 pp. DAI 55:3610B.

Rabin studies children's understanding of how television characters display and handle emotions.

Rasmussen, Jay Beck. "Literacy Responses of Mexican-American Sixth-Grade Students to Authentic Mexican-American and Traditional American Children's Literature." Ph.D. diss. University of Minnesota, 1996. 264 pp. DAI 57:155–56A.

Rasmussen worked with five English-speaking Mexican American sixth-graders while they read traditional American and "authentic Mexican American" fiction and nonfiction written for children.

Read, Ken E. "The King's New Clothes: A Comic Opera in Two Acts" [Original Composition]. D.M.A. University of Kentucky, 1995. 658 pp. DAI 56:2478A.

Reynolds, Sherry Vin. "Effects of Using Children's Books and a Traditional Textbook on Student Achievement and Higher-Level Thinking Skills." Ed.D. diss. Oklahoma State University, 1995. 77 pp. DAI 56:4341A.

Children taught American history using story books did not score perceptively higher on history tests than a control group.

Rochon, François. "Savoirs de le fiction et crises du sujet: Essais d'épistémocritique sur Carroll, Roussel, Calvino." Ph.D. diss. Ecole Polytechnique, 1994. 358 pp. DAI 56:1346A.

Rochon discusses the interface between science and literature and focuses on the two *Alice* books, among others.

Roy, Pierre. "La relation entre les intérêts de lecture et le contenu des Romans pour la jeunesse (Etude de trois collections: 1985 à 1993)." Ph.D. diss. Université de Sherbrooke, 1995. 518 pp. DAI 57:625A.

Scarborough, Nancy Smith. "Author to Author: An Author-Focused Program to Develop Literary Interpretations by Middle School Students." Ph.D. diss. George Mason University, 1995. 248 pp. DAI 56:3073A.

By focusing her study of literature on the role of the author Scarborough hopes to make students "more interested in and more capable of constructing the meaning of what they read."

Sisco, Lisa Ann. "Emerging from the Chrysalis: Isolation and Publication in Nineteenth-Century Literacy Narratives." Ph.D. diss. University of New Hampshire, 1995. 300 pp. DAI 56:3964–65A.

Among other works, Sisco discusses *Little Women.*

Sotto, Carolyn D. "The Comprehension of Riddles by School-Age Children with Normal Language Abilities and School-Age Children with Learning Disabilities." Ph.D. diss. University of Cincinnati, 1994. 154 pp. DAI 55:3411A.

Sotto suggests "the use of riddles for assessment and intervention activities that involve linguistic-based humor to improve language skills."

Tapper, John Michael. "Identity and Media Use in Adolescence: Exploring the Patterns of Everyday Life." Ph.D. diss. University of Wisconsin at Madison, 1996. 221 pp. DAI 56:2922A.

Weber, Kittie Michelle. "A Pilot Study Using Literature as an Alternate Way to Evaluate Piaget's Stages of Development." Ph.D. diss. Union Institute, 1995. 128 pp. DAI 56:3481B.

Weber found the method effective.

Williams, Barbara Yost. "Literary Liaisons: A Girl and Her Books." Ph.D. diss. University of Wisconsin at Madison, 1995. 182 pp. DAI 56:2622A.

The author closely analyzes three months' worth of her fourth-grade daughter's reading and demonstrates that "literature offered characters and situations that provoked thoughtful talk about and consideration of human experiences."

Willoughby, Barbara E. "Effects of Fairy Tale Reconstruction on Midlife Females' Perceptions of Self, World, Future and Preferred Self." Ed.D. diss. University of South Dakota, 1995. 211 pp. DAI 56:4980–81A.

This dissertation in women's studies indicates that there are "implications for use of fairy tales . . . in counseling, self-awareness and [personal] choices."

Contributors and Editors

GILLIAN ADAMS is the editor and publisher of *Children's Literature Abstracts* for the International Federation of Library Associations and the past editor, now an associate editor, of the *Children's Literature Association Quarterly*. Her most recent publication is "Missing the Boat: Countee Cullen's *The Lost Zoo,*" *The Lion and the Unicorn* 21, no. 1 (Winter 1997).

ALIDA ALLISON is an associate professor of English and comparative literature at San Diego State University, where she specializes in children's literature and serves as the director of SDSU's Children's Literature Circle. She is currently at work on a critical analysis of Russell Hoban's major works; her most recent book is *Isaac Bashevis Singer: Children's Stories and Childhood Memoirs.* She is also the author of several books for children.

FRANCELIA BUTLER, founding editor of *Children's Literature,* has published many books on children's literature, including *Skipping Around the World: The Ritual Nature of Folk Rhymes.*

JOHN CECH's most recent books are *The Southernmost Cat* (Simon and Schuster) and his study of Maurice Sendak, *Angels and Wild Things.* He teaches in the English Department of the University of Florida in Gainesville.

PAULA T. CONNOLLY is an associate professor of English at the University of North Carolina at Charlotte, where she teaches courses in American and children's literature. She is currently working on a book-length study of the depiction of American slavery in children's literature.

R. H. W. DILLARD, editor-in-chief of *Children's Literature* and professor of English at Hollins College, is the longtime chair of the Hollins Creative Writing Program and is adviser to the director of the Hollins Graduate Program in Children's Literature. A novelist and poet, he is also the author of two critical monographs, *Horror Films* and *Understanding George Garrett,* as well as articles on Ellen Glasgow, Vladimir Nabokov, Federico Fellini, Robert Coover, Fred Chappell, and others.

LEDIA DITTBERNER teaches elementary school and is currently finishing her master's degree in children's literature at Eastern Michigan University. She plans to pursue a Ph.D. in children's studies.

RACHEL FORDYCE, former executive secretary of the Children's Literature Association, has written five books, most recently *Semiotics and Linguistics in Alice's Worlds* with Carla Marello. She is a professor of English and the dean of humanities and social sciences at Montclair State University.

TINA L. HANLON is an associate professor of English at Ferrum College in Virginia, where she teaches children's literature, linguistics, and general studies courses. She has written essays on folktales, fantasy, Robinsonnades, and picture books.

ELIZABETH LENNOX KEYSER, editor of volumes 22–24 and 26, is an associate professor of English at Hollins College, where she teaches children's literature, American literature, and American studies. Her book *Whispers in the Dark: The Fiction of Louisa May Alcott* (University of Tennessee Press) won the 1993 Children's Literature Association Book Award. She is currently writing the volume on *Little Women* for the Twayne Masterwork series.

ANNE LUNDIN teaches children's literature at the University of Wisconsin at Madison, the School of Library and Information Studies. Her research interests are Walter

Crane, Randolph Caldecott, and Kate Greenaway, about whom she is writing a book to be published in the Children's Literature Association series.

EMER O'SULLIVAN lectures and researches at the Institut für Jugendbuchforschung at the Johann Wolfgang Goethe-Universität, Frankfurt. She has published a book (in German) on the aesthetic potential of national stereotypes in children's literature as well as the study *Friend and Foe: The Image of Germany and the Germans in British Children's Literature from 1870 till the Present,* has co-edited a volume on comparative children's literature, and has written several articles on related topics. She is currently completing a major study on comparative children's literature research.

JOHN RIEDER is a professor of English at the University of Hawaii at Manoa. He has published on English Romanticism, children's literature, and science fiction.

J. D. STAHL is the author of the book *Mark Twain, Culture and Gender* (Georgia University Press, 1994) and of a number of articles about Mark Twain, including "Mark Twain's 'Slovenly Peter' in the Context of Twain and German Culture" in *The Lion and the Unicorn* and "'Lasting Obligations': The Friendship of Samuel Clemens and Mary Mason Fairbanks" in the *Mark Twain Journal.* He teaches at Virginia Tech and in the M.A. program in children's literature at Hollins College.

JAN SUSINA is an associate professor of English at Illinois State University, where he teaches courses in children's and adolescent literature. He has edited *Logic and Tea: The Letters of Charles Dodgson to Members of the G. J. Rowell Family* (1984).

JEANIE WATSON is president and professor of English at Nebraska Wesleyan University. The author of *Risking Enchantment: Coleridge's Symbolic World of Faery* (1990), she has also published articles in children's literature on Christina Rossetti, Tennyson, and Coleridge, as well as on "Little Red-Cap."

IAN WOJCIK-ANDREWS teaches children's literature at Eastern Michigan University. He is currently finishing a book on children's films entitled *Children's Films: History, Ideology, Theory, and Pedagogy.*

NAOMI J. WOOD is an associate professor of English at Kansas State University. She has published articles on George MacDonald, Charles Kingsley, and other nineteenth-century writers for children.

JANE PARISH YANG received her Ph.D. in Chinese literature and language from the University of Wisconsin at Madison. Associate professor and chair of the East Asian Languages and Cultures Department at Lawrence University in Appleton, Wisconsin, she has translated many works of modern Chinese fiction, including Hualing Nieh's *Mulberry and Peach: Two Women of China* (Beacon Press, 1988), which won a 1990 American Book Award. This paper on children's literature stems from her interest in using authentic materials such as children's stories in her beginning Chinese language classes.

YOSHIDA JUNKO is an associate professor of English at Hiroshima University in Japan, where she teaches adolescent literature and American studies. Her research interests center on gender issues in adolescent novels. She has published several books in Japanese, including *Family Quest in American Children's Literature.* She is also a co-translator of Jack Zipes's *The Trials and Tribulations of Little Red Riding Hood* and Jerry Griswold's *Audacious Kids.* Her latest translation, of Zipes's *Fairy Tale as Myth, Myth as Fairy Tale,* will be published in 1998.

Award Applications

The article award committee of the Children's Literature Association publishes a bibliography of the year's work in children's literature in the *Children's Literature Association Quarterly* and selects the year's best critical articles. For pertinent articles that have appeared in a collection of essays or journal other than one devoted to children's literature, please send a photocopy or offprint with the correct citation and your address written on the first page to Gillian Adams, 5906 Fairlane Drive, Austin, Tex. 78731. Papers will be acknowledged and returned if return postage is enclosed. The annual deadline is May 1.

The Phoenix Award is given for a book first published twenty years earlier that did not win a major award but has passed the test of time and is deemed to be of high literary quality. Send nominations to Alethea Helbig, 3640 Eli Road, Ann Arbor, Mich. 48104.

The Children's Literature Association offers two annual research grants. The Margaret P. Esmonde Memorial Scholarship offers $500 for criticism and original works in the areas of fantasy or science fiction for children or adolescents by beginning scholars, including graduate students, instructors, and assistant professors. Research Fellowships are awards ranging from $250 to $1,000 (the number and amount of awards are based on the number and needs of winning applicants) for criticism or original scholarship leading to a significant publication. Recipients must have postdoctoral or equivalent professional standing. Awards may be used for transportation, living expenses, materials, and supplies but not for obtaining advanced degrees, for creative writing, textbook writing, or pedagogical purposes. For full application guidelines on both grants, write the Children's Literature Association, c/o Marianne Gessner, 22 Harvest Lane, Battle Creek, Mich. 49015. The annual deadline for these awards is February 1.

Order Form Yale University Press
P.O. Box 209040, New Haven, CT 06520-9040
Phone orders 1-800-YUP-READ (U.S. and Canada)

Customers in the United States and Canada may photocopy this form and use it for ordering all volumes of **Children's Literature** available from Yale University Press. Individuals are asked to pay in advance. All payments must be made in U.S. dollars. We honor both MasterCard and VISA. Checks should be made payable to Yale University Press.

Prices given are 1998 list prices for the United States and are subject to change without notice. A shipping charge of $3.50 for the U.S. and $5.00 for Canada is to be added to each order, and Connecticut residents must pay a sales tax of 6 percent.

Qty.	Volume	Price	Total amount	Qty.	Volume	Price	Total amount
___	10 (cloth)	$50.00	______	___	20 (cloth)	$50.00	______
___	11 (cloth)	$50.00	______	___	20 (paper)	$18.00	______
___	12 (cloth)	$50.00	______	___	21 (cloth)	$50.00	______
___	13 (cloth)	$50.00	______	___	21 (paper)	$18.00	______
___	14 (cloth)	$50.00	______	___	22 (cloth)	$50.00	______
___	15 (cloth)	$50.00	______	___	22 (paper)	$18.00	______
___	15 (paper)	$18.00	______	___	23 (cloth)	$50.00	______
___	16 (paper)	$18.00	______	___	23 (paper)	$18.00	______
___	17 (cloth)	$50.00	______	___	24 (cloth)	$50.00	______
___	17 (paper)	$18.00	______	___	24 (paper)	$18.00	______
___	18 (cloth)	$50.00	______	___	25 (cloth)	$50.00	______
___	18 (paper)	$18.00	______	___	25 (paper)	$18.00	______
___	19 (cloth)	$50.00	______	___	26 (cloth)	$50.00	______
___	19 (paper)	$18.00	______	___	26 (paper)	$18.00	______

Payment of $________________ is enclosed (including sales tax if applicable).

MasterCard no. ________________

4-digit bank no. ________________ Expiration date ________________

VISA no. ________________ Expiration date ________________

Signature ________________

SHIP TO: ________________

____

____

See the next page for ordering issues from Yale University Press, London. Volumes out of stock in New Haven may be available from the London office.

Volumes 1–7 of **Children's Literature** can be obtained directly from John C. Wandell, The Children's Literature Foundation, P.O. Box 370, Windham Center, Conn. 06280.

Order Form Yale University Press, 23 Pond Street, Hampstead, London NW3 2PN, England

Customers in the United Kingdom, Europe, and the British Commonwealth may photocopy this form and use it for ordering all volumes of **Children's Literature** available from Yale University Press. Individuals are asked to pay in advance. We honour Access, VISA, and American Express accounts. Cheques should be made payable to Yale University Press.

The prices given are 1998 list prices for the United Kingdom and are subject to change. A post and packing charge of £1.95 is to be added to each order.

Qty.	Volume	Price	Total amount	Qty.	Volume	Price	Total amount
___	8 (cloth)	£40.00	___	___	17 (paper)	£14.95	___
___	8 (paper)	£14.95	___	___	18 (cloth)	£40.00	___
___	9 (cloth)	£40.00	___	___	18 (paper)	£14.95	___
___	9 (paper)	£14.95	___	___	19 (cloth)	£40.00	___
___	10 (cloth)	£40.00	___	___	19 (paper)	£14.95	___
___	11 (cloth)	£40.00	___	___	20 (paper)	£14.95	___
___	11 (paper)	£14.95	___	___	21 (paper)	£14.95	___
___	12 (cloth)	£40.00	___	___	22 (cloth)	£40.00	___
___	12 (paper)	£14.95	___	___	22 (paper)	£14.95	___
___	13 (cloth)	£40.00	___	___	23 (cloth)	£40.00	___
___	13 (paper)	£14.95	___	___	23 (paper)	£14.95	___
___	14 (cloth)	£40.00	___	___	24 (cloth)	£40.00	___
___	14 (paper)	£14.95	___	___	24 (paper)	£14.95	___
___	15 (cloth)	£40.00	___	___	25 (cloth)	£40.00	___
___	15 (paper)	£14.95	___	___	25 (paper)	£14.95	___
___	16 (paper)	£14.95	___	___	26 (cloth)	£40.00	___
___	17 (cloth)	£40.00	___	___	26 (paper)	£14.95	___

Payment of £ ________________________________ is enclosed.

Please debit my Access/VISA/American Express account no. ________________

Expiry date ________________________________

Signature ________________ Name ________________

Address ________________________________

See the previous page for ordering issues from Yale University Press, New Haven.

Volumes 1–7 of **Children's Literature** can be obtained directly from John C. Wandell, The Children's Literature Foundation, Box 370, Windham Center, Conn. 06280.